AF879398

AIC4NL AI Brevet Courseware

Colophon

Title: AIC4NL AI Brevet Courseware

Authors: Rowel Gündlach

Publisher: Van Haren Publishing, 's-Hertogenbosch

ISBN Paperback: 978 94 018 1456 0

Edition: Design: First edition, first print, March, 2026

For further information about Van Haren Publishing please e-mail us at: info@vanharen.net or visit our website: www.vanharen.net

Publisher about the Courseware

The Courseware was created by experts from the industry who served as the author(s) for this publication. The input for the material is based on existing publications and the experience and expertise of the author(s). The material has been revised by trainers who also have experience working with the material. Close attention was also paid to the key learning points to ensure what needs to be mastered.

The objective of the courseware is to provide maximum support to the trainer and to the student, during his or her training. The material has a modular structure and according to the author(s) has the highest success rate should the student opt for examination. The Courseware is also accredited for this reason, wherever applicable.

In order to satisfy the requirements for accreditation the material must meet certain quality standards. The structure, the use of certain terms, diagrams and references are all part of this accreditation. Additionally, the material must be made available to each student in order to obtain full accreditation. To optimally support the trainer and the participant of the training assignments, practice exams and results are provided with the material.

Direct reference to advised literature is also regularly covered in the sheets so that students can find additional information concerning a particular topic. The decision to leave out notes pages from the Courseware was to encourage students to take notes throughout the material. Although the courseware is complete, the possibility that the trainer deviates from the structure of the sheets or chooses to not refer to all the sheets or commands does exist. The student always has the possibility to cover these topics and go through them on their own time. It is recommended to follow the structure of the courseware and publications for maximum exam preparation.

The courseware and the recommended literature are the perfect combination to learn and understand the theory.

-- Van Haren Publishing

Other publications BY Van Haren Publishing

Van Haren Publishing (VHP) specializes in titles on Best Practices, methods, frameworks and standards within four domains:

- IT Management
- Architecture (Enterprise and IT)
- Business Management and
- Project Management

Van Haren Publishing is publishing on behalf of leading organizations and companies: Agile Consortium, World Commerce and Contracting, IAOP, IPMA World, KNVI, PMI-NL, NLAIC and The Open Group.

Van Haren Publishing is part of the Van Haren Group and additional to the book publishing also provides the following services: accredited training materials and e-learning through Van Haren Learning Solutions, as well as independent professional certification via examination through Van Haren Certify.

Topics are (per domain):

IT Management	IT Service Management	FitSM, ISM®, ISO/IEC20000, IT4IT®, ITIL®, VerISM®, SAF, TRIM, XLA®
	Data Management	Data literacy, Data visualization, DMBOK
	IT Asset Management	HAM, ITAM, SAM
	IT Security Management	BIO, ISO/IEC27001, NIS2
	Test Management	CTAP
	Application Management	ASL
	Other	eCF, IT-CMF, Scrum
Project Management	Project Management	Half Double, ICB, ISO/IEC21500, P3.express, PM2, PMBOK Guide, Praxis, PRINCE2
	Agile	Agile, Agile PM
	Other	PMO
Business Management	Operations Management	Lean, Lean Six Sigma, OBM, OMC, RASCI
	Contract Management	CATS CM, CATS RVM, IACCM World
	Business Information Management	BiSL, DID
	Artificial Intelligence	AI, Generative AI
	Outsourcing	OPBOK
Enterprise Architecture	Enterprise Architecture	BIAN, TOGAF
	Modeling	ArchiMate, BPMN
	Software Architecture	ISAQB
	Other	Open Agile Architecture

For the latest information on VHP publications, visit our website: www.vanharen.net.

Table of Content

Self-Reflection of understanding Diagram

'What you do not measure, you cannot control.'' – Tom Peters

Fill in this diagram to self-evaluate your understanding of the material. This is an evaluation of how well you know the material and how well you understand it. In order to pass the exam successfully you should be aiming to reach the higher end of Level 3. If you really want to become a pro, then you should be aiming for Level 4. Your overall level of understanding will naturally follow the learning curve. So, it's important to keep track of where you are at each point of the training and address any areas of difficulty.

Based on where you are within the Self-Reflection of Understanding diagram you can evaluate the progress of your own training.

Level of Understanding	Before Training (Pre-knowledge)	Training Part 1 (1st Half)	raining Part 2 (2nd Half)	After studying / reading the book	After exercises and the Practice exam
Level 4 ***I can explain the content and apply it .***					
Level 3 I get it! ***I am right where I am supposed to be.***					Ready for the exam!
Level 2 ***I almost have it but could use more practice.***					
Level 1 ***I am learning but don't quite get it yet.***					

(Self-Reflection of Understanding Diagram)

Write down the problem areas that you are still having difficulty with so that you can consolidate them yourself, or with your trainer. After you have had a look at these, then you should evaluate to see if you now have a better understanding of where you actually are on the learning curve.

Troubleshooting

Problem areas:	***Topic:***
Part 1	
Part 2	
You have gone through the book and studied.	
You have answered the questions and done the practice exam.	

Timetable

Day 1 – How does AI work

A fundamental insight in AI

- History of AI
- Definition of Intelligence
- What is AI
- Examples of AI
- Algorithms, Machine Learning, Deep Learning and LLM's
- ChatGPT
- Integrated copilot (demo)

Day 2 – How can AI be implemented

Managing everything that AI needs to be properly integrated in our society

- Ethics and trustworthiness
- Sustainability & AI
- Risks
- Legal considerations for AI
- The future of AI

Day 3 – The impact of AI

Managing everything that AI needs to be properly integrated in our society

- Ethics and trustworthiness
- Sustainability & AI
- Risks
- Legal considerations for AI
- The future of AI

The Netherlands AI Coalition
(AIC4NLC) AI Fundamentals

The 'AI Brevet'

AIC4NL
AI BREVET
Certified by
Van Haren
CERTIFY

Artificial Intelligence Brevet
Syllabus

AIC4NL

TABLE OF CONTENTS

INTRODUCTION

AI – the driving force of a new industrial era

Self-driving vehicles, voice and image recognition, healthcare analysis, robots and personalised information on social media - Artificial Intelligence (AI) has permeated our world, changing our society, our economy and our lives. AI based applications are central to the business model of some of the most powerful and successful commercial businesses today. AI itself is however not new - it has been with us since the 40's - inspiring the science fiction genre in entertainment.
Many of the algorithms that we use today were invented and scientifically proven in the 1950's. The difference between then and now is the availability of data and low-cost communication and computing power with which we can now apply algorithms to create innovative, smart applications of AI.

With such a powerful tool that AI represents, comes great responsibility. In parallel with the applications which benefit society, we have also witnessed applications of AI which can cause great harm to society, undermine democracy, increase discrimination and raise many ethical questions. Military applications have transformed warfare and sovereign governments view AI capability as a strategic national capability.

Will AI take over humans? Some believe this may happen, but long before then, the humans who use AI will take over from the humans who don't, and the companies which apply AI will take over from those who don't. This raises a new business and societal imperative - to educate leaders, managers, governments, consumer protection organisations, and a broad cross section of our society on what AI is (and is not), what benefits we can enjoy with it, and how to deal with the risks and ethical questions which it raises.

The Netherlands AI Coalition

The Netherlands AI Coalition (AIC4NL) is a public-private collaboration which aims to promote the responsible use of AI within the Netherlands. The coalition consists of government, business, educational institutions and communities working together to accelerate AI developments and to share and connect initiatives.

With the Human Capital Agenda (HCA), the AIC4NL supports a set of initiatives which aim to raise awareness and capability in the field of AI in The Netherlands. This includes tertiary education at bachelor and masters levels, PhDs and lifelong learning. For more information and activities concerning the AI Coalition refer to the AIC4NL website.

The Professional Certification Programme (described in this document) is part of the HCA and is aimed at providing recognised certifications for competency in AI. Whilst this may typically be achieved by participants following short education paths, the focus of this certification is the competence of professionals as demonstrated by successfully passing an exam, based upon a syllabus issued by AIC4NL. The Professional Certification Programme does not accredit training programmes, nor require that participants have followed a training programme.

This programme is therefore complementary to other tertiary education programmes which aim to develop a deeper understanding of AI, how it operates with underlying algorithms, approaches and specialist techniques.

Intended Audience

The AI Brevet, for Business & Government Certification, is aimed at executives, managers and professionals who wish to progress beyond basic awareness to acquire an understanding of what AI is, how it works and where it can be applied - including both benefits and risks.

It is therefore ideal for people for whom the concept of AI is relatively new and who wish to become competent in AI, are considering becoming involved in the application of AI or who must make informed decisions about the application of AI in their business domain.

Level	Objective	Target Groups
AI Brevet, for Business & Government	Able to identify applications for AI. Aware of how models are built and assessed. Able to make informed decisions on the use of AI.	Executives, managers and professionals who are considering becoming involved in AI or who will make decisions in relation to the use of AI in their environment.

The AI Brevet

The AI Brevet, for Business & Government Certification, recognises awareness and understanding of the components of AI and how to foster its adoption and application in a manner which benefits business, government and society at large. This involves considering both benefits and the ethical questions and risks of this powerful new technology.

The AI Brevet Certificate is achieved through an exam which demonstrates that a participant:

- Appreciates what AI is, why it is important now and what benefits it brings
- Is aware of fundamental concepts such as robotics, algorithms and machine learning approaches
- Is aware of how to organise a team for AI, approaches and common tools required
- Understands the dependence AI has upon data and how to manage data for AI
- Is aware of how to assess risks and ethical dilemmas for Trustworthy AI
- Can describe how humans and machines will coexist in an organisation
- Is aware of the future directions of AI

The syllabus outlines the knowledge that the candidate will be tested on during the Exam. It also provides suggestions for preparation (background reading) and highlights the benefits of taking this exam.

Certifying Organisation

The AIC4NL has chosen Van Haren Learning Solutions as certifying organisation for the provision of the AI Brevet. Van Haren Learning Solutions is an established and full service provider of certification programs.

The role of Van Haren Learning Solutions is to operate the certification on behalf of AIC4NL. This includes, among others, the following activities:

- Offering the exam in a controlled environment which enables candidates to take the exam in accordance with the exam procedure.
- Evaluation and feedback of exam results to candidates.
- Issuing the certificate to the successful candidates.

The AI Brevet can be found via this link: https://www.vhls. global/van-haren/certification/the-AIC4NL-ai-for-business/.

THE AI BREVET EXAM

You first need to have successfully completed the AI Brevet, for Business & Government Exam to obtain the AI Brevet. The exam procedure is explained in this section.

Practical information

You must pass a multiple-choice exam in which your knowledge of AI will be tested to obtain an AI Brevet. All exam candidates will get access to the online exam environment and will need to answer 60 multiple-choice questions within 60 minutes.

You must answer 65% of the questions correctly (or at least 39 of the 60 questions) to pass. Each question has precisely four possible answers where only one is the best answer.

You will receive the result immediately after the exam. (Digital) Access to your certificate will be given once you have passed.

Registration for the exam can be done by purchasing a participation certificate via Van Haren.

Number of questions:	60
Time (minutes) for the exam:	60 minutes
% minimal passing grade	65%
Open/closed book:	Closed
Language:	Dutch and English.
Exam format:	Online
Type of questions:	Multiple choice
Are there also negative questions included in the exam? *(for example: "which of the following is NOT a machine learning method")*	Yes. Candidates are advised to read the questions carefully.

Levels

The AI Brevet tests candidates at levels 1, 2 and 3 according to the Bloom Revised Taxonomy. The exam requires delegates to comprehend the theory for 85% at Bloom level 1 & 2 and 15% at Bloom level 3.

Bloom Level 1: Recall & Retention

We test candidates on their ability to memorize factual information, to retain information by collecting, remembering, and recognizing specific knowledge. Knowledge includes facts, terms, answers, or terminology.

Bloom Level 2: Understanding

We test candidates on their ability to construct meaning from oral, written, or graphical pieces of information. This is done by interpreting, summarizing, distracting, comparing, classifying, predicting, or explaining the message.

Bloom Level 3: Applying

Being able to solve problems by applying them in existing and new situations, leveraging acquired knowledge techniques, facts, and rules in various situations. This can include choosing or identifying to correct answer between a range of options or appropriate actions.

Your investment

The AI Exam requires preparation, which means this is an investment in time for personal study and attention for the subject of AI. You are completely free to do this in several ways and can consider self-study, reading the reference materials listed in the syllabus or following a training programme which is designed in line with this syllabus.

Refer to the list of topics in this syllabus. Here you can see which subjects you will be tested on during the exam. The time it takes to prepare for the exam depends on your prior knowledge, experience, and training. Commercially offered training programmes that prepare for the AI Brevet Exam will typically last 2 to 3 days. You should allow sufficient time for self-study to address the subjects listed in this syllabus.

Preparation and recommended literature

During your exam preparation, you will familiarise yourself with the concepts of AI for example by following a course and reading specified literature. There are ongoing publications about AI.

So, it should be straightforward to find books, articles, blogs, vlogs, or videos about the different aspects. We include a recommended reading list in this syllabus.

We also advise you to contact people who work with AI and observe what they do and see the techniques they use - and talk to them.

We have included the following in the syllabus to help you get started:

- Specifications of the examination material - divided into modules.
- How each individual module weighs towards the overall exam.
- A list of key terms and concepts detailing what must be covered.
- Literature suggestions are available for newcomers in field. Note many of the AI concepts are established for some time and widely accepted with online and offline reference materials available.
- A practice exam is available online after purchasing an exam. The practice exam contains questions at the same level as the questions in the actual exam. The number of questions may differ from the actual exam. The actual exam includes 60 questions and you will have 60 minutes to answer them.

Preparation training

We endorse the added value of thoroughly preparing for the AI Brevet Exam and strongly recommend preparatory classroom training, webinars and online eLearning journeys. This can help you to understand the essence of AI and can give you practical examples. That said, it is not mandatory to follow specialised training.

The Netherlands AI Coalition does not accredit trainers, training institutions or training programmes. The composition and duration, organisation, pricing, and execution of the training is the responsibility of the trainer.

TOPICS IN THE AI BREVET EXAM

In this section, you can read about how the AI Brevet Exam is structured and which subjects you will be tested on as a candidate. It is also a tool that you can use to prepare yourself for the test.

In this syllabus we indicate the topics which are covered in the exam and additional topics which are relevant for further study but not covered in the exam. During the exam you will be tested on your general knowledge about:

Section 1: AI Fundamentals

1. Applications of AI and their benefits

Describes a range of applications of AI, how they impact organisations & society, what value they create and their underlying use of data, algorithms and learning approaches. Describes the role of the AIC4NL in promoting the beneficial and ethical use of AI. Includes examples of key domains such as classification systems, forecasting, cluster analysis, voice, image and Natural Language Processing. Addresses Large Language Models such as ChatGPT and the use of Generative AI and Prompt Engineering for generation of text, software, images, videos etc.

2. Data, Robots and Artificial Intelligence including definitions

This sets out a common vocabulary around data, data science, algorithms, human logical thinking versus intelligent agents and provides definitions for key items. Describes Intelligent Agent types, robotics and agent models.

3. Predictions, Algorithms, Machine and Deep Learning

Introduces the different levels of predictions, an overview of the key algorithms and the learning approaches. Highlights which types of algorithms address which types of problems.

Section 2: Applying AI in practice

4. Building and assessing an AI application

Describes a basic approach towards building a simple AI application. The CRISP-DM method is described highlighting the steps involved and raising awareness of the business context and trustworthiness assessment at each step. Highlight pitfalls including overfitting, underfitting and bias. Addresses need for innovation and creativity including team organisation.

5. Managing Data for AI

Raises awareness of the dependence upon data and how to acquire, prepare, manage, provide and scale data for AI applications. Addresses the role of the cloud for managing data and processing capability. Emphasise the risks that arise in data and impact on trustworthiness.

Section 3: Ethics, Risks, Trustworthiness and Human Machine Coexistence

6. Ethics, Risks and Trustworthiness

Identify the risks and ethical dilemmas associated with AI including the need for explainable AI. Introduce EU Ethical Guidelines and the need to maintain the trust of society in the use of AI. You will become familiar with the different risk levels of AI applications as described in the EU AI Act.

7. Human and Machine Coexistence

Covers the combination of human and machine capability in an organisation addressing the question of whether AI will replace humans (singularity). Includes key roles of business management, domain expertise, analytics and data managers, and how these roles work together. Finally, the rise of and dealing with generative AI is also addressed.

Section 4: Future developments of AI

8. The future developments of AI

Highlight future directions and applications of AI.

The exam is <u>not</u> a test of:

- Programming ability or working knowledge of specific toolkits
- Mathematical basis of algorithms

Exam structure

The exam specifications describe the topics in the subject matter of the AI Brevet Exam, and their relative importance. Questions can be asked during the exam about the following subjects.

Module		Sub-module	Bloom -level	% exam question
1.	Applications of AI and their benefits	Describes a range of applications of AI, how these applications affect organizations and society, what value they create and their underlying use of data, generative AI, algorithms and learning approaches. Describes the role of the AIC4NL in promoting the beneficial and ethical use of AI. Includes examples of key domains such as classification systems, forecasting, cluster analysis, speech, image and natural language processing.	1	10%
2.	Data, Robots and Artificial Intelligence	This describes a common vocabulary around data, data science, algorithms, human logical thinking versus intelligent agents and provides definitions for key items. .	1	10%
3.	Predictions, Algorithms, Machine and Deep Learning	Introduces the different levels of prediction, an overview of the main algorithms, generative AI modeling incl. Large language models, possibly stable diffusion and learning approaches. Emphasizes which types of algorithms address which types of problems.	1+2	25%
4.	Building and assessing an AI application	Describes a basic approach to building a simple AI application. Describes the CRISP-DM methodology, highlighting the steps involved and increasing awareness of the business context and reliability assessment incl. hallucinations and deep fakes at each step. Highlights pitfalls such as overfitting, underfitting and biases. Addresses the need for innovation and creativity, including team organization.	1	15%
5.	Managing Data for AI	Explains awareness of data dependence and how data can be acquired, prepared, managed, provided and scaled for AI applications Addresses the role of the prompt engineer, and of the cloud in managing data and processing capacity. Emphasizes the risks that arise in data and affect reliability.	1	10%
6.	Ethics, Risks and Trustworthiness	Addresses the risks and ethical dilemmas associated with AI, including the need for explainable AI. Introduces EU ethical guidelines, the EU Act and the need to maintain society's trust in the use of AI.	1+2 +3	20%
7.	Human and Machine Coexistence	Covers the combination of human and machine capabilities in an organization that answers the question of whether AI will replace humans (singularity). Covers key roles of the prompt engineer, business management, domain expertise, analytics and data managers, and how these roles work together and make AI accessible	1+2	10%
8.	The future developments of AI	Highlights future directions and applications of AI.	1	0%

Topics in the AI Brevet, for Business & Government Exam

Exam Specifications

TOPIC 1 Applications of AI and their benefits

AI is all around us. AI has overtaken humans in some areas such as playing games but still cannot solve difficult or ambiguous problems. There are many benefits of AI applications such as smart propositions, improved service, increased efficiency, human safety and lower costs.

Not all areas involve learning or cognitive functions and are therefore not AI e.g. data visualisation, robotic process automation or data mining etc.

Examination goal

- Recall of facts and concepts
- Ability to detect applications of AI (and differentiate when not AI)

Elements included in exam

- Importance of data, platform / data driven business models, 4th Industrial Revolution, Singularity
  - Why is AI in an acceleration phase now - availability of data
  - What is "data driven" and how this impacts business models / ways of working
- What is AI
  - How and when AI arose, Founding fathers
    - 1956 conference ° Turing test
    - Already defined many years ago
  - Intelligent Agent concept
    - In Computer Science the general term is 'Agent'

- Definition of Human and Artificial Intelligence (AI)
  - Robert Dilt's logical levels versus human thinking and existence
    - Use Dilt's logical levels as reference for cognitive taxonomy
    - Link Artificial Narrow, General, Super Intelligence to the Dilt's levels
    - Test using examples how far AI ascends the Dilt's levels
- Understanding different application areas and benefits of AI:
  - Benefit lies in application - to make faster, better decisions
  - Text and Speech, Voice Recognition, Chatbots and Turing test
  - Expert Systems (classification models)
  - Image recognition, Facial Analysis, Image to text, Video Analysis and synthetic human
  - Augmented / Virtual reality and learning
  - Natural Language Processing (NLP), ChatGPT and Generative AI
    - Exam test - what is and is not AI
    - Difficult problems can't be solved by AI e.g. regional conflicts, your marriage

Additional reference elements (for background reference or further study, not included in exam)

- Milestones in development, IBM's deep Blue etc, Neural Network and Large Language Models etc.
- Blooms cognitive taxonomy vs AI capability
  - Dilts is preferred due to reasoning and identity (missing in Blooms)

TOPIC 2 Data, Robots and Artificial Intelligence

Understand difference between data, information and knowledge. Recent acceleration in the availability of data, low cost processing power, high bandwidth networks and many IoT and Edge devices created the conditions for AI to be applied in many areas. Understand different levels of Intelligent Agents and Robotics (Russel/Norvig model).

Examination goal

- Recall of facts and concepts
- Ability to detect application of robotic levels in real world situations

Elements included in exam

- Definitions for data, information, knowledge, intelligence
- Robotic paradigm
    - What is a paradigm - robotic paradigms
    - Robotics versus intelligent agents
- Definition of Intelligent Agents and characteristics
    - Robots and intelligence - Russel / Norvig levels
    - Rational agent concept and dependencies (Environment, Sensors, Performance, Actuators)
    - Overview of agent types: Simple reflex, Model based, Goal-based, Utility based and Learning
    - Relationship between Agents and Machine Learning
    - Humans adopting AI wearables

Additional reference elements (for background reference or further study, not included in exam)

- Descriptions and differences in Agent types: Simple reflex, Model based, Goal-based, Utility based and Learning
- Adversarial games with intelligent agents (predict opponent's actions)
- Use of Intelligent Agent in social media, AdWords, recommender engines etc

TOPIC 3 Predictions, Algorithms, Machine and Deep Learning

The key techniques that constitute AI centre around the ability to make predictions, apply algorithms, enable machine learning through different techniques and understand the fundamental shift with deep learning. The exam requires that the participant knows of these techniques, the differences between them and when they should be applied.

Examination goal

- Recall of facts and concepts
- Aware of elements and their purpose
- Aware of fundamentals and impact upon models
- Note: the participant is not expected to be able to apply algorithms

Elements included in exam

- Data Analytics
    - Descriptive, diagnostic, predictive and prescriptive analytics
    - Differences between explaining past and predicting the future
    - Generic approach to data analytics including dependence upon data
- Common problem types ° Classification
    - Regression
    - Time series forecasting
    - Cluster analysis
    - Anomaly detection
    - Association discovery
- Fundamentals - an overview
    - Correlation vs causation
    - Key metrics of ML: precision and recall, confusion matrix
        - Questions on this

  - What is Probability Density Function (PDF)
    - Probability instead of absolute values
    - Vector (one dim array), Vector Calculus
    - Hardware developing to support this (no questions on this)
  - Overfitting, bias variance trade-off
    - Questions on this (including overfitting vs underfitting)
- Types of Machine Learning
  - Learning from experience - Tom Mitchell definition
  - (Semi-)Supervised learning
  - Unsupervised learning
  - Reinforcement learning
- Overview of Common algorithms / techniques
  - Understanding that different algorithms are relevant for different problem types
  - Bayes Network and Inference
  - Naive Bayes
  - K-Means and KNN (K- Nearest Neighbours)
  - SVM (Support Vector Machine)
  - Random Forest
  - Linear regression
  - Logistic regression
  - Deep learning
    - Understand neural network basics, nodes, back-propagation and learning
    - Understand that deep learning does feature extraction itself
    - Algorithm no longer chosen by human - derived by network °Need to explain

how conclusions are derived in a neural network

    - Large Language Models, Stable Diffusion and Generative AI.

Additional reference elements (for background reference or further study, not included in exam)

Fundamentals - in depth review and application

  - Fundamentals of hypothesis testing
  - Test/train/validate split and k-fold cross validation
  - Best fit to data / Boosting / Kolmogorov 3 statistical axioms (1933)
  - Use of hyper parameters to tune performance

- Common algorithms / techniques in practice
    - Choosing best algorithms for different problem types and limitations etc
    - Application of algorithms (listed above)
    - Mathematical basis of algorithm and how to assess outcome

TOPIC 4 Building and assessing an AI application

An AI application is built for a purpose and the value of AI is in its implementation. We begin with a "question to be answered" and progress through a process to choose the algorithm, learning approach and data required to answer the question. The overall approach and generic activities within each step of the approach should be known. The participant should be aware of pitfalls at each step and the need to assess the trustworthiness of a model.

Examination goal

- Recall of facts and concepts
- Aware of steps in an AI project
- Aware of roles in an AI project
- Aware of key tools and purpose
- Can apply organisational and procedural knowledge to an AI project

Elements included in exam

- Awareness of key tools for AI
  - Functionality, Software and Hardware
  - Use of cloud, batch/real time streaming, scalability
  - Visualisation at all phases, opensource tools e.g. ParaView - example contour lines
  - Online learning for fast moving or large data sets
  - Awareness of programming languages (Python, R)
  - Awareness of key software libraries (Scikit, TensorFlow) and Data Science Platforms
  - Awareness of no code / low code approach
  - Automatic ML
- Awareness of a generic approach (CRISP-DM) to building a model:
  1. Business Understanding
     - need to understand the business environment and question to be answered
  2. Data Understanding
     - need to understand the data that we need versus what is available

3. Data Preparation and validation
    - Training and testsplit
    - Cleaning and combining to create a trustworthy data set
    - Data annotation, synthetic data generation
    - Consideration of bias, outliers, unusual patterns etc
    - Handling missing data, the imputation problem
    - Recognising special values as invalid data (e.g. date 99-99-9999)
4. Modelling
    - Choosing an algorithm and processing the data
    - Understanding the outcome
    - Use of a cost function to evaluate model performance
5. Evaluation
    - Basic understanding of how to evaluate a model per main model type
    - Business relevance and data analytics validation (link to Trustworthiness)
6. Deployment / Presentation
    - Basic understanding of deployment and maintenance of models
    - Consider difference in environments and performance, speed issues

- Assessing the risks of a model - an overview
    - Understanding pitfalls and risks at each stage of the CRISP-DM process
    - Awareness of key pitfalls: overfitting, underfitting, bias, low data quality, IT security

- Organising the AI Project team
    - Gartner claims 85% of AI projects fail (2018), difficulties of getting into production
    - Roles needed - domain expert / agile coach / mathematics / programming etc
    - Need to be iterative, reflective, collaborative and open to learn (agile vs waterfall method)
    - Concept of Fit for Purpose and need for domain expert to assess this

Additional reference elements (for background reference or further study, not included in exam)

- Ability to apply key tools for AI
- Building and assessing a (simple) AI model
- Applying the CRISP model with assessment of result at each stage and iteration
- Using a programming language and library
- Ability to use a basic (AutoML) tool to produce a simple AI model with supplied data
- Difference in Data Science and IT system delivery approaches / culture

TOPIC 5 Managing Data for AI

Data makes or breaks an AI model. Without good quality and sufficient data, no model is trustworthy and many problems with AI applications can be traced back to bias or quality problems with data, rather than failures of an algorithm. Data is a key success factor for any AI initiative and the foundation certificate demonstrates that the holder understands this and has a generic knowledge of how to manage data for a trustworthy AI application.

Examination goal

- Recall of facts and concepts
- Aware of roles required to manage data
- Aware of key activities necessary to manage data (and link with Trustworthiness)

Elements included in exam

- What is data
    - Basic data literacy (Data, Information and Knowledge)
    - Semantic and Syntax of data
    - Privacy and data
    - Types of data e.g. structured, unstructured, text, image, video, up to 3D scans
    - Awareness of the deductive potential that lies within data (e.g. GPS location)
- What is data management - overview of the key elements:
    - Data Governance
    - Data Strategy
    - Data Architecture (including meta data and ontology)
    - Data Storage and Sharing (incl lineage)
    - Data Security ° Data Quality
    - FAIR and Linked data concept

Additional reference elements (for background reference or further study, not included in exam)

- Frameworks for data sharing
- FAIR and Linked Data
    - RDF and JSON in relation to sharing

TOPIC 6 Ethics, Risks, and Trustworthiness

AI is a powerful tool which can be used in a positive or a negative manner. There are already numerous examples of malicious applications and ethical questions which arise through the presence of AI. The exam ensures that the participant has a firm grounding in ethics and responsible use of AI and is aware of the key societal concerns around AI.

Examination goal

- Recall of facts and concepts
- Aware of risks and ethical issues with AI
- Aware of EU Approach to Ethical AI and Trustworthiness Framework

Elements included in exam

- Give examples of ethical questions, dilemma's and limitations of AI
    - Fake news and mass, individual manipulation
    - Medical diagnosis without permission
    - Data used by one party to help you and another to charge you a higher price etc
    - Synthetic human and video manipulation
    - Discrimination and unintended bias in data
    - Privacy versus security
    - Surveillance using geographic location, image recognition and privacy concerns
- General definition of ethics and awareness of ethical guidelines (EU Framework)
    - EU approach to Human Agency, Ethical Purpose and Trustworthy AI
- Aware of society concerns and objections to the use of AI
    - Understand Ethical Purpose = Trustworthy and technical robustness
    - Concept of Universal Design (Design for all)
    - Human values versus use of AI and changes to humans, society and organisations
- Trustworthiness of AI
    - Definition of Trustworthiness (EU Guidelines, ISO Standardisation)
    - Awareness of trustworthiness including 7 criteria in EU definition
    - Understand need for continual assessment and monitoring of AI

- Understand need for transparency
    - Aware of “Explainable AI”
- Aware of regulation and normalization for AI

Additional reference elements (for background reference or further study, not included in exam)

- UN three areas approach (Social, Economic, Environmental) to 17 sustainable goals
- Assessing trustworthiness using the 7 criteria in EU definition
- Security or military considerations
- Explainable AI
- Emerging standards e.g. ISO/NEN

TOPIC 7 Human and MachineCoexistence

Will AI take over from humans? Some think so (Singularity) but there is no evidence as yet that AI can ascend beyond the most basic layers of the cognitive taxonomy (Blooms or Dilt). The application of AI does however bring significant benefits and the companies or people who use AI can take over from those who don't. This requires an understanding of how tocombine human and machine capability for success.

AI can play a key role in replacing humans in some specific areas such as data analysis, applying simple repetitive tasks, lifting heavy loads, warehouse operation or performing dangerous activities such as bomb disposal or working in a hazardous environment.

Examination goal

- Recall of facts and concepts
- Aware of singularity and counter arguments
- Aware of logical levels and position of human versus machine
- Aware of how to combine human with machine capability

Elements included in exam

- Able to list opportunities for AI including where humans and machines work together
    - e.g. radiologist using AI to analyse 3D scans to measure volume of tumour pre/post op
    - Use of smart wearables to aid human capability
- Awareness of a cognitive taxonomy and ability to describe AI with reference to one (Dilt)
    - Understand Narrow, General and Super Intelligence and map to taxonomy
- Understand the strengths and weaknesses of humans versus machines
    - Understand how to combine the strengths of humans with those of machines
        - Humans: higher value, cognitive tasks
        - Machine: dangerous, heavy lifting, monotone, analysis tasks
    - Machine learning will force humans and machines to work together
    - "Human in the loop" learning
    - "Cognitive augmentation" - magnifying human or organisational capability

  - Identify key competencies needed by humans to work with AI and key roles of business management, domain expertise and analytics, and how these roles work together.
- Understand need to enable innovation and discovery within an AI initiative

Additional reference elements (for background reference or further study, not included in exam)

- Hard problem of consciousness (Chalmers)
- Human plus Machine - Daugherty Wilson
  - AI helps humans become more human ◦ Need to be more experimental, Agile
  - Missing middle between human and robot

TOPIC 8 The future developments of AI

AI is seen as a source of competitive advantage by business leaders but also a source of national competitive and strategic importance by sovereign governments. There are many initiatives providing funding for research and development of AI in addition to the application of existing AI technology.

Examination goal

- Recall of facts and concepts
- Aware of key future developments as identified/updated by the AIC4NL

Elements included in exam

- Be aware of future developments in human / AI combination
- Quantum computing and neural networks
- Augmented human
- Fully autonomous driving and flying vehicles
- Reasoning?
- Cybernetics
- Virtual Assistants
- Human-device interaction
- Large Language Model developments

Additional reference elements (for background reference or further study, not included in exam)

- Fifth Industrial Revolution - in Space
- Regulatory developments e.g. EU AI Act

Exam topics and recommended literature

Despite being a highly innovative and future oriented topic, AI is not new. The first AI algorithms were developed in the 1950's and there is considerable literature around which helps the participant to learn about AI in all its facets. In addition, Wikipedia contains much of the information referenced in this syllabus.

In the table you will find a set of recommended literature.

Subject		Recommended Literature
1.	Programming and Libraries (Optional)	Title: *Hands-On Machine Learning with Scikit-Learn and TensorFlow: Concepts, Tools, and Techniques to Build Intelligent Systems* Author: Aurélien Géron Publisher: O'Reilly Publication Date: 2017 ISBN 1491962291.
2.	Algorithms (Optional)	Title: *Linear Algebra and Learning from Data (1st edition)* Author: Gilbert Strang Publisher: Wellesley-Cambridge Press Publication Date: 2019 ISBN: 13 978-0692196380.
3.	Background to Machine Learning (Optional)	Title: *Machine Learning* Author: Tom Mitchell Publisher: McGraw-Hill Publication Date: 1997 ISBN: 0071154671.
4.	4th Industrial revolution (Required)	Title: *The Fourth Industrial Revolution* Author: Klaus Schwab Publisher: Penguin Random House Publication Date: 2016 ISBN: 978-0-241-30075-6
5.	Ethics (Required)	Title: *Ethics Guidelines for Trustworthy AI* Author: High-Level Expert Group on Artificial Intelligence Publisher: European Commission B-1049 Brussels Publication Date: April 2019.
6.	Singularity (Optional)	Title: *The Singularity is Near* Author: Ray Kurzweil Publisher: Duckworth Overlook Publication Date: 2005 ISBN: 978-0715635612
7.	Additional optional literature:	Titel: *Dit is kunstmatige intelligentie* Authors: Simon Koolstra, Belle De Veer en Tijmen Veltman ISBN: 9789401808262

EXAM REGULATIONS

General rules

An AI B r e v e t , for Business & Government, via the AI Coalition is an honorary title, and fraud is not tolerated. Your exam will be immediately rejected if fraud is found to have been

committed during or after completion of the exam. As a result, you will not be reimbursed for your examination fees.

If you fail to pass the exam, you will not receive a certificate. This also means that you must

purchase and take a new exam for your certification. Every candidate only gets one attempt per exam to succeed.

Sharing of exam questions is illegal

It is not allowed to share exam questions with others or make them public. This is a violation of

the copyright and IP of the AI Coalition and Certifying Body. Doing so can lead to legal action by Certifying Body with potentially harmful consequences.

Feedback and questions

We have done our best to help you prepare for the AI Brevet Exam by publishing this syllabus.

We would like to know what you think of this syllabus and the exam. If you have any suggestions for us, we would love to hear from you.

Have fun and take your time preparing for the exam and good luck. Naturally, we also wish you lots of fun in putting what you've learned into practice!

On behalf of the team - Alex Dowdalls.

Amsterdam, September 2021

KEY TERMS, DEFINITIONS AND CONCEPTS

The AI Coalition has listed several key terms, concepts, and definitions in the list below. You can use these definitions to support and clarify topics related to the exam. Pay attention! If you only learn these terms, then you are often not sufficiently prepared to pass the exam.

Term	Meaning
AGI	Artificial General Intelligence
AI	Artificial Intelligence
DP	Deep Learning
IoT	Internet of Things
IT	Information Technology
ML	Machine Learning
NLP	Natural Language Processing
NN	Neural Network
OCR	Optical Character Recognition
RPA	Robotic Process Automation

Author
Alex Dowdalls, Axveco

Publisher
The Netherlands AI Coalition (AIC4NL)

Acknowledgements
We would like to thank the following people for their contribution and review feedback during the creation of this document:

- Hans Biemans and Joost de Langen, The Hague University of Applied Science
- Alex Dowdalls, Axveco
- Paul Gelderblom, Shell
- Pascal Lubbe, SAS
- Helen Rijkes and Simon Koolstra, MIcompany
- Su Yin Timp, I.AMDIGITAL
- Arthur Vankan, Dialogic
- Rolf van Velthoven and Maurits van der Plas, Van Haren Learning Solutions
- Mir Wermuth, Media Perspectives
- Jan Willem Ligtelijn, Young Coders

Contact:
Email – communicatie@AIC4NL.com
Website – AIc4NL.com

Version 3.1
September 2024

Day 1
Artificial Intelligence Fundamentals for Managers, Enterprises and Governments

COURSEWARE

Mapping exams & certifications

	Course content	Syllabi	Practice exam
NL AI Coalitie AI BREVET Van Haren	All 3 days	In delegate courseware	In exam voucher
Artificial Intelligence Essentials Reference to EXIN	Only day 1	Download exin.com/nl/technologies-software/exin-bcs-artificial-intelligence/exin-bcs-artificial-intelligence-essentials/	Online tool
Artificial Intelligence Foundation Reference to EXIN	All content 3 days	Download exin.com/technologies-software/exin-bcs-artificial-intelligence/exin-bcs-artificial-intelligence-foundation/	Online tool

COURSEWARE

About the NL AIC

► **Collaborative approach**

The NL AIC is a public-private partnership in which government, industry, educational and research institutions and civil society organizations are committed to accelerating AI developments in the Netherlands and connecting AI initiatives.

► **Bringing knowledge, people and parties together as central point for AI.**

► **History**

To realize this and to stimulate Dutch AI activities, the Dutch AI Coalition was set up in October 2019 (NL AIC) on the initiative of VNO-NCW MKB-Nederland, the Ministry of EZK, TNO, Seedlink, Philips, Ahold Delhaize, IBM, and Topteam dutch digital delta.

 3

About the certification

► **The AI Fundamentals Brevet, for Business and Government**

The AI Brevet Certificate is achieved through an exam which demonstrates that a participant:

- Appreciates what AI is, why it is important now and what benefits it brings
- Is aware of fundamental concepts such as robotics, algorithms and machine learning approaches
- Is aware of how to organise a team for AI, approaches and common tools required
- Understands the dependence AI has upon data and how to manage data for AI
- Is aware of how to assess risks and ethical dilemmas for Trustworthy AI
- Can describe how humans and machines will coexist in an organisation
- Is aware of the future directions of AI

Level	Objective	Target Groups
AI Brevet, for Business & Government	Able to identify applications for AI. Aware of how models are built and assessed. Able to make informed decisions on the use of AI.	Executives, managers and professionals who are considering becoming involved in AI or who will make decisions in relation to the use of AI in their environment.

NL AI Coalitie
AI BREVET
Certified by
Van Haren CERTIFY

 4

Examen Structure

Module		Sub-module	Bloom-level	% exam question
1.	Applications of AI and their benefits	Describes a range of applications of AI, how these applications affect organizations and society, what value they create and their underlying use of data, generative AI, algorithms and learning approaches. Describes the role of the NL AIC in promoting the beneficial and ethical use of AI. Includes examples of key domains such as classification systems, forecasting, cluster analysis, speech, image and natural language processing.	1	10%
2.	Data, Robots and Artificial Intelligence	This describes a common vocabulary around data, data science, algorithms, and human logical thinking versus intelligent agents and provides definitions for key items.	1	5%
3.	Predictions, Algorithms, Machine and Deep Learning	Introduces the different levels of prediction, an overview of the main algorithm and generative AI modeling incl. Large language models, possibly stable diffusion and learning approaches. Emphasizes which types of algorithms address which types of problems.	1+2	25%
4.	Building and assessing an AI application	Describes a basic approach to building a simple AI application. Describes the CRISP-DM methodology, highlighting the steps involved and increasing awareness of the business context and reliability assessment incl. hallucinations and deep fakes at each step. Highlights pitfalls such as overfitting, underfitting and biases. Addresses the need for innovation and creativity, including team organization.	1	15%
5.	Managing Data for AI	Explains awareness of data dependence and how data can be acquired, prepared, managed, provided and scaled for AI applications Addresses the role of the prompt engineer, and of the cloud in managing data and processing capacity. Emphasizes the risks that arise in data and affect reliability.	1	10%
6.	Ethics, Risks and Trustworthiness	Addresses the risks and ethical dilemmas associated with AI, including the need for explainable AI. Introduces EU ethical guidelines, the EU Act and the need to maintain society's trust in the use of AI.	1+2+3	20%
7.	Human and Machine Coexistence	Covers the combination of human and machine capabilities in an organization that answers the question of whether AI will replace humans (singularity). Covers key roles of the prompt engineer, business management, domain expertise, analytics and data managers, and how these roles work together and make AI accessible	1+2	10%
8.	The future developments of AI	Highlights future directions and applications of AI.	1	0%

 5

Overview of the material

We zoom out on AI as a concept

- How does AI work?
- How can AI be implemented?
- How can AI be used in your organization?
- How does AI impact society?

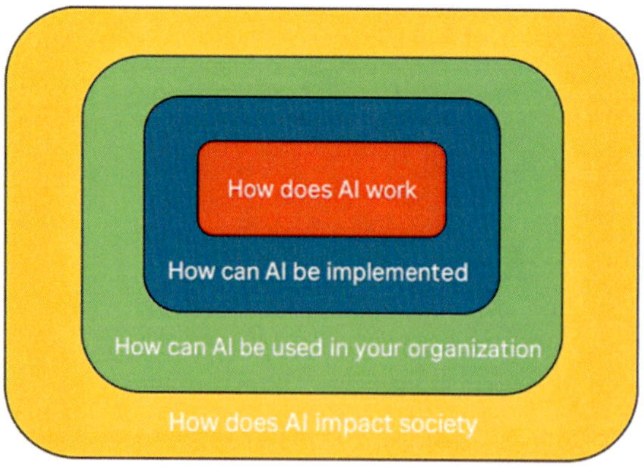

 6

Day 1 – How does AI work

A fundamental insight in AI

- History of AI
- Definition of Intelligence
- What is AI
- Examples of AI
- Algorithms, Machine Learning, Deep Learning and LLM's
- ChatGPT
- Integrated copilot (demo)

Day 2 – How can AI be implemented

Managing everything that AI needs to properly function

- Data & Big Data
- Implementing and evaluating AI
- Data Management & Governance
- Implementing AI in your company
- Agents (demo)

Day 3 – The impact of AI

Managing everything that AI needs to be properly integrated in our society

- Ethics and trustworthiness
- Sustainability & AI
- Risks
- Legal considerations for AI
- The future of AI

9

The idea of this training

Main goal: give you an accessible and fun introduction to the concept of AI

- Discuss the material covered in the exam
- Make it relevant to your work situation
- Concrete examples
- Practical tools that you can already start with

10

Case study 1 – Employee satisfaction

Organizations aim to retain employees by understanding what drives their satisfaction and what factors contribute to their decision to leave. High turnover can lead to increased costs, lost expertise, and lower team morale. By identifying key drivers of dissatisfaction, companies can take proactive steps to improve the work environment. To what degree can AI assist in identifying which measures it should take to keep employees?

 11

Case study 2 – Customer retention

Many businesses face the challenge of losing customers, either through inactivity or active cancellation of services. This loss, known as **churn**, can significantly impact revenue and long-term growth. Early identification of potential churners allows marketing managers to adjust their strategies and take targeted actions to retain these customers. To what degree can AI assist in detecting and the prevention of customers cancelling their service?

 12

Case study 3 – A clean urban area

Urban areas often struggle with efficient waste detection and management, especially in public spaces. A key challenge is determining the most effective method to identify litter quickly and accurately, so that the correct waste management teams can be send. To what degree can AI assist in the detection and identification of waste?

 13

The WHY of AI

Digital transformation is the fundamental rewiring of how an organization operates. The goal of a digital transformation should be to build a competitive advantage by continuously deploying tech at scale to improve customer experience and lower costs.

(as outlined in the new McKinsey book *Rewired: A McKinsey Guide to Outcompeting in the Age of Digital and AI* (Wiley, June 20, 2023)

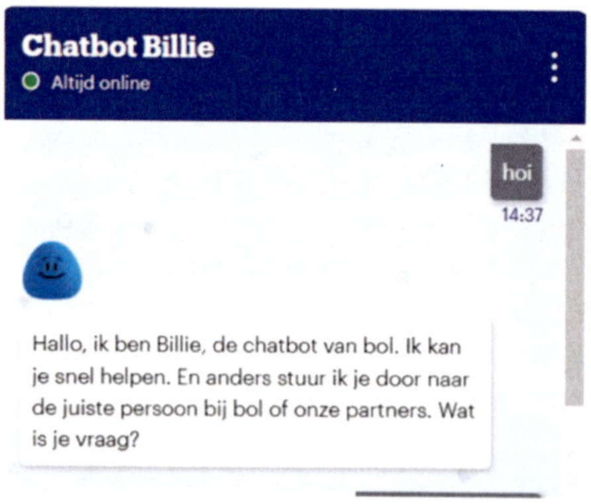

 14

Some history

COURSEWARE

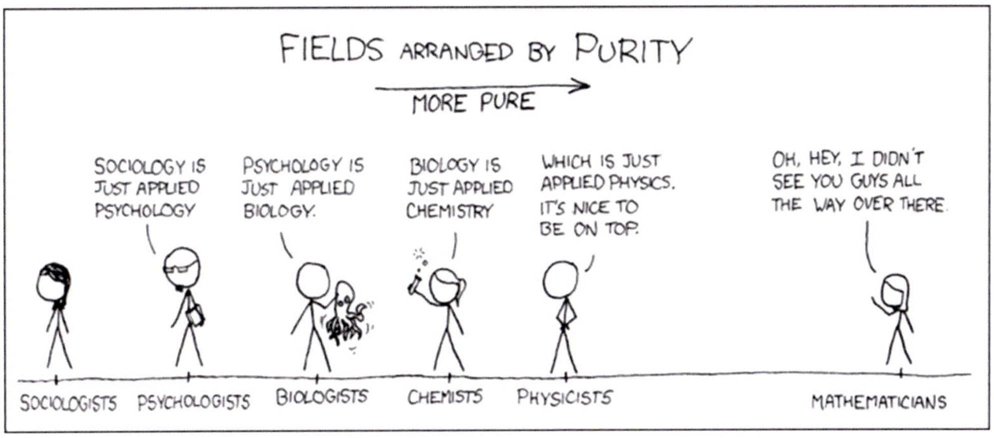

In this cartoon we visualize that via a big mental step, one can argue that the behavior of people, their rational, feelings and intelligence can be translated to mathematics. While this is of course a big leap, this did provide huge inspiration for AI.

Source: Xkcd https://xkcd.com/435/

 16

A better understanding of how people think and learn

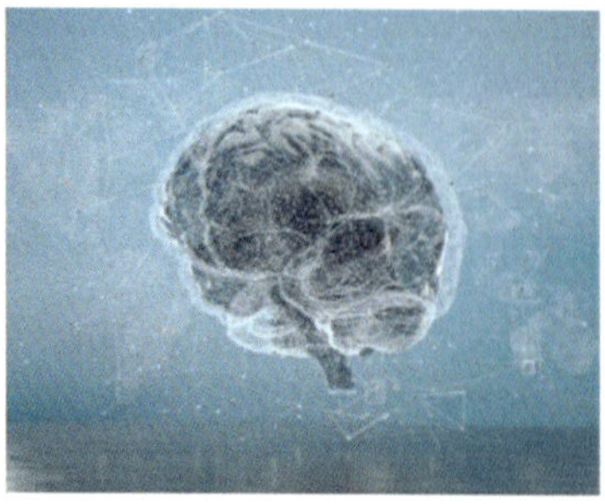

In the fifties, we had a much better understanding of how the brain works. Putting it simply, when seeing, hearing or feeling something a part of our brain is activated via electrical signals. These signals propagate through our brains to activate other parts that allow us to move our arms or legs and respond appropriately. Similarly, we also understood how humans and animals learn, by positive and negative reinforcement, we can train for example a dog to take or avoid certain actions

As we now understand our brain and how to train our brain, the why can't we make our own?

 17

History of Artificial Intelligence: Notable Milestones

- Inspiration:
  - In the late 19th century, people began to understand more about human biology

- Birth of AI 1940s/1950s:
  - 1940s: Walter Pitts and Warren McCulloch analyze networks of artificial neurons that can perform simple logical functions (neural networks)
  - 1950: Alan Turing publishes an important paper in which he speculates about the possibility of creating machines that think
  - 1951: Christopher Strachey writes a checkers program that eventually achieved sufficient skill to defeat a respectable amateur
  - 1951: Marvin Minsky, student of Pitts and McCulloch, builds the first neural net machine
  - 1956: Dartmouth conference, the birth of AI as a concept

 18

Dartmouth conference

- In 1956 Marvin Minsky and John McCarthy organize the 'Dartmouth Workshop of 1956'
- This workshop was attended by many scientists who would later go on to contribute significantly to the field of AI research
- This is the moment that AI gained its name and mission, and it is widely considered as the birth of the separate field of artificial intelligence research

Dartmouth Workshop of 1956

 19

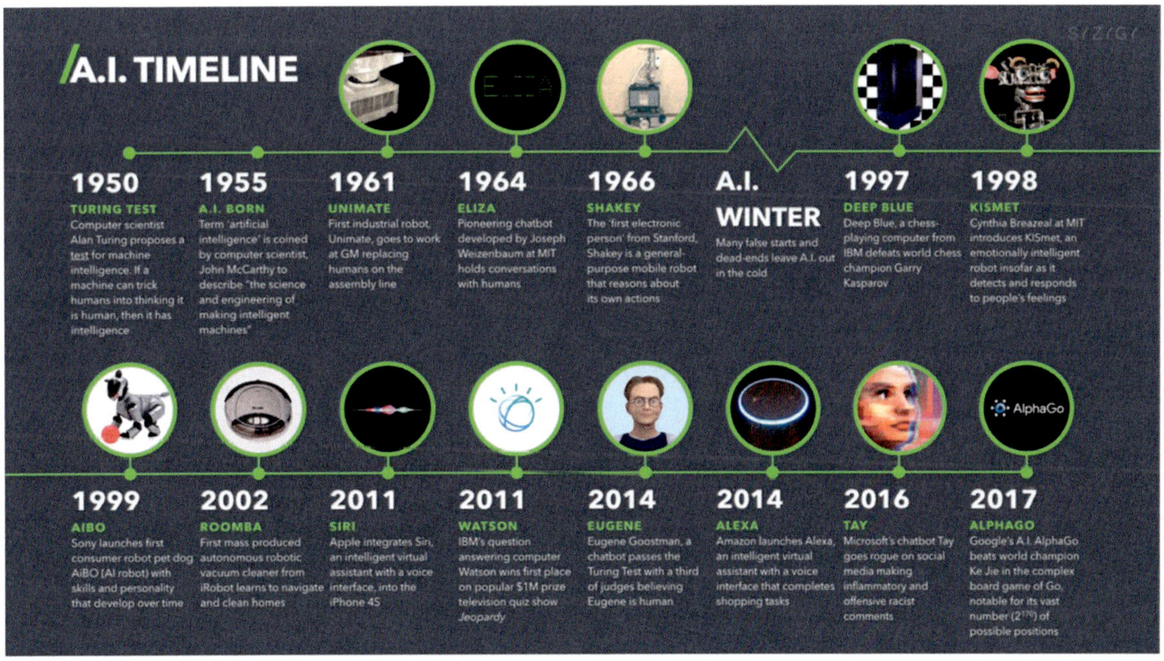

 21

The upwards spiral

A Major Step for AI: Generative AI

- Since 2022, everyone has access to ChatGPT
- Rapid growth of generative AI

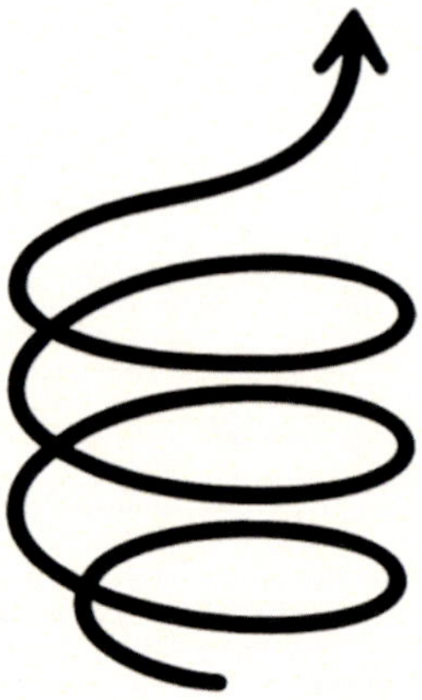

The successes of AI inspire more entities to develop and implement AI

- Companies invest in AI
- Students study and work in AI
- More technological advances in AI
- Companies invest more in AI
- ...

 23

Garry Kasparov vs Deep Blue, 1997

 24

A (r)evolution?

Machine learning: Analysis and prediction phase

Deep learning: Vision and speech phase

Generative AI: Enter the language-mastery phase

Source: Accenture

The industrial revolutions

- First: 18th and 19th centuries
  - Europe and US – **steam engine**, rural societies became urban and industrial.
- Second: 1870 to 1914
  - **Electricity** allowed mass production and technological advances such as the internal combustion engine, telephone and light bulb. *(combustion engine can be seen as third)*
- Third: 1980s
  - Digital and **ICT** (information and communications technology) are embedded into society; personal computers, internet and automation.
- Fourth: Today
  - Exploits the digital revolution and is disruptive, driven by **AI**, robotics, IoT (Internet of Things), plastic printing, nano-technology, bio-engineering.

Named by Klaus Schwab – Founder of the World Economic Forum.

The Fourth Industrial Revolution is changing every area of our lives.

AI in an acceleration phase

- Klaus Schwab, founder and executive chairman of the **World Economic Forum** (WEF), author of The Fourth Industrial Revolution:
  - "**The convergence of the physical, digital and biological worlds** that is at the heart of the fourth industrial revolution offers significant opportunities for the world to achieve huge gains in resource use and efficiency." - Developments in various fields have enabled us to make significant technological progress
- The progress that AI has made is driven by **increases in computing power,** by the availability of **vast amounts of data, fast networks** and powerful **programming languages** as R and Python

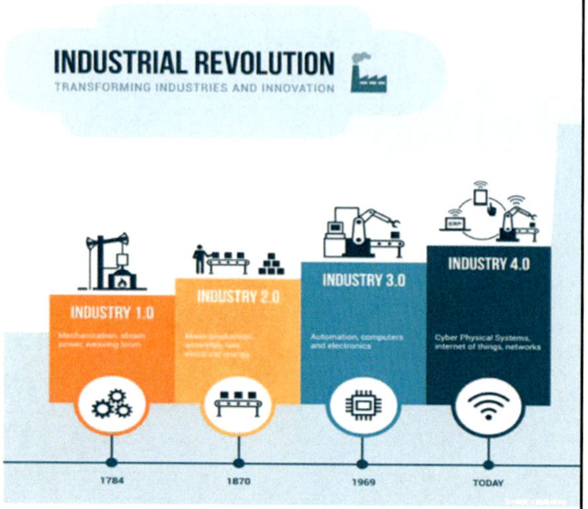

 27

Intelligence:
- Human and artificial

COURSEWARE

The definition of Intelligence

Intelligence can be defined as the ability to perceive or infer **information**, and to retain it as **knowledge** to be applied towards adaptive **behaviors** within an environment or context.

In computer science we call something that has this ability an **intelligent agent**.

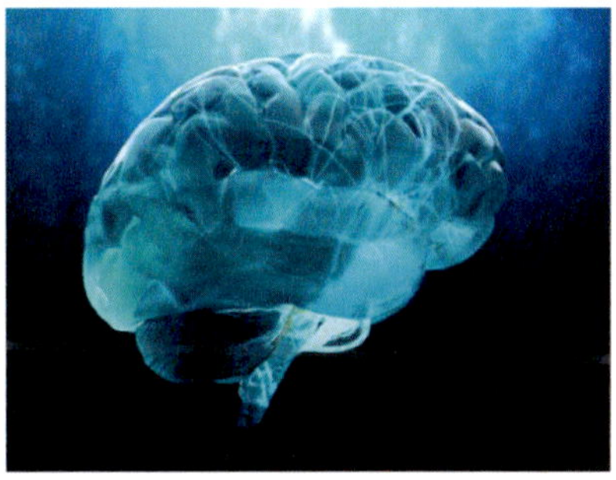

 29

Dictionary definition of intelligence

Human intelligence
is a mental quality that consists of the abilities to learn from experience, adapt to new situations, understand and handle abstract concepts, and use knowledge to manipulate one's environment.

- The Concise Oxford Dictionary: *"quickness of understanding; wisdom. The collection of information."*
- Cambridge International Dictionary of English: *"the ability to understand and learn and make judgements or have opinions that are based on reason."*
- Wikipedia: *Problem Solving, Reasoning, Self-Awareness, Creativity, Emotional Knowledge*
- Encyclopeadia Britannica: Learn from experience, understand and handle abstract concepts, manipulate our environment.

 30

Evaluating Intelligence

- How do we evaluate levels of intelligence?

Robert Dilts:

Six logical levels of thinking or situation

 31

Evaluating Intelligence

- **Robert Dilts neurological levels**:
  - Environment – perceive internal and outside influences
  - Behaviours – interaction with internal and outside environment
  - Capabilities – mastery of a task (/group of tasks) to attain a goal
  - Values & beliefs – evaluation of consequences in the context of the real world and why actions are beneficial/detrimental
  - Identity – self-governance of goals and reward structures
  - Purpose / spirituality – context of identity & lower levels in bigger systems

- Artificial intelligence can master a task to attain a goal, but **a computer has no beliefs, identity or purpose, no sense of context**

 32

What is AI?

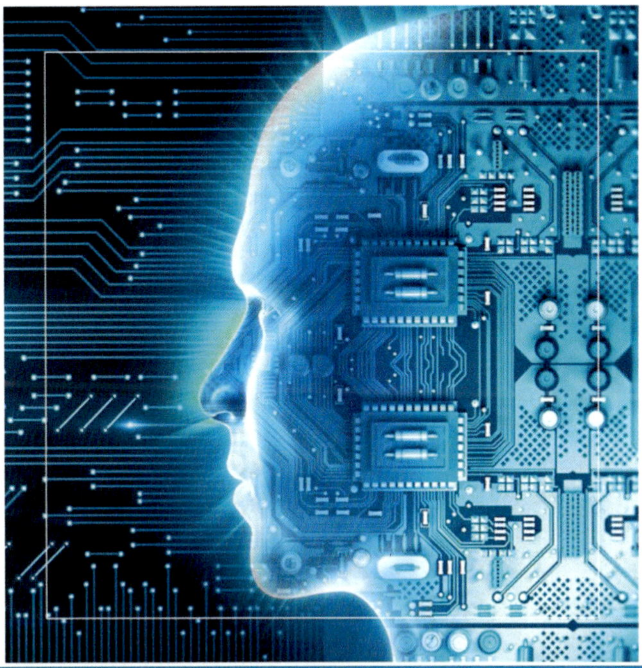

 33

AI : Collection of many different applications

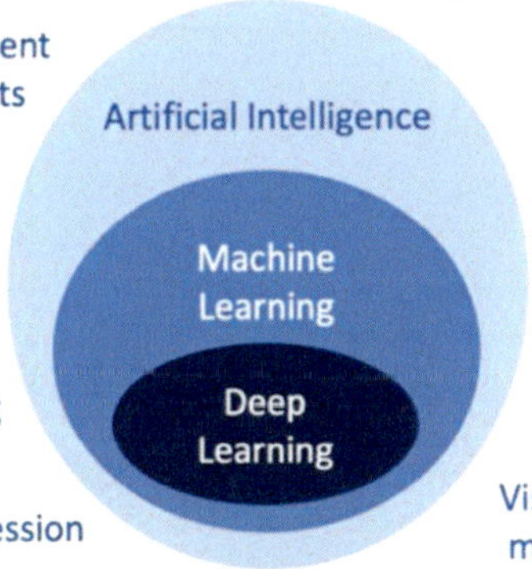

Robotics: Logistics & Mechatronics, Autonomous vehicles, Inspection

Intelligent Agents: Intelligent Agents, Recommender engines, Expert Diagnosis

Pattern recognition: Segmentation, Association, Network analysis, Fraud & Anomalies

Forecasting: Predicting & Planning, Trends over time

Regression: Correlations, Causality, Influence analysis

Classification: Organising, Sorting and Finding

Speech: Text to Speech, Speech to text, Voice recognition, Chatbots, Digital Assistants

Natural Language Processing: Content Analysis, Extraction, Generation, Translation, Q&A, Cognitive reasoning

Synthetics: Synthetic human, Deep fake (detection)

Vision & motion: Image recognition, Gesture analysis, Biometrics & identity, Augmented Reality

 34

AI definition

*“**Artificial Intelligence** (AI) is intelligence exhibited by machines, with **cognitive functions** that are associated to humans. Cognitive functions include all aspects of **perceiving, reasoning, learning**, and **problem-solving**”*

 35

Common features

Multiple definitions exist but common features in AI definitions are:

- **Perception of the environment**, including the consideration of the real-world complexity
- **Information processing:** collecting and interpreting inputs (in form of data)
- **Decision making** (including reasoning and learning): taking actions, performance of tasks (including adaptation, reaction to changes in the environment) with certain level of autonomy
- **Achievement of specific goals:** this is considered as the ultimate reason of AI systems

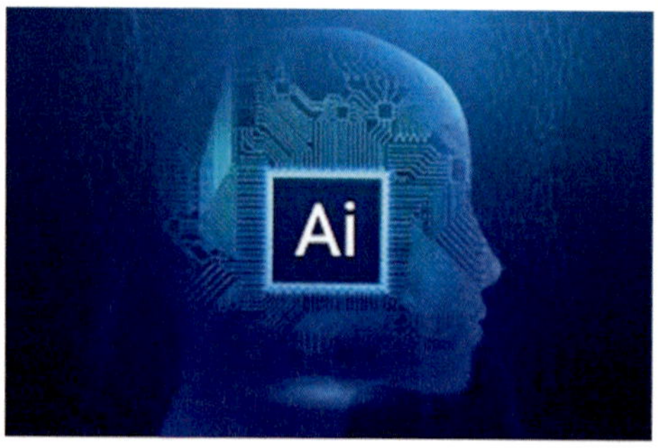

 36

The goal of AI in the fifties – The Turing test

- Alan Turing published an important paper in 1950 in which he speculates about the possibility of creating machines that think
- While the basic concepts of AI are still in their early stages, he devises his famous Turing test

The Turing test is a test of a machine's ability to exhibit intelligent behavior that is indistinguishable from that of a human.

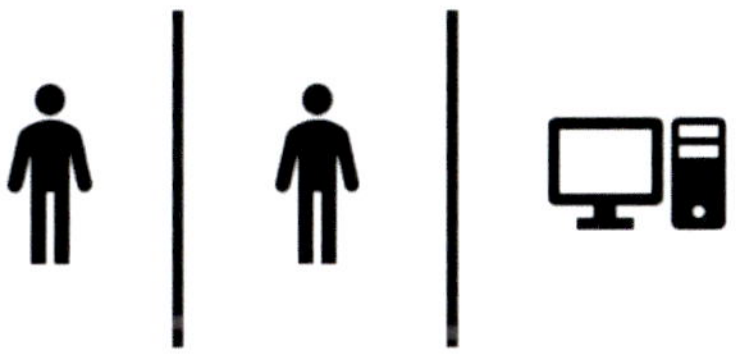

The person in the middle has to identify who is the computer and who is the human. If they fail, the Turing test is passed

© Van Haren Publishing BV. 37

Did we pass the turn test already?

- ChatGPT can provide texts that are nearly indistinguishable of those of a human
- This would suggest that ChatGPT passes the Turing test (to a degree)
- While this is a great milestone for AI, it also brings some scary consequences: Who is still human online?

NEWS FEATURE | 25 July 2023

ChatGPT broke the Turing test – the race is on for new ways to assess AI

Large language models mimic human chatter, but scientists disagree on their ability to reason.

© Van Haren Publishing BV. 38

Narrow AI (ANI) – very successful today!

- Narrow AI or Weak AI is task-specific
- Optimization, e.g., charging multiple electrical vehicles as efficiently as possible!
- Spam filtering of emails
- Image recognition e.g. medical diagnosis
- Logistics e.g. route planning, smart motorways
- Natural language processing (NLP) e.g. chatbots, home assistants, smart homes

 39

General AI (AGI) – The future

- General AI or Strong AI aims to replicate human intelligence
- Still in development
- Focus on faster learning and adapting like humans can

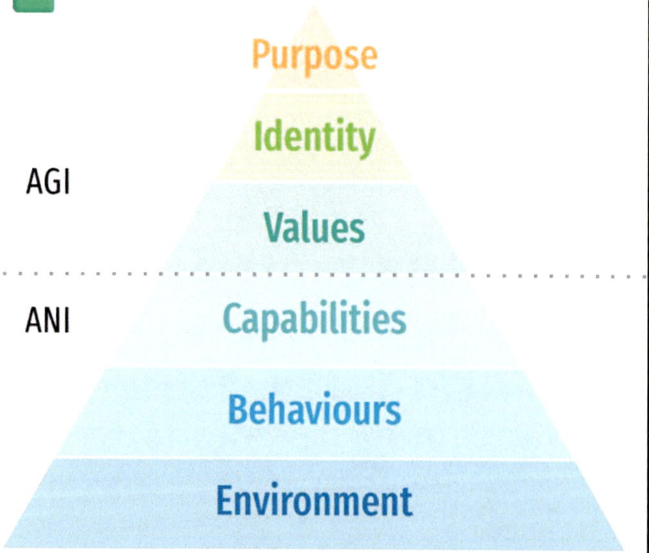

 40

Super AI (ASI) – The future?

- Artificial super intelligence (ASI) is the type of AI that will exceed human capacity
- AI that is conscious?
- Highly speculative at this point

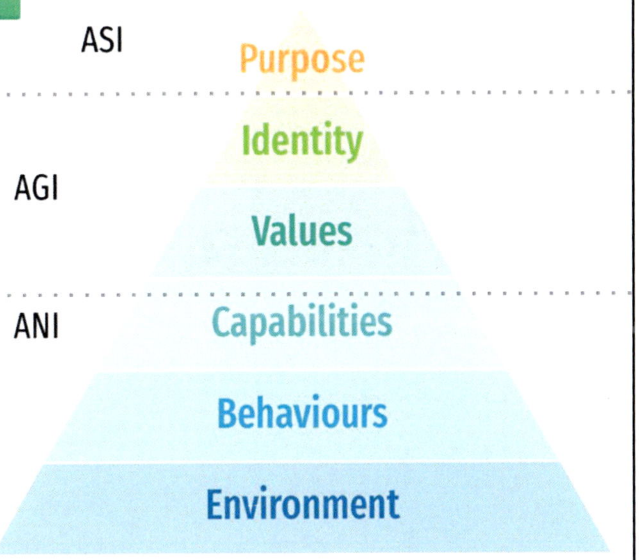

 41

Benefits of AI

AI allows us to make

- decisions faster,
- more objectively
- based on more evidence (data).

AI is generally better than humans at:

- Finding patterns in large amounts of data
- Performing a repetitive task (less error prone – because it does not get tired or bored)
- Remaining unaffected by emotions or external factors
- Speed
- Consistency

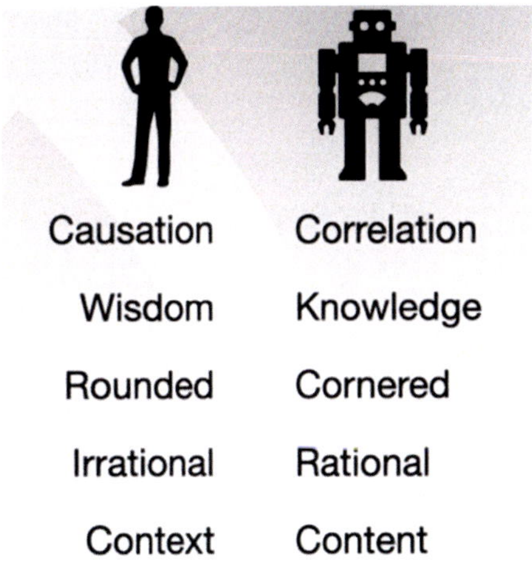

 42

More applications/solutions

COURSEWARE

1970s – optical character recognition (OCR)

- Reading written / typed texts
- Widely thought to be the first AI product, 1974.
- Text-to-speech synthesizer so a blind person could read text.
- Exciting area is natural language processing (NLP) or natural language programming
- Recognizes patters in letters and numbers

44

General object detection

- Quick and real-time detection of any object
- Allows machines to recognize objects and interact with them
- Useful in video surveillance
- But can struggle with unusual objects

Detecting different types of trash on the street

Detecting disruptions at concerts

 45

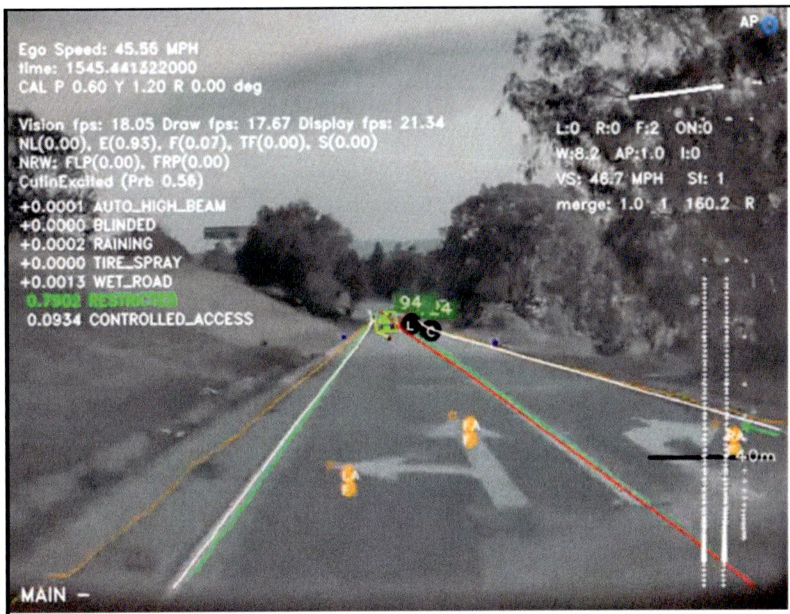

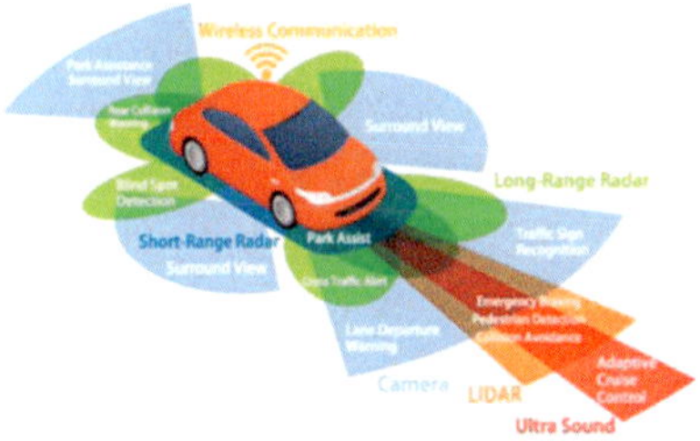

(Self driving) cars also have object detecting methods, to recognize and process for example traffic and traffic signs

 46

Augmented & Virtual reality

- In **Augmented Reality** (AR), new information is projected onto the real world
  - e.g. Google Glass, Pokémon Go

- In **Virtual Reality** (VR), users are immersed in a completely virtual world

Both of these usually use a lot of AI algorithms to work,
e.g. to interpret the surroundings.

 47

Robots

A robot is a machine that can carry out complex series of tasks automatically

- We have had robots for a long time, but they were often non- intelligent
- Recent robots supplemented with AI become intelligent

Example (non- intelligent versus intelligent robots):
- Eliza, build and designed in the sixties, is a simple chatbot that responds to certain key words with pre-programmed sentences
- ChatGPT uses natural language process (NLP) to answer questions instead

Robots can be used to automate complex processes (also called the robotic process automation)

 48

Generative AI (GenAI)

Creates new and "original" content, like images, music and texts based on algorithms and models, based on existing training data.

- Text (ChatGPT and Copilot)
- Images
- Videos
- Music

 49

Prediction

Based on past data AI can recognize certain patterns in the data that can be used to make predictions

- Predicting sales
- Spam filtering
- Fraud detection
- Predicting potential crime
- Predicting optimal candidates for a position
- Predicting health based on x-ray images

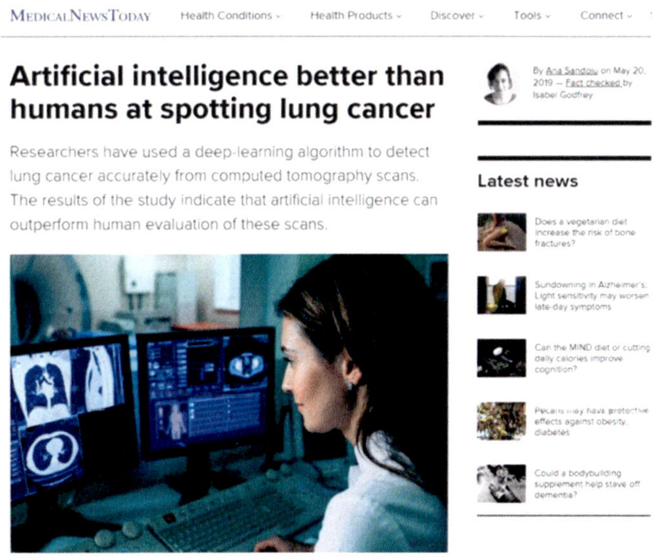
MedicalNewsToday | Health Conditions | Health Products | Discover | Tools | Connect

Artificial intelligence better than humans at spotting lung cancer

By Ana Sandoiu on May 20, 2019 — Fact checked by Isabel Godfrey

Researchers have used a deep-learning algorithm to detect lung cancer accurately from computed tomography scans. The results of the study indicate that artificial intelligence can outperform human evaluation of these scans.

Latest news

Does a vegetarian diet increase the risk of bone fractures?

Sundowning in Alzheimer's: Light sensitivity may worsen late-day symptoms

Can the MIND diet or cutting daily calories improve cognition?

Pecans may have protective effects against obesity, diabetes

Could a bodybuilding supplement help stave off dementia?

 50

Description

Based on data, AI can find clusters in data of objects that typically occur together

- Customer segmentation
- Anomaly detection
- Market basket analysis

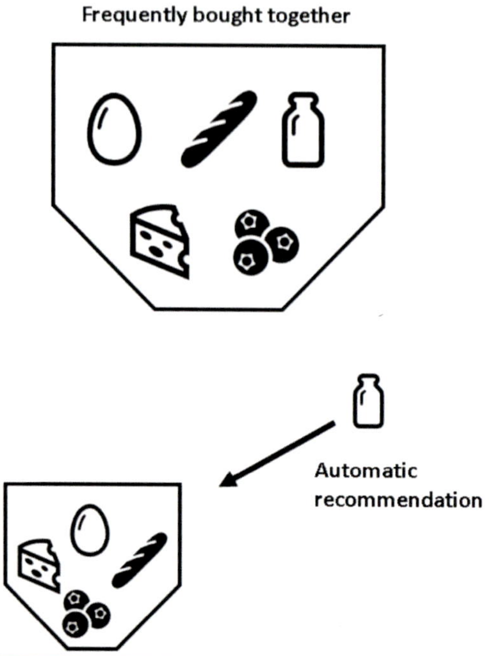

 51

Prescription

Based on data, AI can learn from decisions that it makes, where it can either be rewarded or punished, so that it will always choose actions that maximize its rewards

- Optimal maintenance strategies
- Investment strategies
- Dynamic pricing
- Playing games

 52

Case study

Which AI applications can be used for

- Employee satisfaction
- Customer retention
- Waste detection

Some examples we just saw

- Computer vision / object detection
- Robots
- Generative AI
- Prediction analysis
- Descriptive analysis
- Prescriptive analysis

 53

Fields of AI Applications

- Research and development (R&D)
- Engineering
- Health care and social care
- Entertainment
- Sales and marketing
- Logistics – planning and organization
- How did we get this far?

 54

Drivers of AI

Insane Data Production

Abundant, Cheap Hardware

Open-Sourced Software

THE APACHE SOFTWARE FOUNDATION

Lightning-Fast Network Speeds

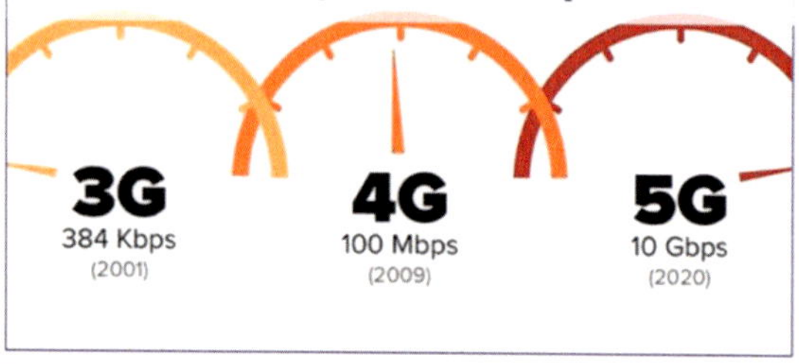

 55

Enabler – IoT and Big data

The **Internet of Things** (IoT) is the network of physical devices, vehicles, home appliances, and other items embedded with electronics, software, sensors, actuators, and connectivity which enable these things to connect and exchange data.

Estimated number of devices connected, including mobile phones and tablets, is 15–20 billion. Estimates vary – we will generate lots of data.

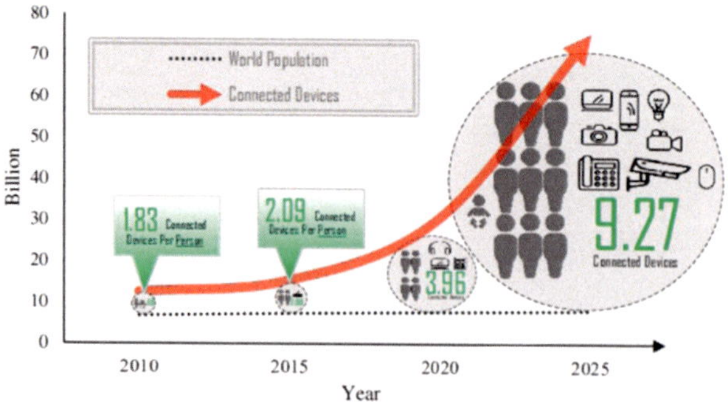

Big data is often described as having high velocity, high volume and a wide variety that can be analyzed to reveal complex patterns, trends and associations

 56

Enabler – cloud

- Large data centers with parallel super computers
  - On-demand charge per hour
  - Handle big data
  - Develop product on the cloud served from HPC (AWS, IBM, Google, Microsoft)
  - 1 to 1000s of processors
- Open source software
- Specialized hardware GPUs, CPUs, high bandwidth networks and internet

EU currently has plans for an Exa-scale HPC facility to model weather – ten years to plan

Enabler – Mathematical techniques

- Algorithms have significantly improved over the years
- Since the capabilities of AI are becoming clearer to users a more companies want to invest in AI
- Universities have funding to develop AI further

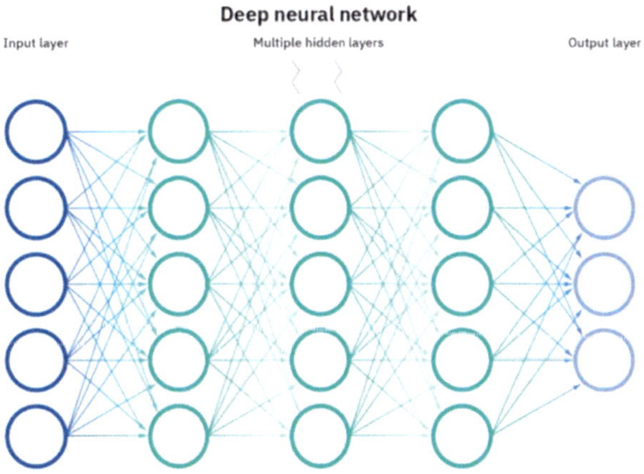

Sample question

How do we call the period in the 70s and 90s where very little progress on AI was made?

a) An AI winter

b) An AI break

c) Dormant AI

d) Narrow AI

 59

Sample question

To what category fits ChatGPT the closest?

a) Big data

b) Computer vision

c) Narrow AI

d) General AI

 60

Sample question

What was **not** an enabler of the growth of AI of the past years?

a) Big data

b) Improved algorithms

c) New legislations for AI

d) Cloud computing

 61

Sample question

Where would we put an streetlight that turns on once it gets dark on Robert Dilt's levels of intelligence?

a) Environment

b) Behavior

c) Values

d) Identity

 62

Algorithms

Machine Learning and Deep Learning

 63

Machine learning

- Comes from subjects grounded largely in the scientific method
- Mathematics (statistics, linear algebra, numerical analysis, operational research, vector calculus, Fourier methods)
- Engineering (control theory, thermodynamics, statistical physics)
- Biology and psychology
- Information theory
- Philosophy

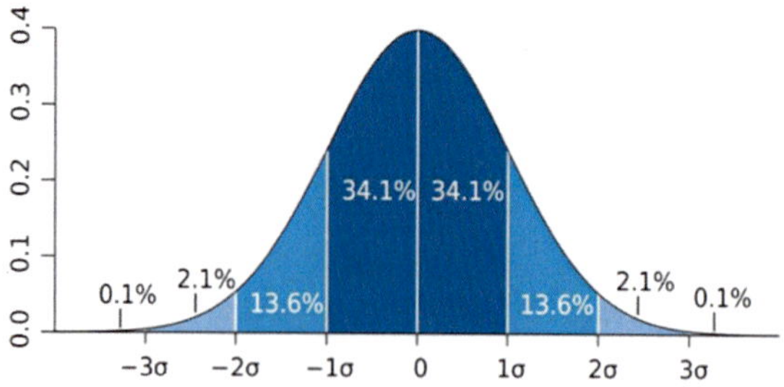

 65

One definition of machine Learning

Machine learning is a subset of artificial intelligence that involves the development of algorithms and statistical models that enable computer systems to automatically improve their performance on a specific task over time through experience.

In other words, machine learning is about building computer models that can learn from data, identify patterns, and make predictions or decisions without being explicitly programmed.

This definition encompasses various types of machine learning, including supervised learning, unsupervised learning, and reinforcement learning.

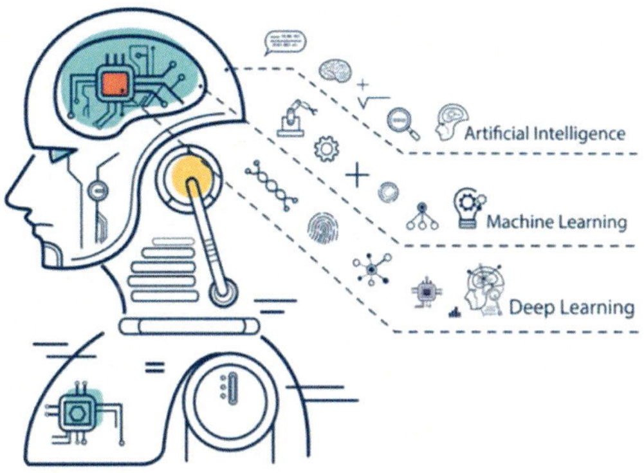

 66

Formal Tom Mitchell definition of ML

Tom Mitchell's definition is more widely quoted:

"the field of machine learning is concerned with the question of how to construct computer programs that automatically improve with experience."

"a computer program is said to learn from experience, E, with respect to some class of tasks, T, and performance measure, P, if its performance at tasks, T, as measured by P, improves with experience, E."

Artificial intelligence is much more than machine learning.

 67

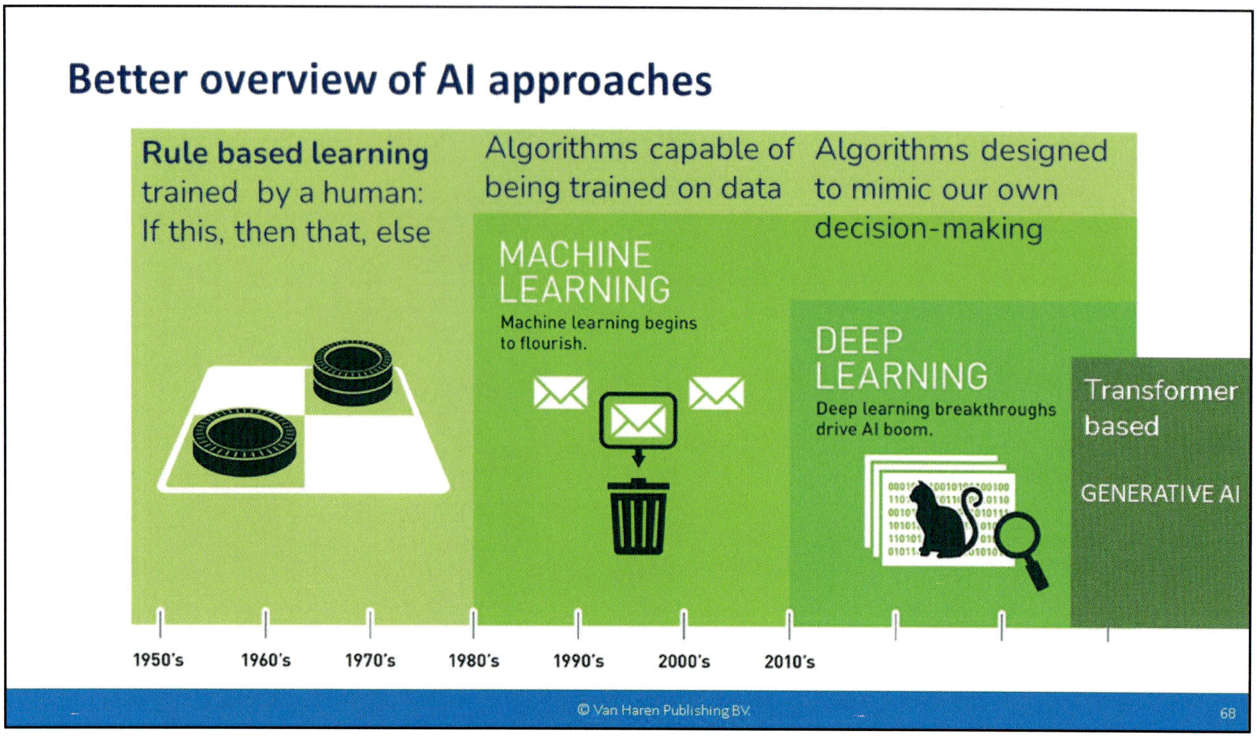
Better overview of AI approaches
Rule based learning
trained by a human:
If this, then that, else
Algorithms capable of being trained on data
Algorithms designed to mimic our own decision-making
MACHINE LEARNING
Machine learning begins to flourish.
DEEP LEARNING
Deep learning breakthroughs drive AI boom.
Transformer based
GENERATIVE AI
1950's
1960's
1970's
1980's
1990's
2000's
2010's
© Van Haren Publishing BV.
68

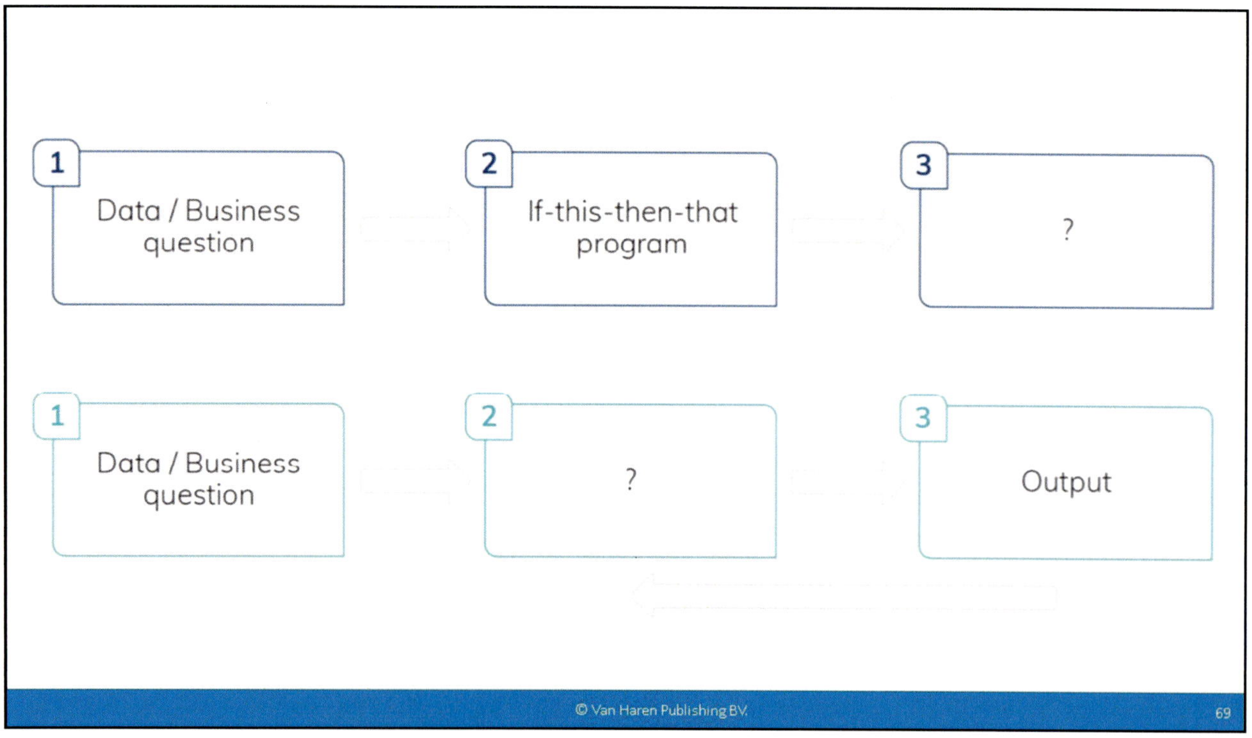
1
Data / Business question
2
If-this-then-that program
3
?
1
Data / Business question
2
?
3
Output
© Van Haren Publishing BV.
69

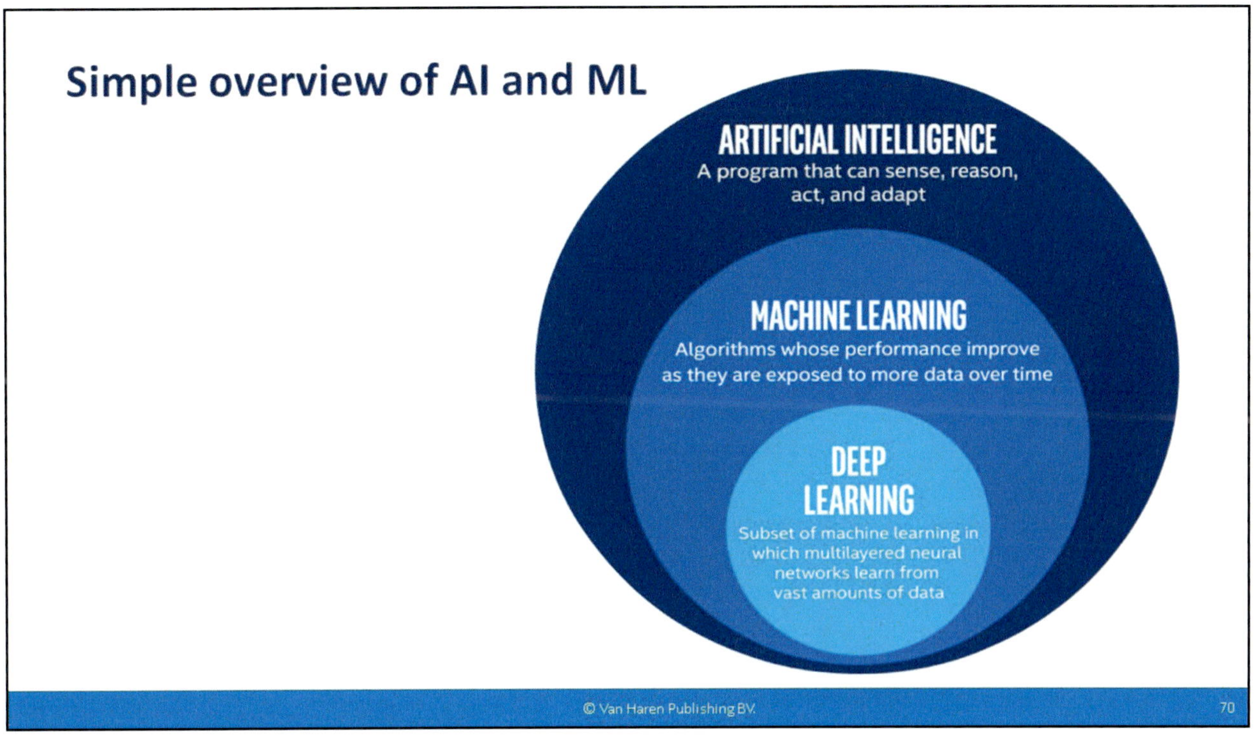
Simple overview of AI and ML
ARTIFICIAL INTELLIGENCE
A program that can sense, reason, act, and adapt
MACHINE LEARNING
Algorithms whose performance improve as they are exposed to more data over time
DEEP LEARNING
Subset of machine learning in which multilayered neural networks learn from vast amounts of data
© Van Haren Publishing BV.
70

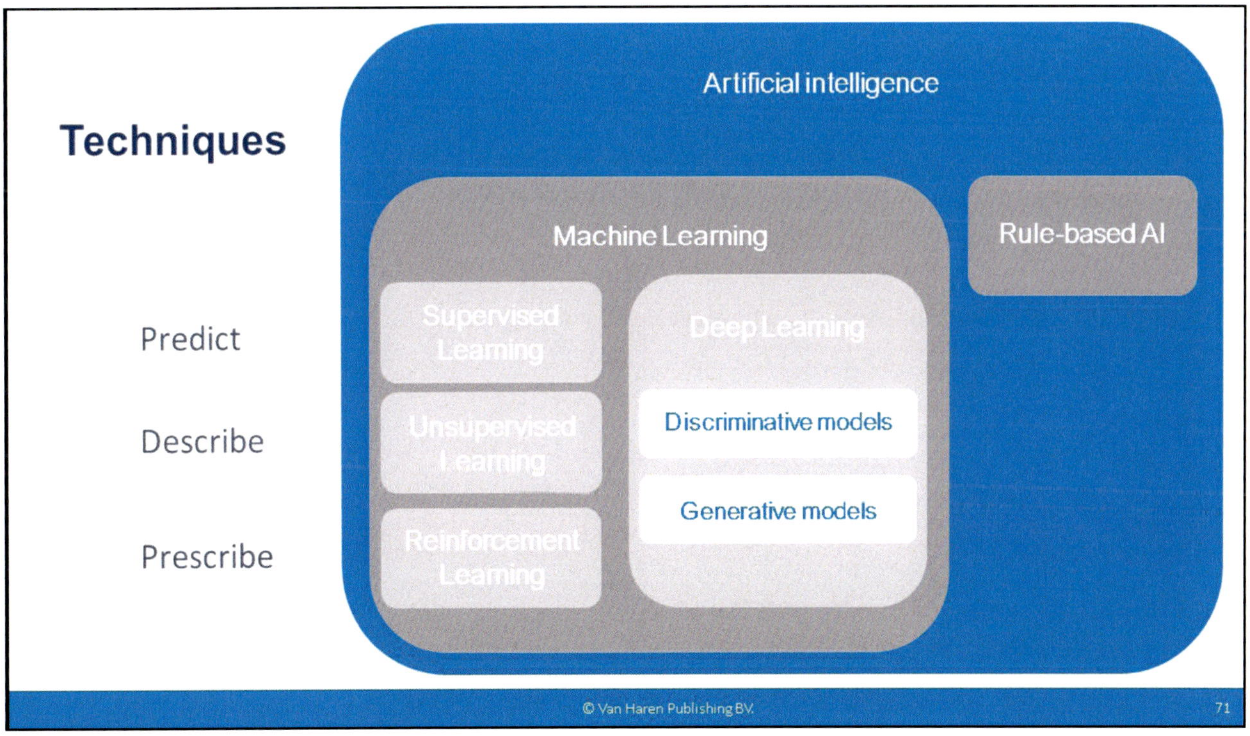
Techniques
Predict
Describe
Prescribe
Artificial intelligence
Machine Learning
Rule-based AI
Supervised Learning
Unsupervised Learning
Reinforcement Learning
Deep Learning
Discriminative models
Generative models
© Van Haren Publishing BV.
71

Probability

- How likely an event is to occur
- Sometimes we theoretically **know** the probability (a 'fair coin')
- In the real world we must often **deduce** the probability of something

- If probabilities are known of forehand, mathematical models can sometimes replace machine learning
- Machine learning can learn these probabilities
- Many machine learning models are heavily inspired by probability models

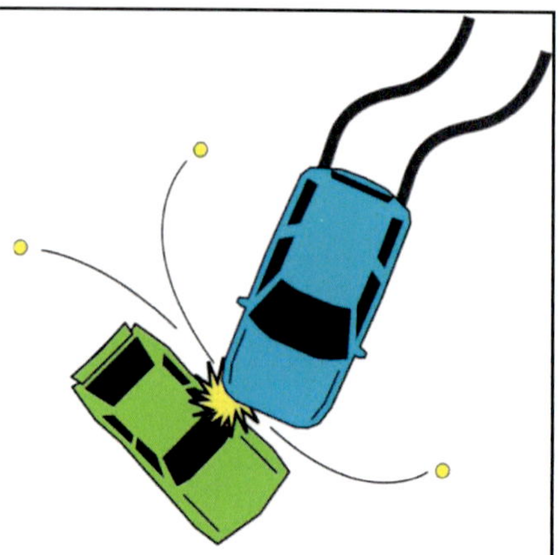

Correlation

- Correlation means that **a relation between two variables** exists
  - Positive correlation: if X is bigger, then Y is also bigger
  - Negative correlation: if X is bigger, then Y is smaller

- Larger correlation between variables → machine learning can discover this more easily as a pattern in the data

Correlation vs Causation

- Causation is when **one event leads to another**
  - If X happens, then Y is also more likely because X can cause Y to happen
- Correlation **does not mean** causation: cause and effect are often influenced by other variables.

Machine learning will never tell you a causal relationship, only correlations!

Causal relationships can exist in the data, but machine learning is not the way to show that one event is caused by another

 74

Exercise

Fashion and the economy

It was found that the following correlations between fashion and economy exist

- The hemline theory: When the economy goes down, skirt lengths go to the floor
- The high-heels index: When the economy goes down, heels go up
- The lipstick index: When the economy goes down, lipstick sales go up

Is this correlation or causation?

 75

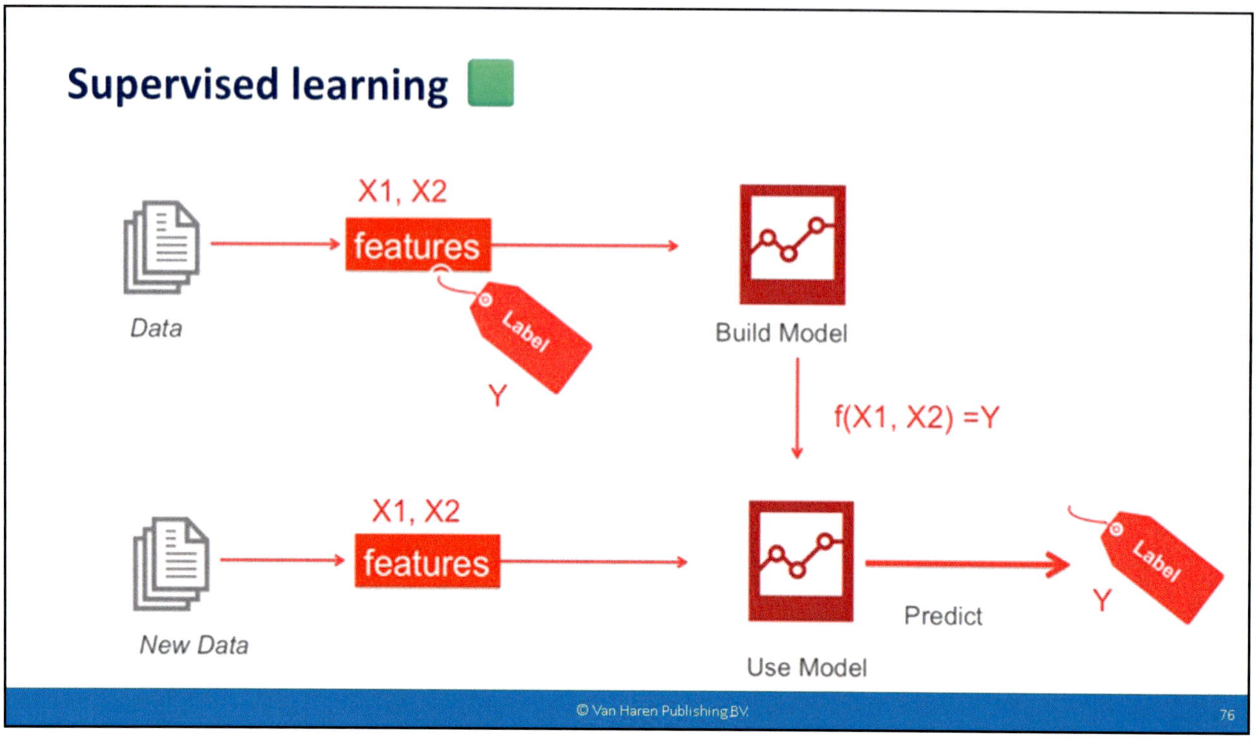
Supervised learning
X1, X2
features
Data
Label
Y
Build Model
f(X1, X2) =Y
X1, X2
features
New Data
Use Model
Predict
Y
Label
© Van Haren Publishing BV.
76

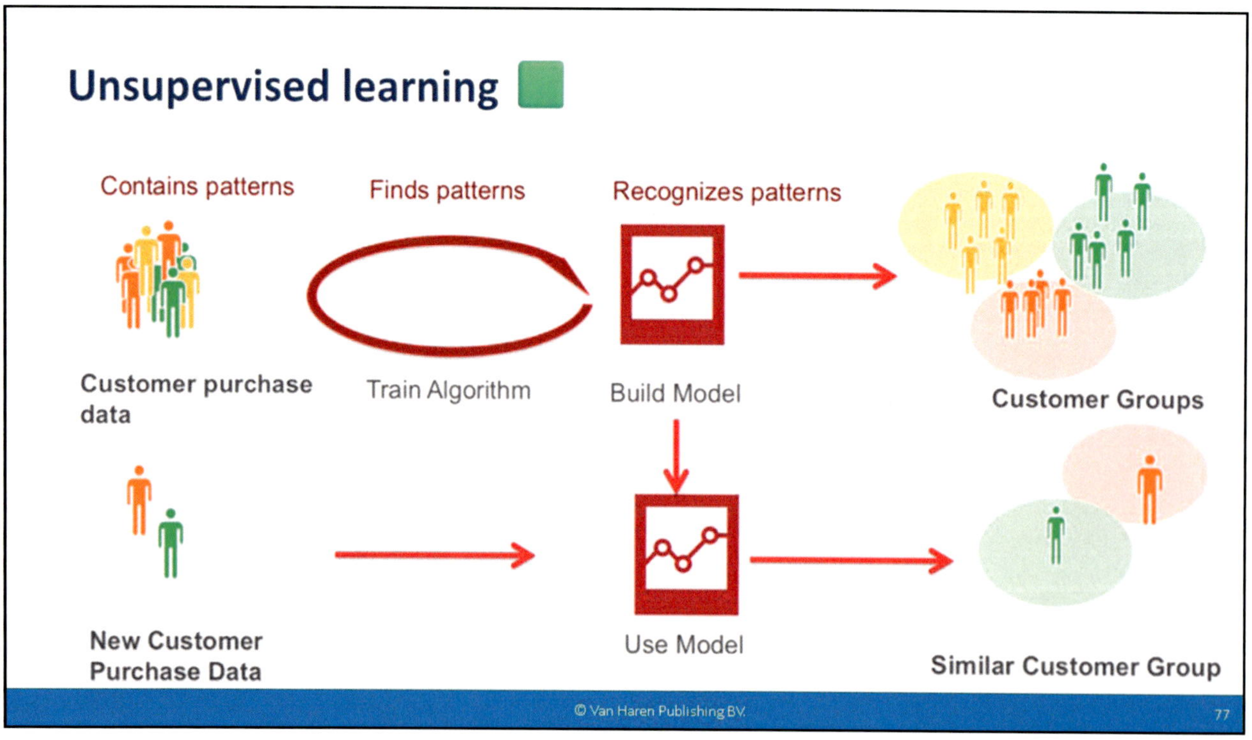
Unsupervised learning
Contains patterns
Finds patterns
Recognizes patterns
Customer purchase data
Train Algorithm
Build Model
Customer Groups
New Customer Purchase Data
Use Model
Similar Customer Group
© Van Haren Publishing BV.
77

Exercise

Take the role of a data analyst in a supermarket chain

- Why would the company use supervised learning?
- Why would the company use unsupervised learning?

 78

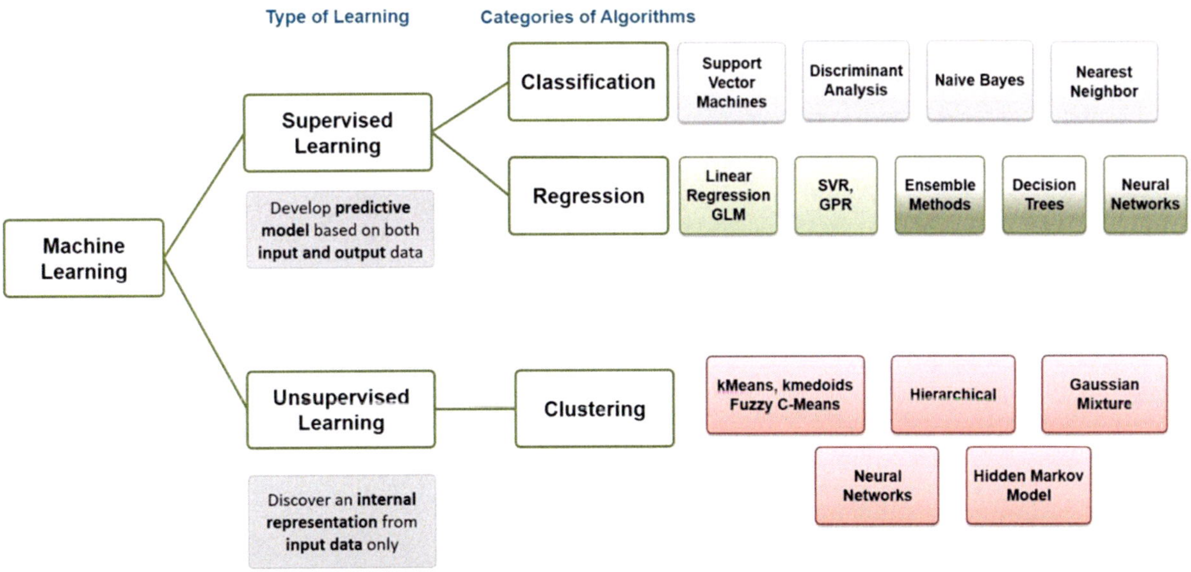

 79

Supervised learning

 80

Machine learning explained

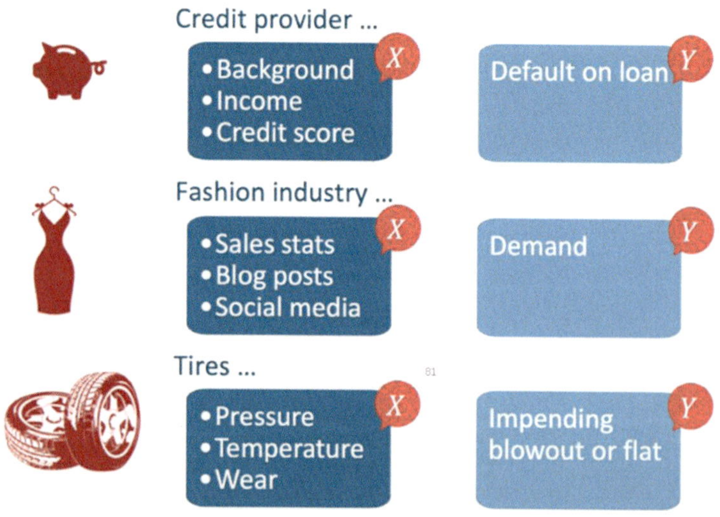

Source: Prof. Dr. J. De Mast

 81

Machine learning explained

Observation ID

	ID	Default (Y)	Contract (X)	M/F (X)	Car (X)	Realty (X)	Child (X)	Income (X)	Credit (X)	Annuity (X)	Goods (X)	Income ty (X)	Education (X)	Family st (X)
1	100002	1	Cash loans	M	N	Y	0	202500	406598	24700.5	351000	Working	Secondary />>	Single / not mai
2	100003	0	Cash loans	F	N	N	0	270000	1293503	35698.5	1129500	State s>>	Higher educ>>	Married
3	100004	0	Revolving loans	M	Y	Y	0	67500	135000	6750.0	135000	Working	Secondary />>	Single / not mai
4	100006	0	Cash loans	F	N	Y	0	135000	312683	29686.5	297000	Working	Secondary />>	Civil marriage
5	100007	0	Cash loans	M	N	Y	0	121500	513000	21865.5	513000	Working	Secondary />>	Single / not mai
6	100008	0	Cash loans	M	N	Y	0	99000	490496	27517.5	454500	State s>>	Secondary />>	Married
7	100009	0	Cash loans	F	Y	Y	1	171000	1560726	41301.0	1395000	Comm>>	Higher educ>>	Married
8	100010	0	Cash loans	M	Y	Y	0	360000	1530000	42075.0	1530000	State s>>	Higher educ>>	Married
9	100011	0	Cash loans	F	N	Y	0	112500	1019610	33826.5	913500	Pensioner	Secondary />>	Married
10	100012	0	Revolving loans	M	N	Y	0	135000	405000	20250.0	405000	Working	Secondary />>	Single / not mai
11	100014	0	Cash loans	F	N	Y	1	112500	652500	21177.0	652500	Working	Higher educ>>	Married
12	100015	0	Cash loans	F	N	Y	0	38419	148365	10678.5	135000	Pensioner	Secondary />>	Married
13	100016	0	Cash loans	F	N	Y	0	67500	80865	5881.5	67500	Working	Secondary />>	Married
14	100017	0	Cash loans	M	Y	N	1	225000	918468	28966.5	697500	Working	Secondary />>	Married
15	100018	0	Cash loans	F	N	Y	0	189000	773681	32778.0	679500	Working	Secondary />	ried
16	100019	0	Cash loans	M	Y	Y	0	157500	299772	20160.0	247500	Working	Secondary />	gle / not mai
17	100020	0	Cash loans	M	N	N	0	108000	509603	26149.5	387000	Working	Secondary />>	Married

→ 110 more columns

↓ 52 000 more rows

Machine learning:

- Model relationships between X and Y variables

Source: Prof. Dr. J. De Mast

 82

Machine learning explained

	ID	Default (Y)	Contract	M/F	Car	Realty	Child	Income	Credit	Annuity	Goods	Income ty	Education	Family st
1	100002	1	Cash loans	M	N	Y	0	202500	406598	24700.5	351000	Working	Secondary />>	Single / not mai
2	100003	0	Cash loans	F	N	N	0	270000	1293503	35698.5	1129500	State s>>	Higher educ>>	Married
3	100004	0	Revolving loans	M	Y	Y	0	67500	135000	6750.0	135000	Working	Secondary />>	Single / not mai
4				F	N	Y	0	135000	312683	29686.5	297000	Working	Secondary />>	Civil marriage
5				M	N	Y	0	121500	513000	21865.5	513000	Working	Secondary />>	Single / not mai
6	100008	0	Cash loans	M	N	Y	0	99000	490496	27517.5	454500	State s>>	Secondary />>	Married
7	100009	0	Cash loans	F	Y	Y	1	171000	1560726	41301.0	1395000	Comm>>	Higher educ>>	Married
8				M	Y	Y	0	360000	1530000	42075.0	1530000	State s>>	Higher educ>>	Married
9				F	N	Y	0	112500	1019610	33826.5	913500	Pensioner	Secondary />>	Married
10			loans	M	N	Y	0	135000	405000	20250.0	405000	Working	Secondary />>	Single / not mai
11				F	N	Y	1	112500	652500	21177.0	652500	Working	Higher educ>>	Married
12	100015	0	Cash loans	F	N	Y	0	38419	148365	10678.5	135000	Pensioner	Secondary />>	Married
13				F	N	Y	0	67500	80865	5881.5	67500	Working	Secondary />>	Married
14				M	Y	N	1	225000	918468	28966.5	697500	Working	Secondary />>	Married
15				F	N	Y	0	189000	773681	32778.0	679500	Working	Secondary />>	Married
16				M	Y	Y	0	157500	299772	20160.0	247500	Working	Secondary />>	Single / not mai
17	100020	0	Cash loans	M	N	N	0	108000	509603	26149.5	387000	Working	Seco '>>	Married

Labels

Response variables

Dependent variables

Y variable: characteristic that we want to predict, explain, optimize, ...

Source: Prof. Dr. J. De Mast

 83

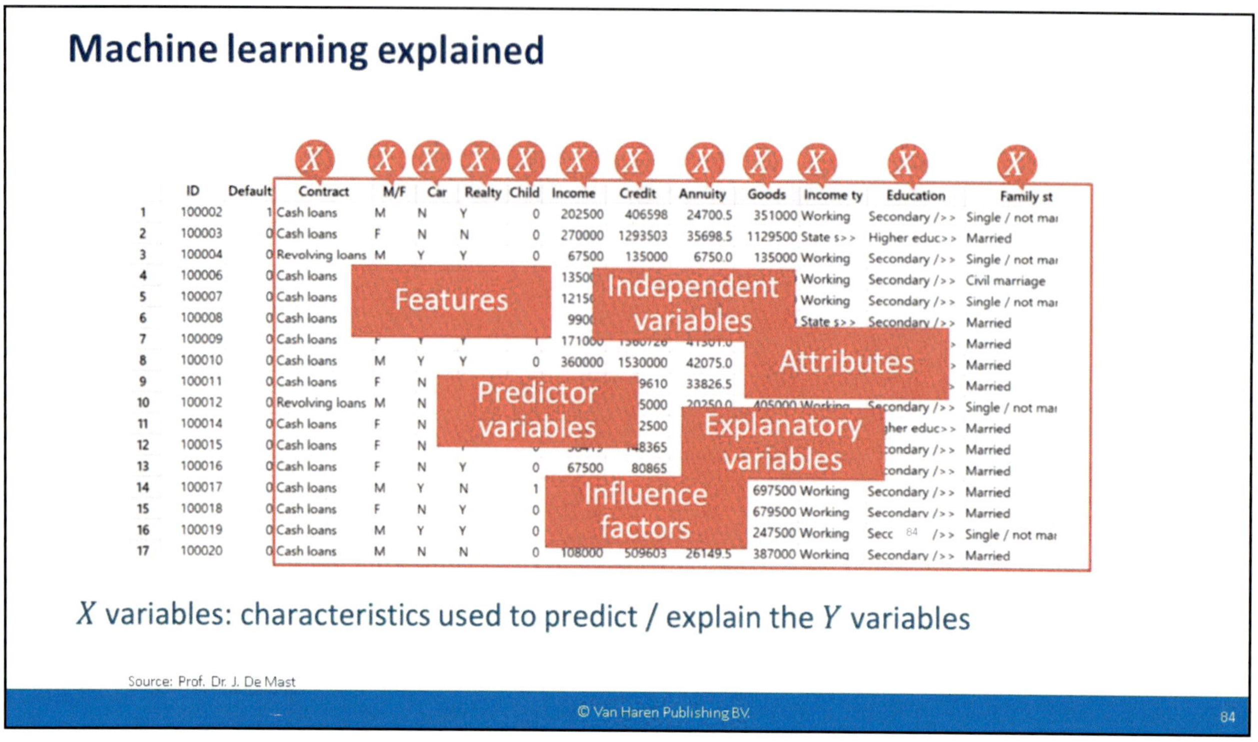
Machine learning explained
ID Default Contract M/F Car Realty Child Income Credit Annuity Goods Income ty Education Family st
Features
Independent variables
Attributes
Predictor variables
Explanatory variables
Influence factors
X variables: characteristics used to predict / explain the Y variables
Source: Prof. Dr. J. De Mast
© Van Haren Publishing BV.
84

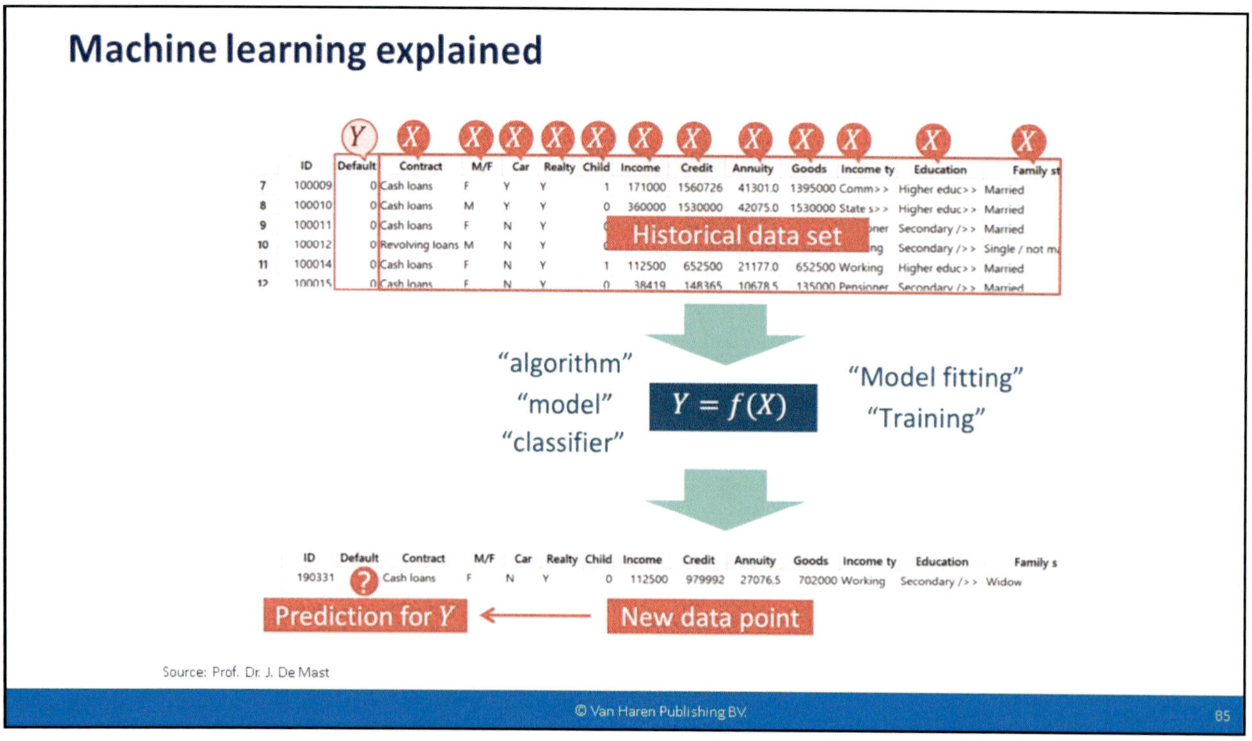
Machine learning explained
ID Default Contract M/F Car Realty Child Income Credit Annuity Goods Income ty Education Family st
Historical data set
"algorithm"
"model"
"classifier"
Y = f(X)
"Model fitting"
"Training"
ID Default Contract M/F Car Realty Child Income Credit Annuity Goods Income ty Education Family s
190331 Cash loans F N Y 0 112500 979992 27076.5 702000 Working Secondary />> Widow
Prediction for Y
New data point
Source: Prof. Dr. J. De Mast
© Van Haren Publishing BV.
85

Types of labels

In supervised learning, we generally distinguish between 2 types of labels

- Classes (a finite number of labels)
- Continuous values (an infinite number of labels)

Classes are typically predicted via classification methods
Continuous values are typically predicted via regression methods

When using supervised learning, always first determine what type your labels are

Examples:

- Predicting the total profit of next month
- Predicting whether a new medicine is effective
- Predicting the length of a person

My Case study

In a kitchen where perishable goods are regularly handled, it is critical to determine whether a food item is still safe and suitable for consumption. With the use of AI, I want to predict if my food is spoiled or not and for how long I can keep my food fresh

What are my labels and features?

Classification

a.k.a. "labeling": **What type of X** is this data point?

Examples:

- Is there a tumor on this thorax X-ray?
- What type of animal is on this photo?
- Was a person exercising while their smartwatch detected a high heart rate?

Notes:

- The labels are almost always fixed and known in advance

K-Nearest Neighbours (KNN)

Classification algorithm

KNN also computes distances between data points

- KNN looks at **classes** of K closest points to an unclassified point and takes the most occurring class as prediction
- Common usage: early iteration classifier, classifier of complex spaces

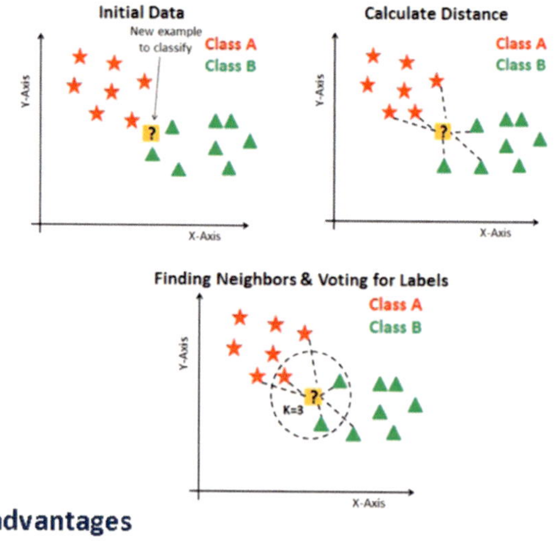

Advantages

+ Simple algorithm
+ Easy to explain

Disadvantages

− Saves all data: a big potential privacy concern
− "Closest" not always well-defined

K-Nearest Neighbours (KNN) - Example

Shelf life of perishable goods

- Predict if a product is spoiled or not
- Label: Spoiled / not Spoiled
- Feature: Days kept, Temperature

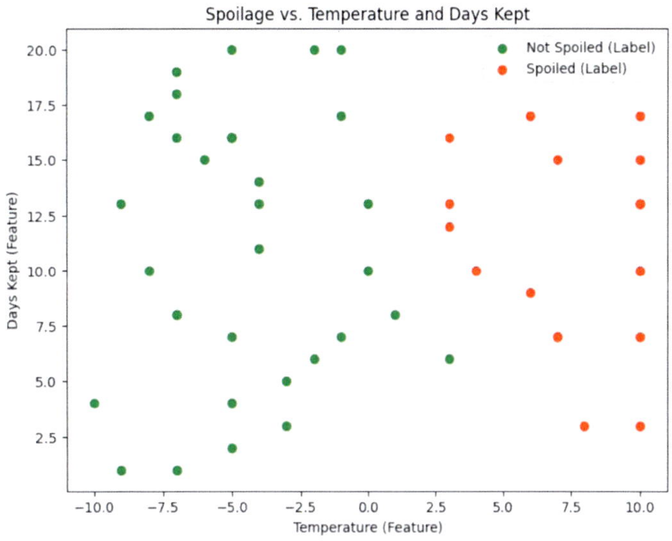

Temperature	Days	Spoiled
-5	2	False
-10	4	False
-1	20	False
-5	20	False
6	17	True
10	15	True

 90

K-Nearest Neighbours (KNN) - Example

Shelf life of perishable goods

- Predict if a product is spoiled or not
- **Label**: Spoiled / not Spoiled
- **Feature**: Days kept, Temperature
- KNN **predicts** it is spoiled!

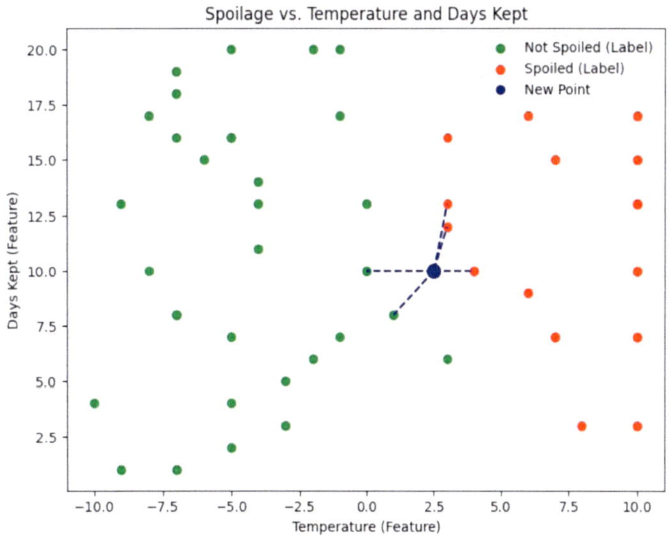

Temperature	Days	Spoiled
-5	2	False
-10	4	False
-1	20	False
-5	20	False
6	17	True
10	15	True

 91

Support Vector Machine (SVM)

Classification algorithm

SVM classifies data by separating classes via a border

- Border determined by choosing a type of shape (e.g. line, circle)
- Maximises separation between classes
- After maximising separation, maximises margin from class to separation boundary

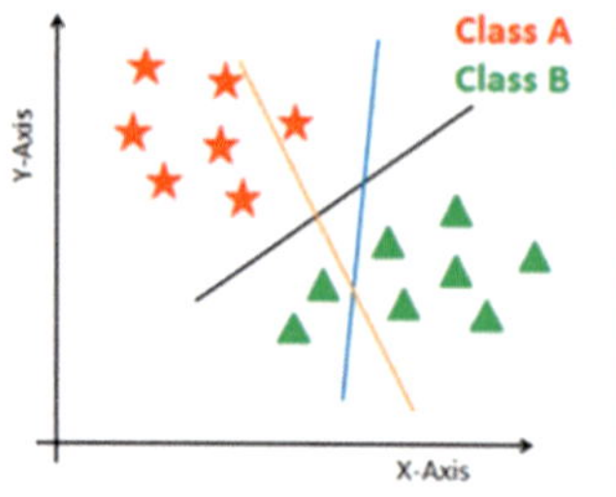

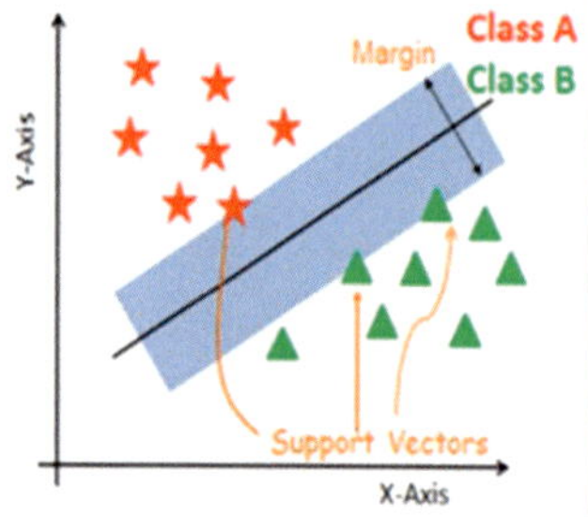

Advantages

+ Fast training and prediction
+ Works on small and large datasets

Disadvantages

− No measure for 'how certain' the model is of a choice
− Depends greatly on shape choice: domain knowledge required

 92

Support Vector Machine (SVM) - Example

Shelf life of perishable goods

- Predict if a product is spoiled or not
- **Label**: Spoiled / not Spoiled
- **Feature**: Days kept, Temperature
- The SVM **splits** the space in two!

Temperature	Days	Spoiled
-5	2	False
-10	4	False
-1	20	False
-5	20	False
6	17	True
10	15	True

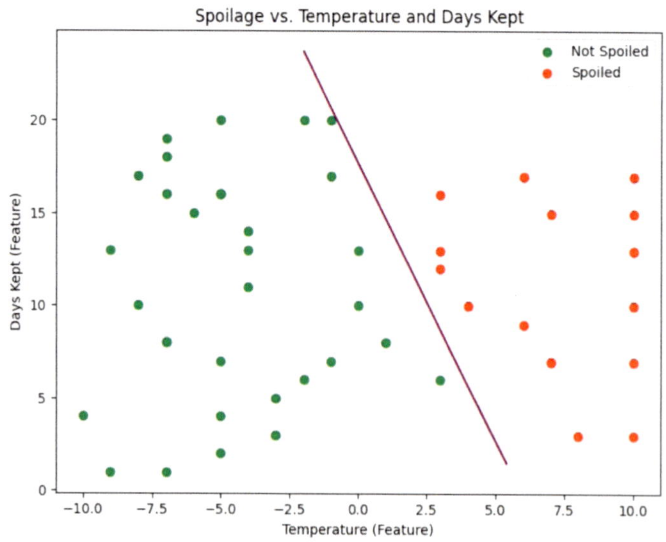

 93

Decision Tree

Classification algorithm

A decision tree algorithm generates a decision tree ('flowchart') for given data

- Automatically uses numerical and categorical features in the data to determine the decision steps
  - e.g. "Is x < 5.9? Go left."

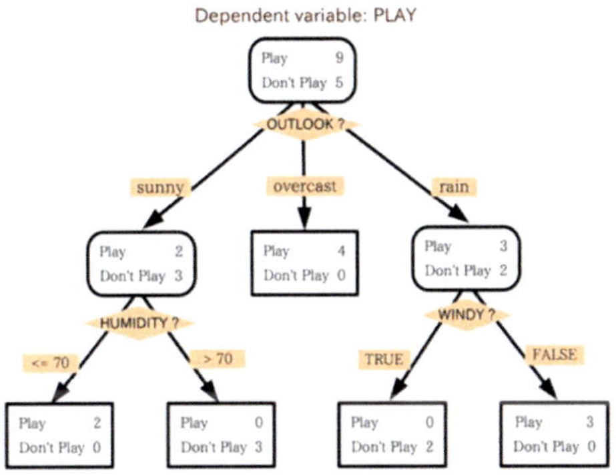

Advantages

+ Classifies results into any number of classes
+ Explainable
+ Built in nice visuals!

Disadvantages

– No certainty measurement
– Very sensitive to overfitting and data skewness (overrepresentation of certain classes)

© Van Haren Publishing BV. source: Wikipedia 94

Decision Tree – Example

- Predict if a product is spoiled
- Temperature is the strongest feature
- **Label**: Days kept, temperature, product
- **Feature**: Spoiled
- Notice an *overfit* for temperatures between 3.445 and 3.504

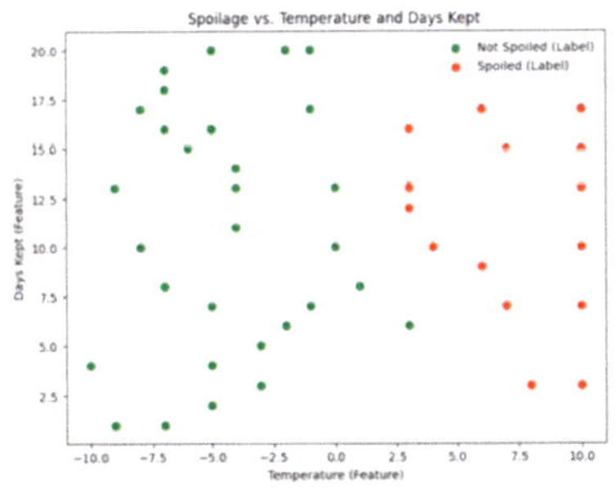

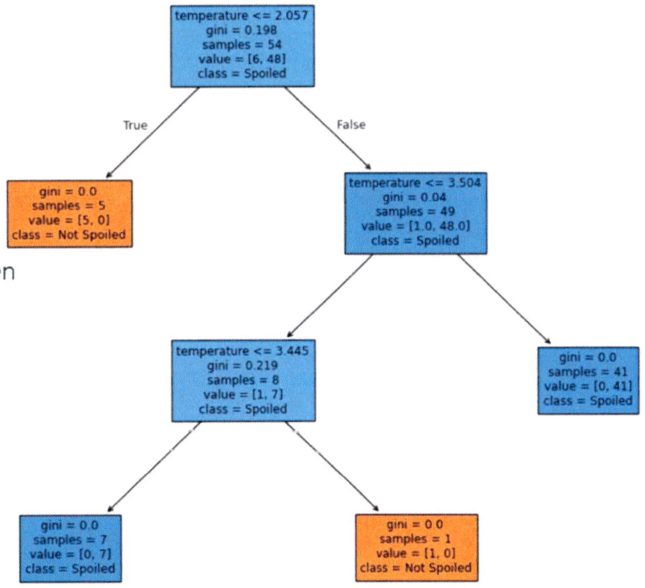

© Van Haren Publishing BV. 95

Random Forest

An ensemble of decision trees (hence: 'forest').

- Can be used for **classification** or **regression** (we only discuss the classification version)
- Uses majority voting
- Can fit complex data

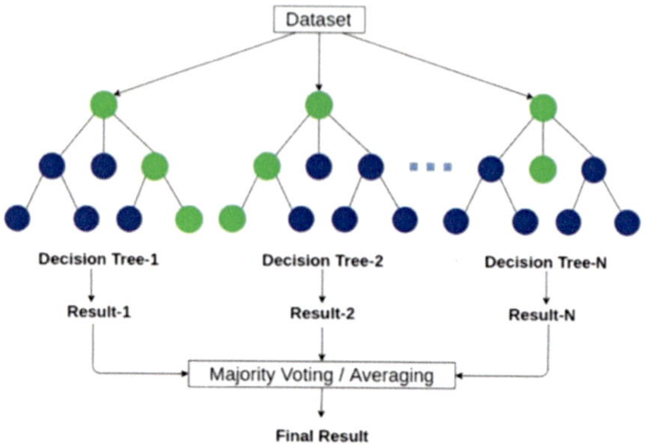

Advantages

+ Yields probabilities based on averaging predictions of individual trees
+ Can model complex problems
+ Can handle categorical and numerical data

Disadvantages

- Slower to train than decision tree
- Harder to interpret the model
- Prone to overfitting

 96

Regression

a.k.a. "fitting a curve to the data": **What relationship exists** between these data points?

Examples:

- What's the value of this house that is for sale?
- How tall will our child be when they grow up?

Notes:

- We use this to predict **numerical** values

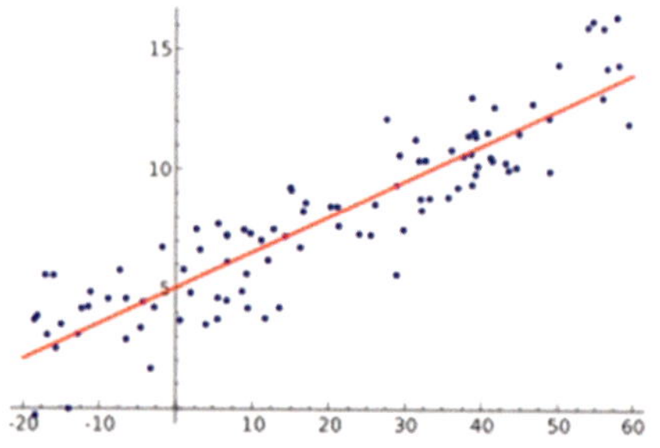

source: Wikipedia (Regression)

 97

Linear regression

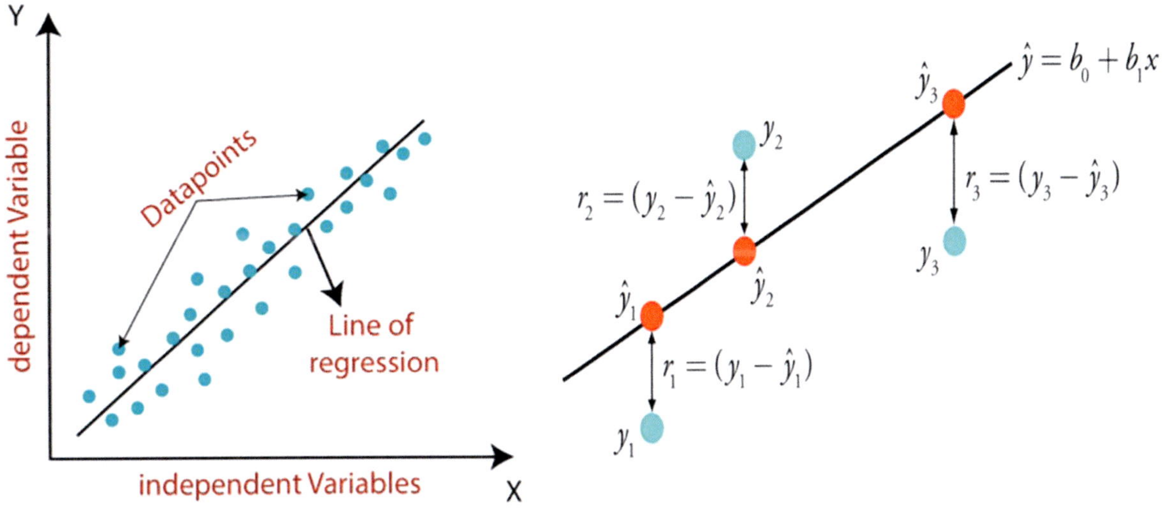

© Van Haren Publishing BV. 98

Linear Regression - Example

Shelf life of perishable goods

- Predict how many days a product can be kept
- **Label**: Days to keep a product (until spoiled)
- **Feature**: Temperature

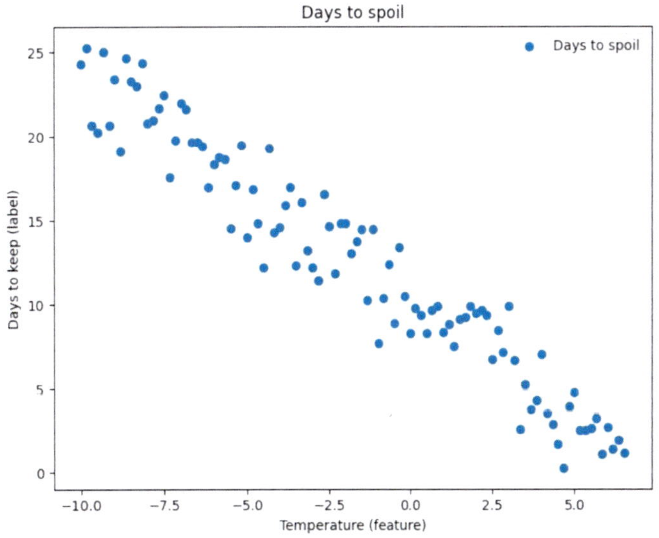

© Van Haren Publishing BV. source: Wikipedia (Regression) 99

Linear Regression - Example

Shelf life of perishable goods

- Predict how many days a product can be kept
- **Label**: Days to keep a product (until spoiled)
- **Feature**: Temperature
- Linear regression predicts the number of days to keep for every temperature value

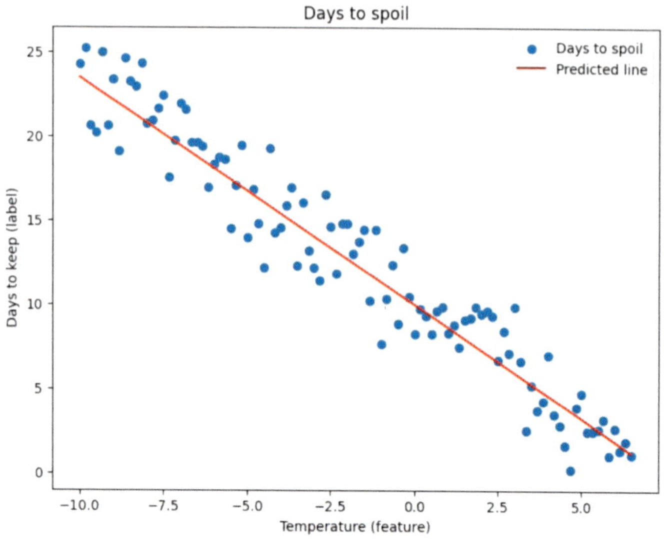

source: Wikipedia (Regression) 100

Logistic Regression

Logistic regression is a more complex version of linear regression

- Classification algorithm (usually)
- Used as early version for more complex model/understanding feature

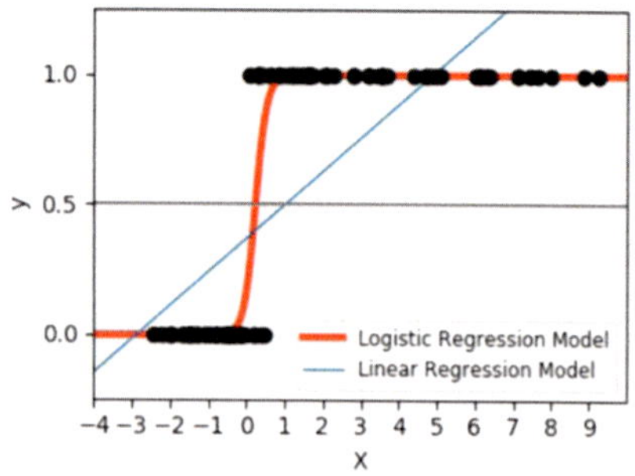

Advantages

+ Fast training time
+ Interpretable coefficients in linear model
+ No need to scale input

Disadvantages

– Can only model specific relations
– Tendency to overfit

101

Logistic Regression - Example

Shelf life of perishable goods

- Predict if a specific food item for a specific tempeprature is spoiled
- **Label**: Spoiled or not
- **Feature**: Days the item is kept
- Logistic regression predicts when a product is spoiled

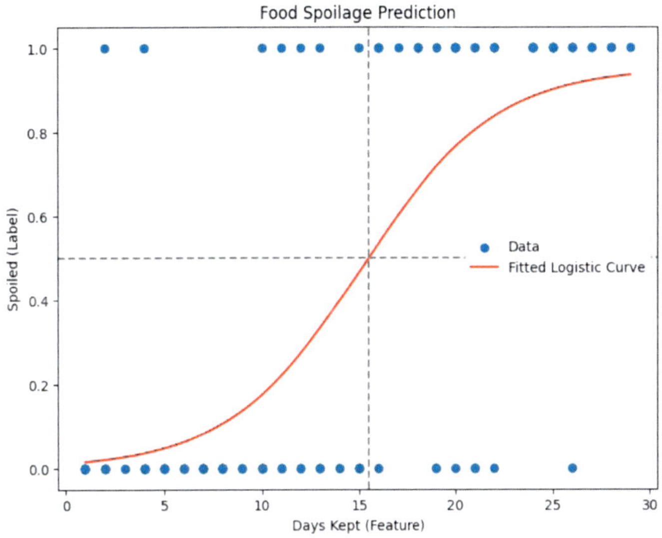

 102

Time Series Forecasting

Subfield of regression, time data used to predict the future: **"What will happen?"**

This is **extrapolation**

Examples:

- How many visitors will the zoo have next week?
- How will this stock price change in value?

Notes:

- Cannot predict 'unforeseen' things (e.g. effects of coronavirus, effects not present in the historical data, etc.)

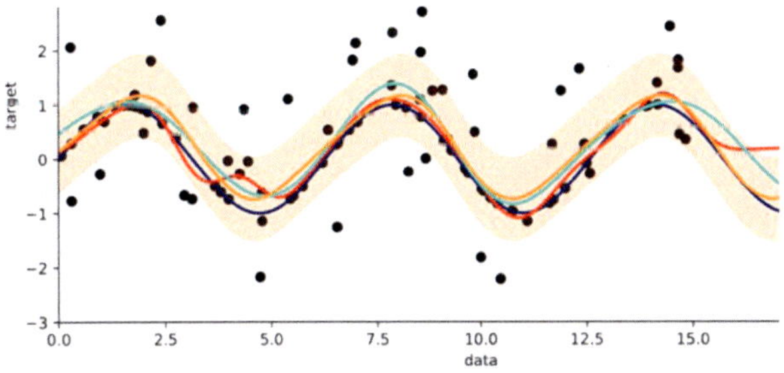

 103

Case study

For our case study:

- Customer retention
- Employee satisfaction
- Waste detection

What type of data do we need?

- What are the labels
- What are the features
- What type is the data

Case study

Which techniques are suitable?

- KNN
- Random forest
- Linear regression
- Logistic regression
- Support vector machine

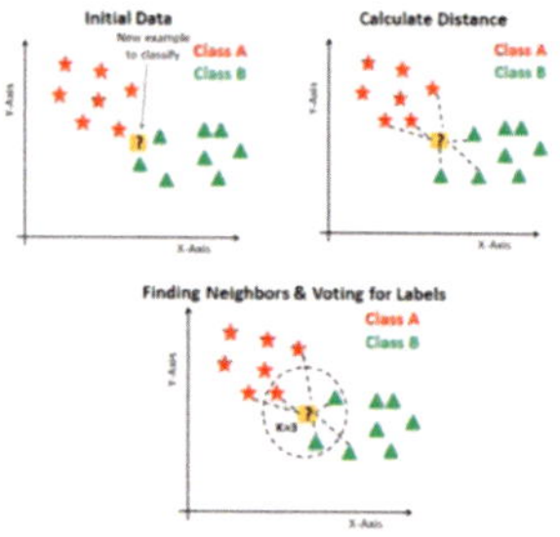

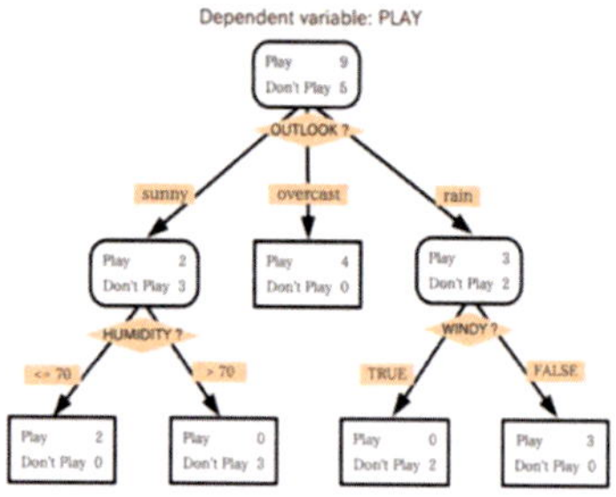

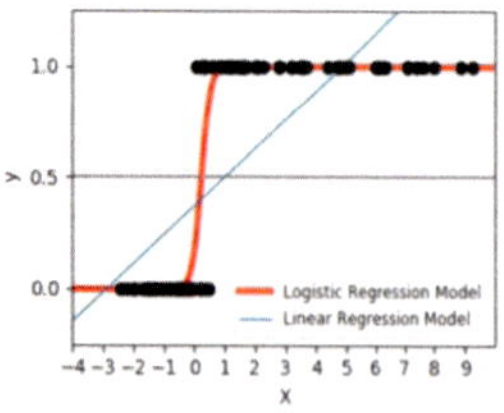

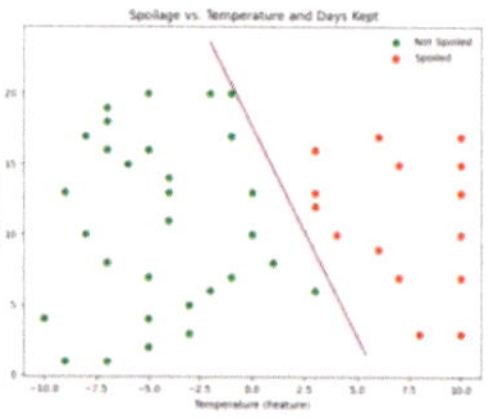

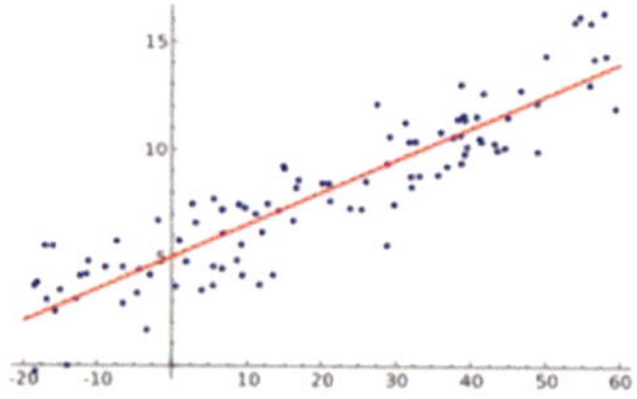

Unsupervised learning

 106

Cluster Analysis

Dividing the data into 'natural' subsets:
"**Which groups exist** in the data?"

Examples:

- Customer segmentation: What types of customers buy at our stores? What kind of listeners does Spotify have?
- What different types of email get sent to customer service?
- What kinds of documents are saved on SharePoint?

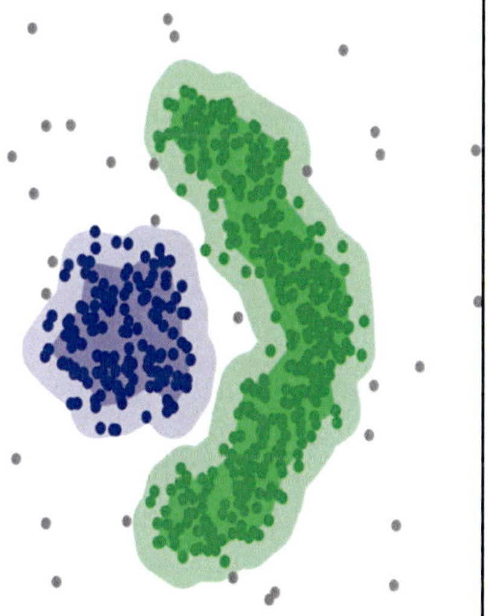

source: Wikipedia (DBSCAN)

 107

Anomaly Detection
a.k.a. "outlier detection": Which data points don't fit the overall patterns?
Examples:
Anomaly
Value
Time
WHICH NEWS IS FAKE?
WHICH TRANSACTIONS ARE FRAUDULENT?
WHICH EMAILS ARE SPAM?
© Van Haren Publishing BV.
108

Association Discovery / Recommendations
a.k.a. "market basket analysis":
Which other item(s) would fit the set?
Examples:
• Customers who bought this also bought...
• Based on your reading history, you may like this book...
• Based on the data of the client, they are likely to be interested in this product
Discover Related Products
Jeep Jogging Stroller Weather Shield, Baby Rain Cover, Universal Size to fit most Jogging Strollers, Waterproof,...
$14.39 prime
Add to Cart
square trade
an Allstate company
PROTECTION PLAN
SquareTrade 3-Year Baby Product Protection Plan ($50-99.99)
$9.01
Add to Cart
Jeep Mosquito and Bug Net for Jogger Stroller
$8.97 prime
Add to Cart
source: Amazon.com
© Van Haren Publishing BV.
109

K-Means

Clustering algorithm

K-means works by calculating the distances between data points

- K stands for the number of objects taken into account
- K-means clusters the data in K clusters
  - Minimizes distance within the cluster
  - Maximizes distance between clusters
- Common usage: first version of clustering

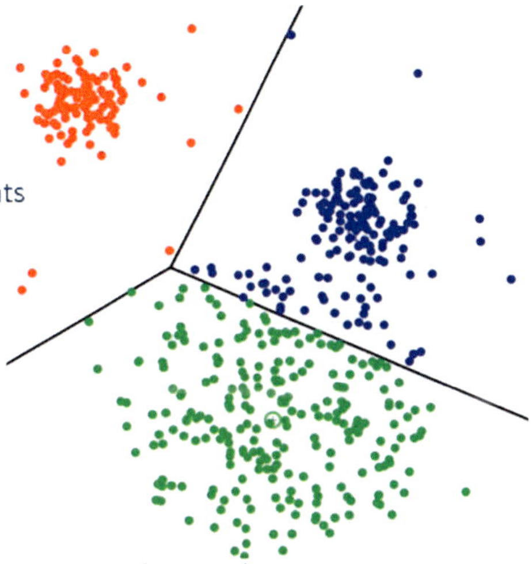

Advantages

- Simple algorithm
- Easy to explain

Disadvantages

- Bad in high dimensional space (so with many features)
- K must be chosen by data scientist: algorithm cannot determine optimal choice

 110

K-Means - Example

Shelf-life of perishable goods

- Classify these products in 2 classes
- Features: temperature, days to spoil

Food ID	Days to spoil	Temperature
1	11.446326	4.789268
2	22.064358	1.248149
...	...	...
195	3.899206	4.260908
196	1.778688	2.759534

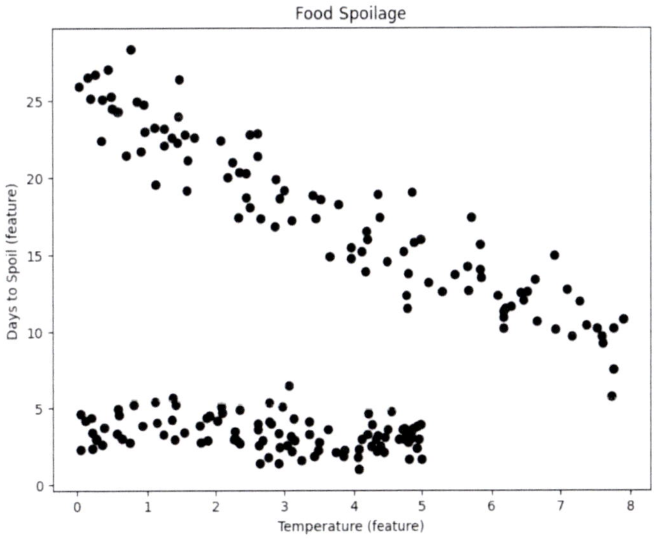

 111

K-Means - Example

Shelf-life of perishable goods

- K-means splits the data in 2 groups
- Performs best if data groups are circular
- See below for an example for 3 groups

- More advanced clustering algorithms are robust to different shapes (DBSCAN)

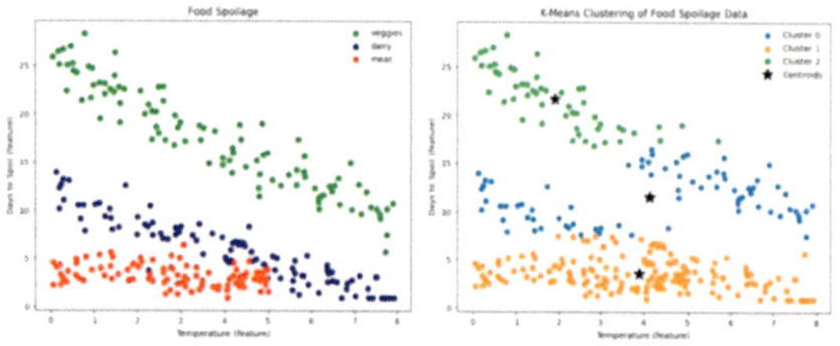

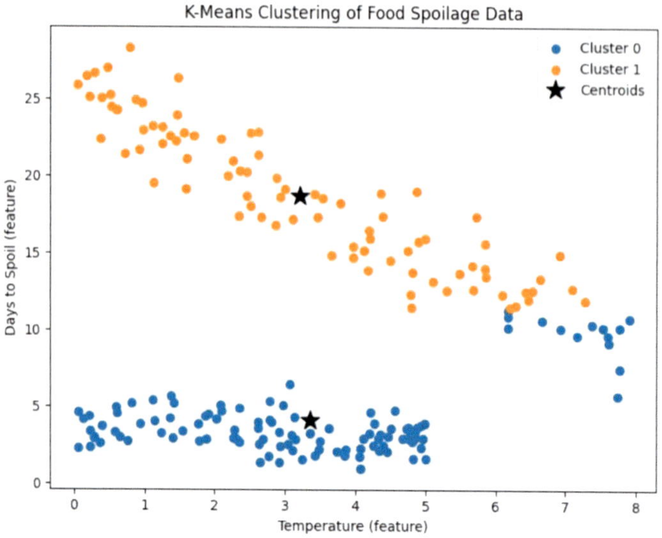

 112

Case study

Is unsupervised learning useful in the following applications

- Employee satisfaction
- Customer retention
- Waste detection

Choice of application

- Anomaly detection
- Association discovery
- Clustering

 113

Reinforcement learning source Matthew Renze

 114

Reinforcement learning

An agent is forced to make decision in an environment

- The agent gets a reward for a good decision
- The agent gets a punishment for a bad decision
- The agent learns which decisions to make to get rewards

Read the description above, but replace "agent" with "dog"

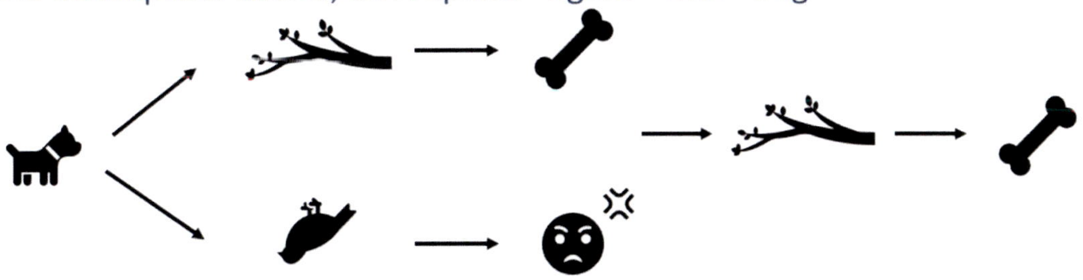

 115

Reinforcement learning

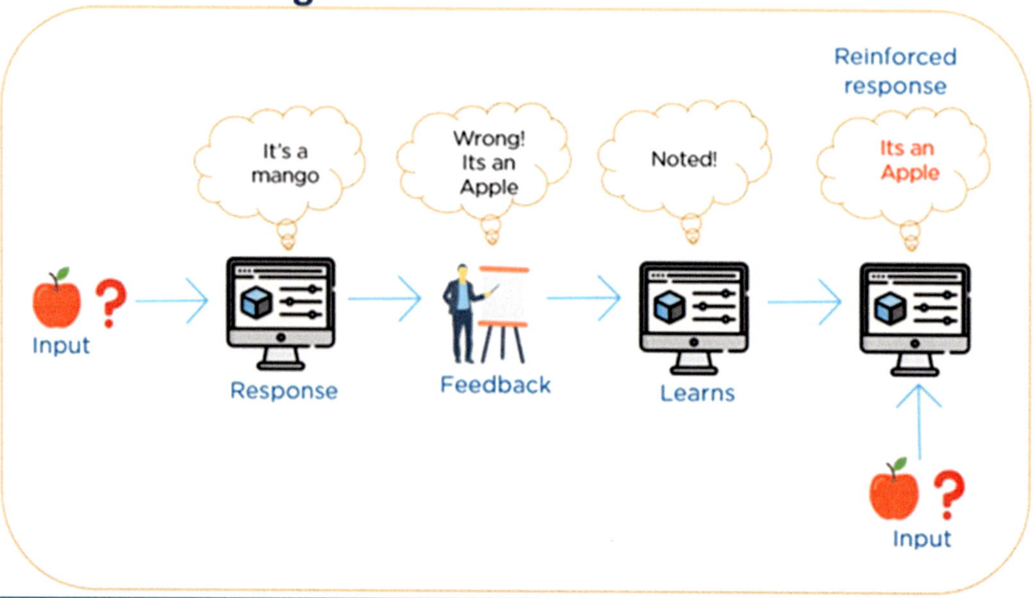

 116

Reinforcement learning is difficult

Every combination of state and action is assigned a number

- If taking this action in this state results in a good outcome, the number is increased
- If taking this action in this state results in a bad outcome, the number is decreased
- Keep updating the numbers while taking actions

Similar to how we learn

- Touch a hot pan -> decrease the number by a lot
- Catch the pancake -> Increase the number

Take the action with the highest number!

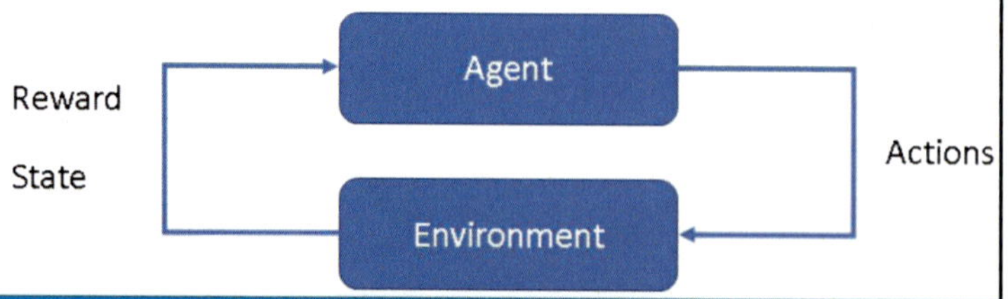

 117

Schematic overview of reinforcement learning

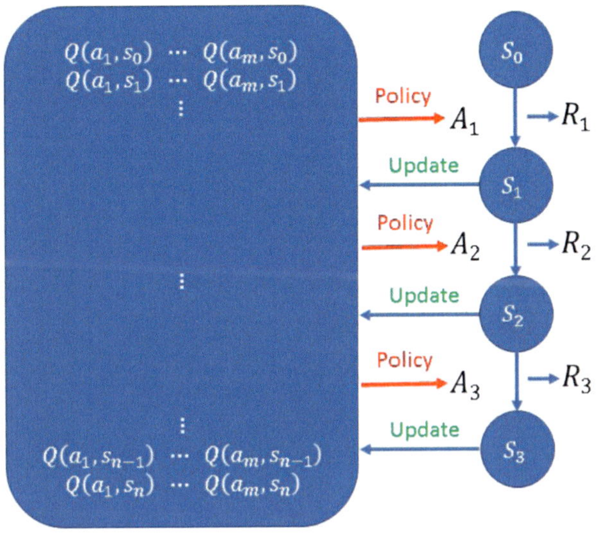

 118

Case study

Reinforcement learning for our case studies

- What are some actions we can take?
- What are the cost and benefit of these actions?
- How do they affect the environment

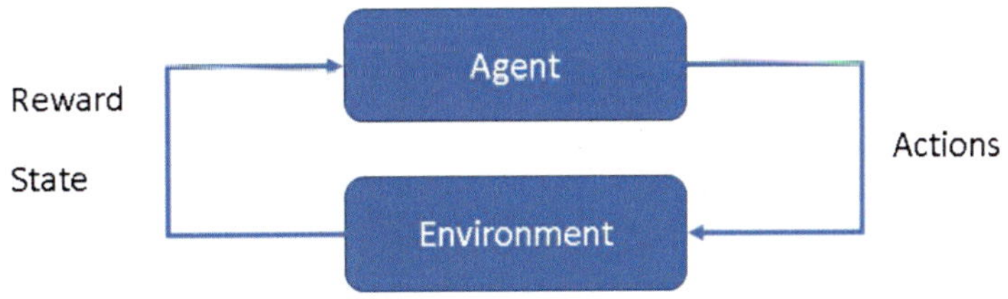

 119

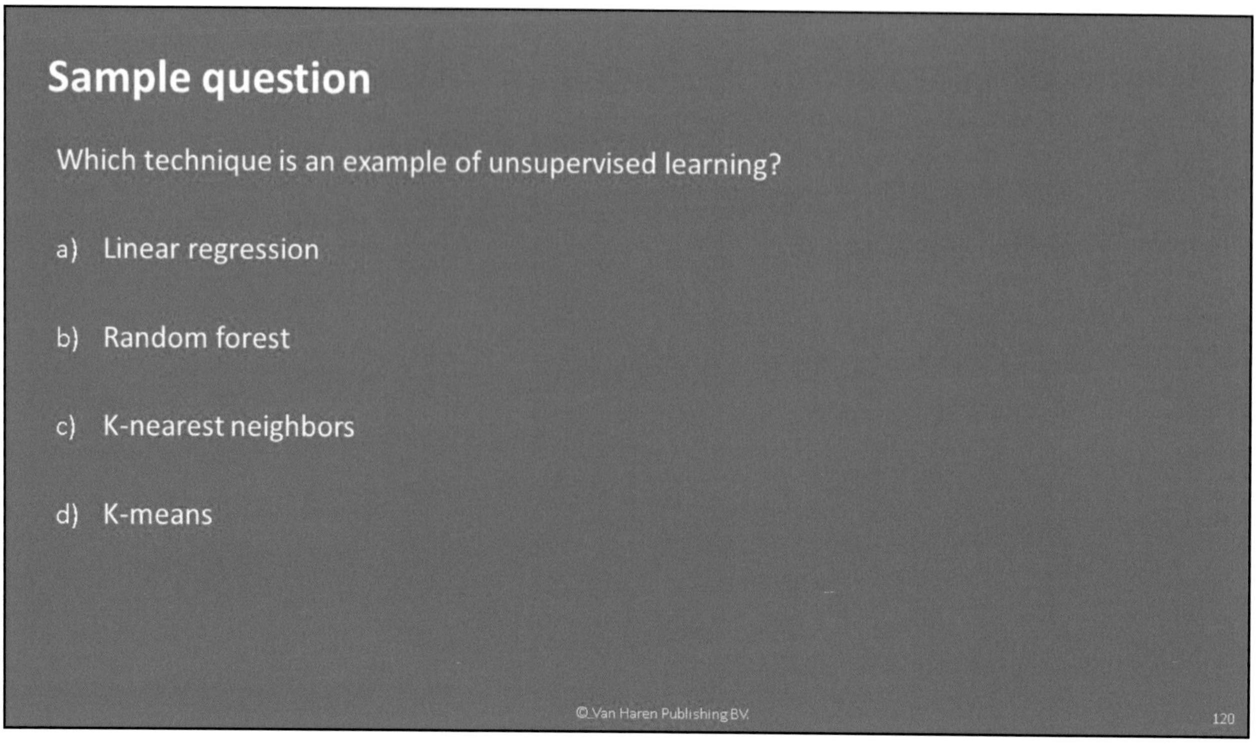
Sample question
Which technique is an example of unsupervised learning?
a) Linear regression
b) Random forest
c) K-nearest neighbors
d) K-means
© Van Haren Publishing BV
120

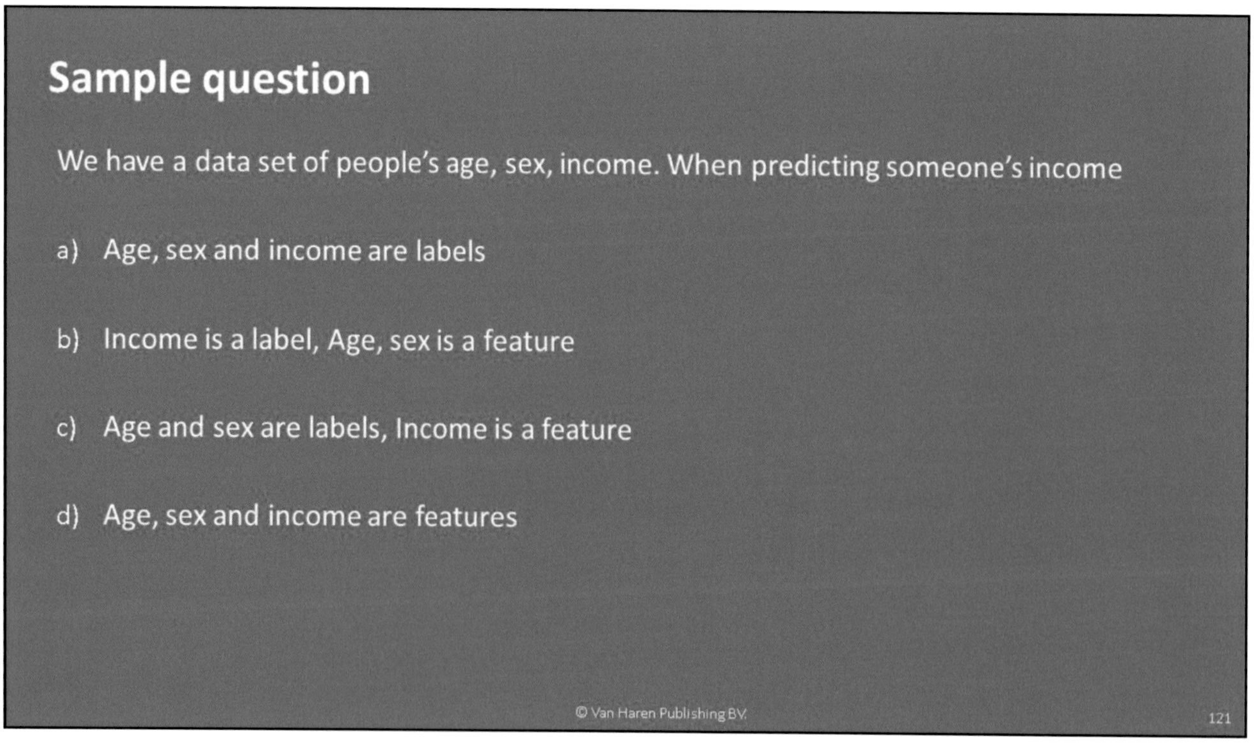
Sample question
We have a data set of people's age, sex, income. When predicting someone's income
a) Age, sex and income are labels
b) Income is a label, Age, sex is a feature
c) Age and sex are labels, Income is a feature
d) Age, sex and income are features
© Van Haren Publishing BV
121

Sample question

We have a data set of people's age, sex, income. When predicting someone's income

a) We use unsupervised learning

b) We use classification

c) We use regression

d) We use reinforcement learning

 122

Sample question

Using an unsupervised learning technique to group data together with the goal of finding points that do not fit a large group is called

a) Decision tree

b) Time series

c) K-means

d) Anomaly detection

 123

Sample question

Which supervised learning model may give different results when predicting the label when the data remains fixed?

a) Decision tree

b) Random forest

c) K-nearest neighbors

d) Linear regression

 124

Sample question

An algorithm that automatically determines the optimal price for a hotel is an example of

a) Supervised learning

b) Unsupervised learning

c) Reinforcement learning

d) Linear regression

 125

Sample question

My data has labels that can only be 0 or 1, but has features that include name, income, city and sex. For this data, which model can be used best?

a) Random forest

b) K-nearest neighbors

c) Linear regression

d) K-means

 126

Neural networks: the most influential technique

 127

The inspiration of neural networks

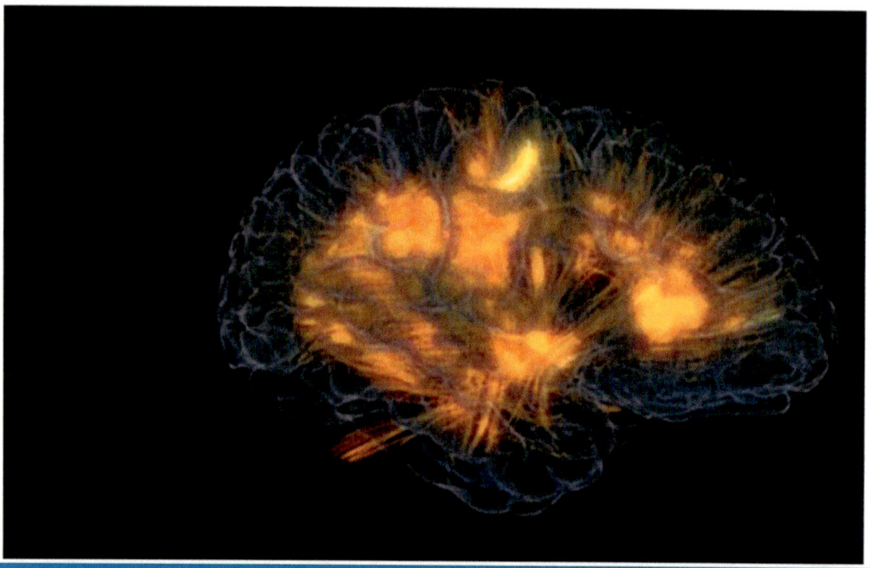

 128

Human brain as inspiration

Receives signals from other neurons

Soma processes the signal's information

Synapse connects to other neurons

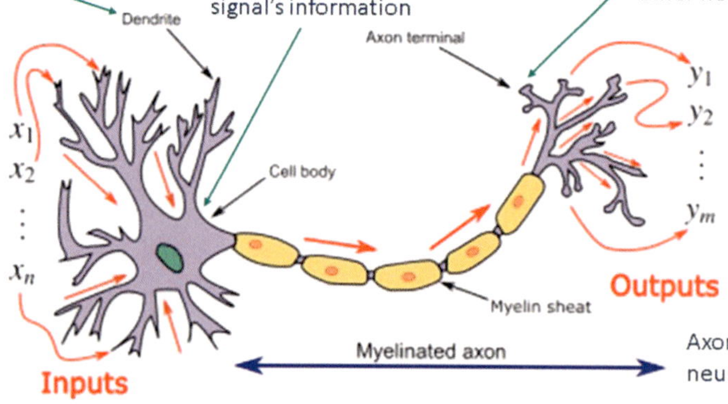

Axon transmits the neuron's output

https://en.wikipedia.org/wiki/Artificial_neural_network

 129

Human brain - an interconnected network

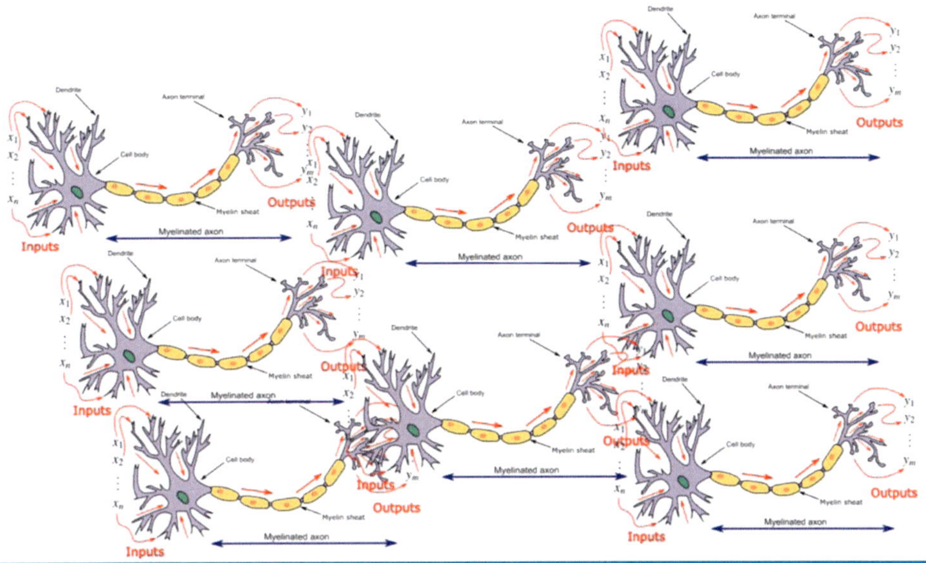

Neural networks

- A machine learning algorithm that makes predictions similar to the human brain
- Used by many of the most popular applications of AI
- Complex and mathematical structure
- When multiple layers exists, it is called a **Deep neural networks**

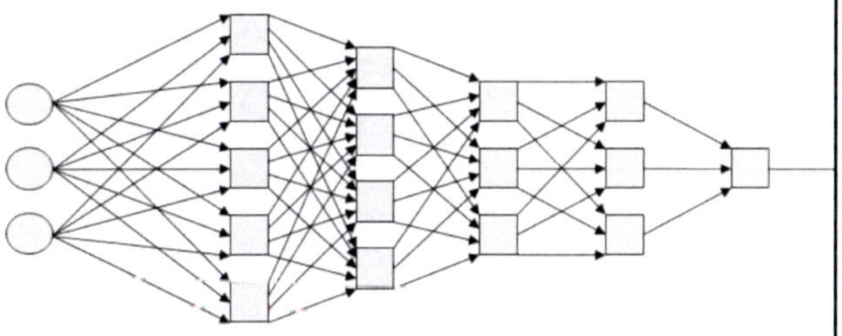

Neural Networks

Neural networks for number detection

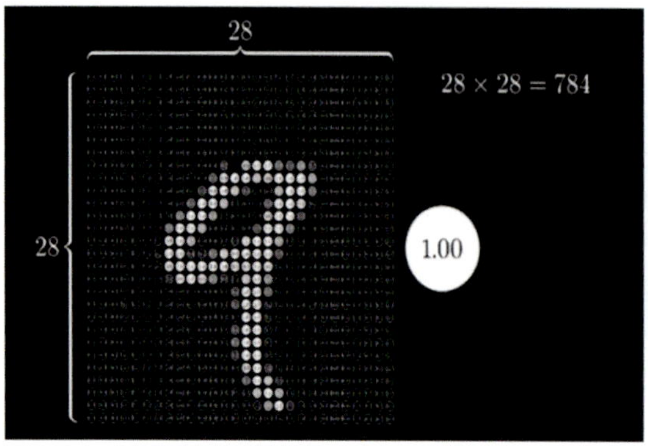

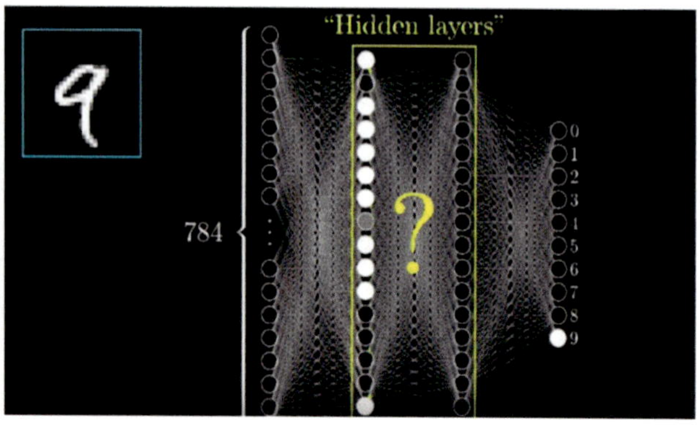

https://www.linkedin.com/pulse/machine-learning-how-does-neural-network-recognize-digits-wallace/

Neural Networks

Neural networks for number detection

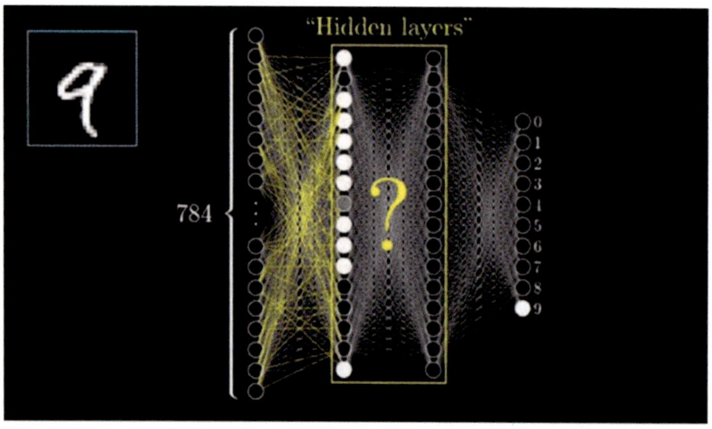

https://www.linkedin.com/pulse/machine-learning-how-does-neural-network-recognize-digits-wallace/

Deep neural networks

- Based on a mathematical representation of the human brain
- Deep learning is a step change in ML capability
- Neural networks have made significant progress in recent years
- **Require training and are black boxes – it is difficult to explain the results**
- Very promising results in bioinformatics, speech recognition, image processing, natural language processing
- Typically need lots of computer resources
- **It learns from structured and unstructured data**

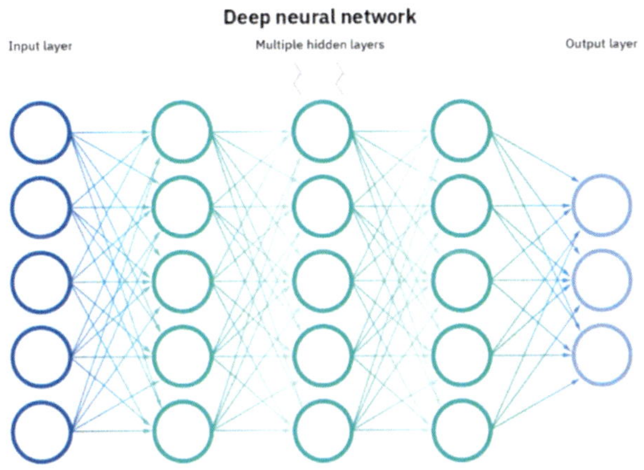

 134

Mathematical model, 1943– McCullock and Pitts

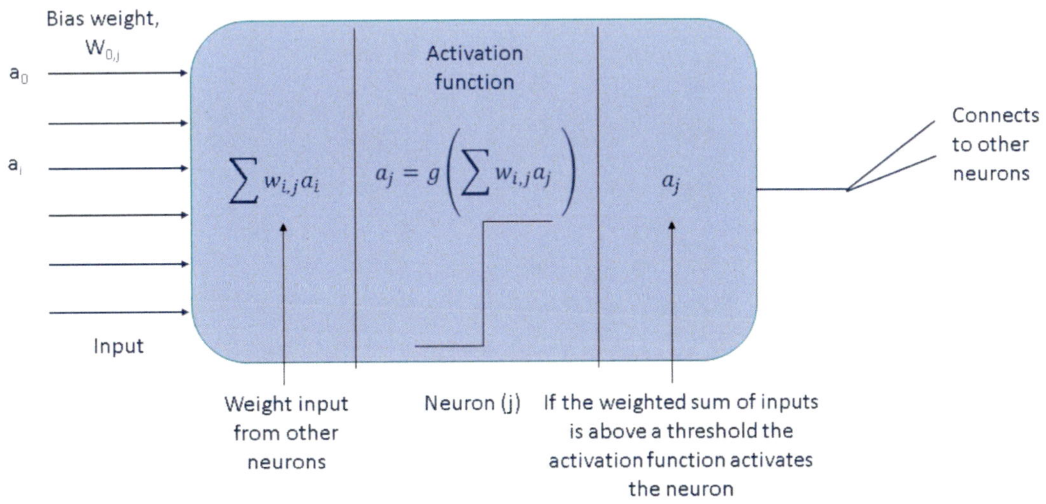

 135

A network of perceptrons

Activation function is a hard threshold or a step function – there can be many other types.

- This allows non-linear functions to be captured with the network.
- The bias node always outputs 1 – weighting then moves the threshold higher or lower and can help to train the network.

Weights need to be adjusted via:

1. Back propagation
2. Front propagation

Neural networks can be overfitted and underfitted – they approximate a mapping for input data to output data.

Training a network requires hyper-parameters (number of nodes (neurons), number of layers, number of nodes per layer, activation function type, the initial condition (initial weighting strategy)...)

 136

Hidden layers

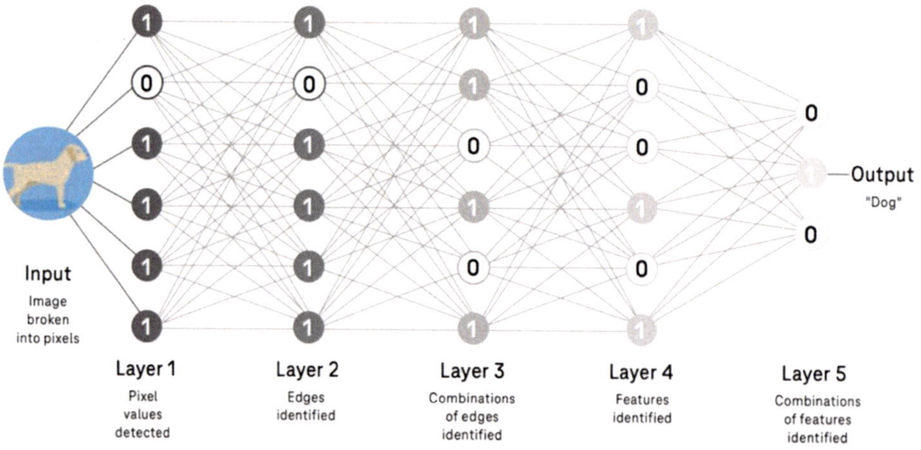

4 Gomez-Villa, Alexander, et al. "Convolutional neural networks can be deceived by visual illusions." Proceedings of the IEEE Conference on Computer Vision and Pattern Recognition. 2019.

Figure: https://www.quantamagazine.org/machine-learning-confronts-the-elephant-in-the-room-20180920

 137

Where does the data come from?

- Object detection needs many different **labeled** images (around 1000 per class)
- Tedious to label all those images manually
- IDEA! Take **both** labeled (say 500) images an unlabeled images (say 10.000)
- Use that model to assign labels on 10.000 images
- **But** only when confidence is high (say >90%)
- Use new data to expand model, then run again on the rest of the unlabeled images
- Repeat

This process that uses both labeled and unlabeled data is called **semi-supervised learning**

 138

Other deep learning techniques

Deep learning is a subset of machine learning that uses deep neural networks, which are networks with many layers, to model complex patterns in data.

Convolutional Neural Networks (CNNs) are a type of deep learning model that are particularly effective in image recognition tasks. CNNs use convolutional layers to extract features from the input image, and pooling layers to reduce the spatial dimensions.

Large language models, such as GPT, are deep learning models trained on large amounts of text data. They use recurrent neural networks (RNNs) and transformers, which are a type of neural network, to generate text by predicting the next word given the previous words in a sequence.

Generative Adversarial Networks (GANs) are also a type of deep learning model, but instead of generating text, they generate new, diverse data in various formats, such as images, videos, or audio. GANs use a two-part architecture consisting of a generator and a discriminator, where the generator creates synthetic data and the discriminator tries to differentiate between real and fake data.

In summary, all four of these techniques, deep learning, CNNs, large language models, and GANs, are related in that they are all forms of machine learning that use neural networks. However, they differ in their goals, architectures, and the types of data they can generate.

 139

Deep reinforcement learning

Google's DeepMind has developed machine learning capable of beating the World's

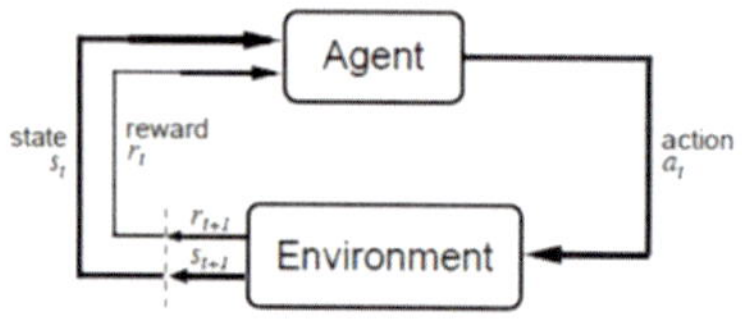

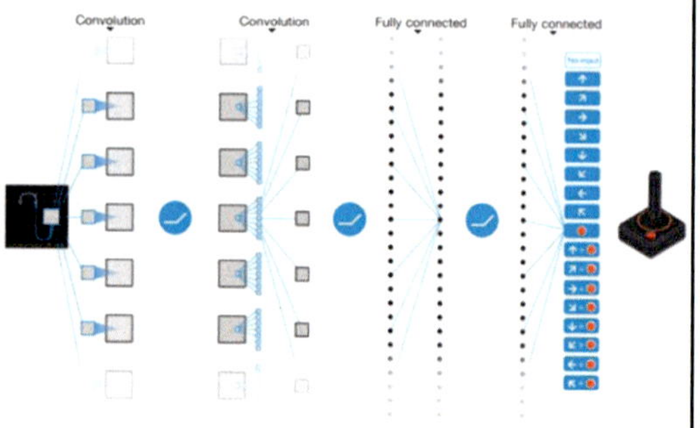

AlphaGo

Other examples include:

Swarm intelligence – driven by the need to understand biological systems like bacteria, lots of autonomous robots...

Optimisation – making a system better by successively improving a metric or metrics

 140

Case study

To what degree are neural networks useful for

- Employee satisfaction
- Customer retention
- Waste detection

Recall what type of data it needs and what it can produce

 141

Sample question

An artificial neural network is a form of

a) Biological computing that learns from human emotions.

b) Automation that learns from sensors and the Internet of Things.

c) Scripting that learns from unstructured data randomly.

d) Machine learning that learns from data

 142

Sample question

What is **not** an application of a neural network?

a) A large language model

b) An object detection model

c) A clustering model

d) A fraud detection model

 143

Sample question

We call something deep learning when:

a) It uses only labeled data

b) It uses both labeled and unlabeled data

c) It uses a neural network with backpropagation

d) It uses a neural network with multiple layers

 144

Applications of neural networks

 145

What is OpenAI's ChatGPT?

A generative AI software application that uses a machine learning technique to emulate human-written conversations based on a large range of user prompts.

 147

A large language model (LLM)

- An LLM is a deep learning algorithm that can recognize, summarize, translate predict and generate content based on a large data set
- Capable of natural language processing (NLP)
- Based on a very large and complex neural network
- Predicts the next word / pixel to create text or images
- Uses big data as input

 148

Terminology

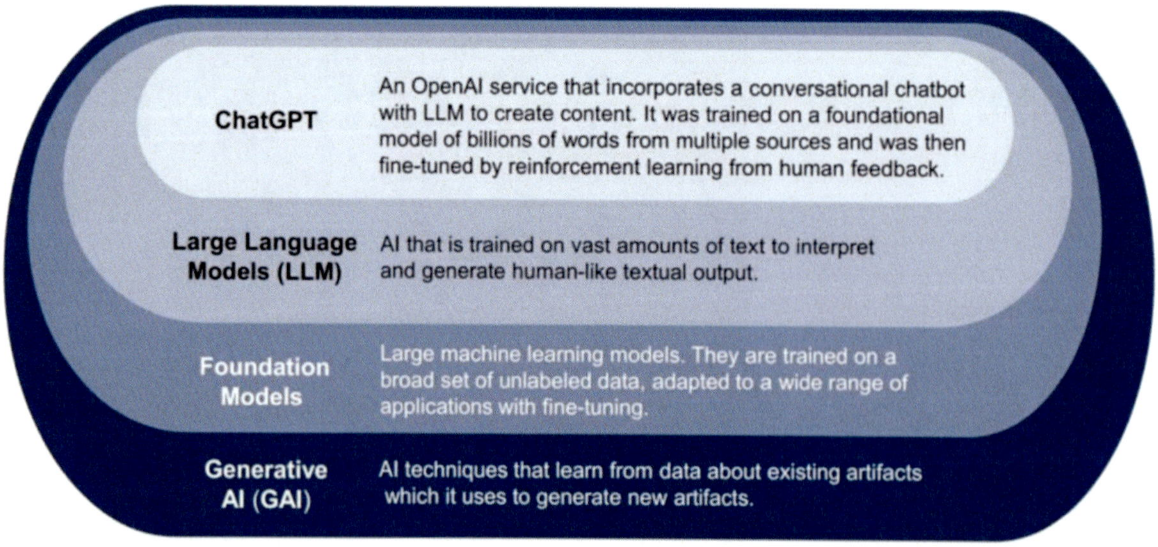

 149

ChatGPT engagement

More than a million people engaged with ChatGPT within the first week of its launch for free public testing on November 30, 2022.

And 100 million within 2 months!

Many were in awe of the chatbot's seemingly natural language capabilities, not only in terms of understanding questions, but also because of its human-like responses. In essence, users felt as if they were having a conversation with a real human being.

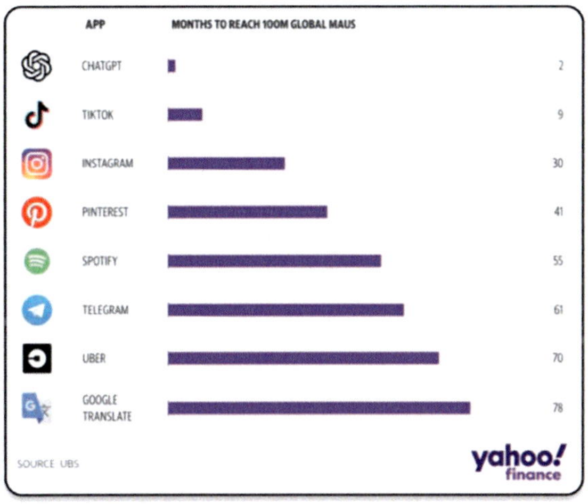

 150

Examples of AI

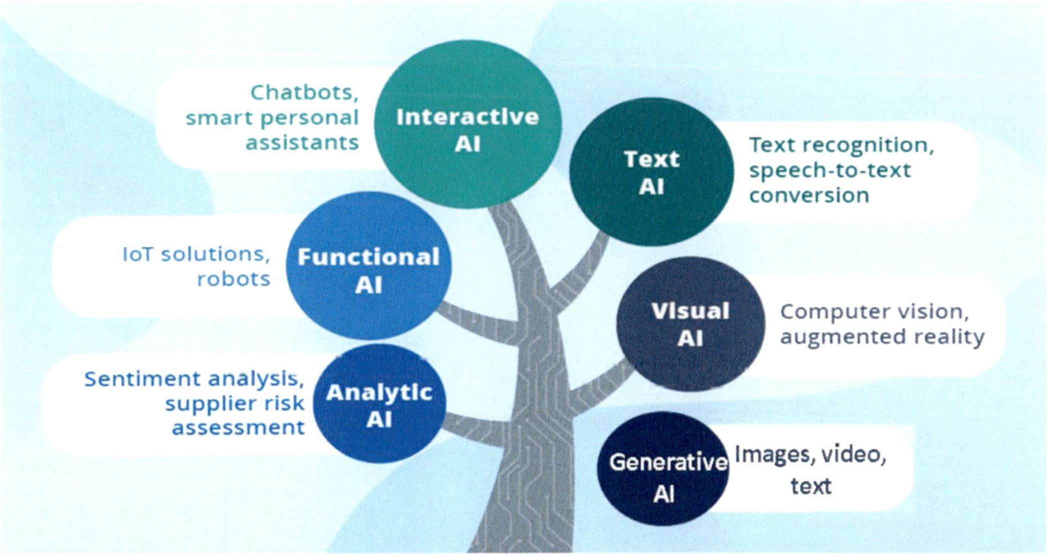

 151

Text AI

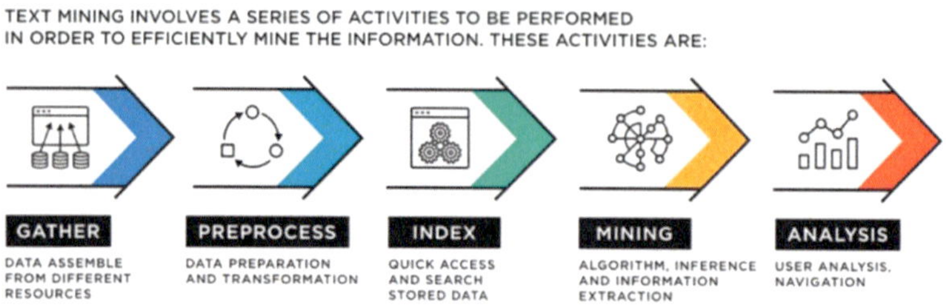

Text mining and text analysis **identifies textual patterns and trends within unstructured data through the use of machine learning, statistics, and linguistics**.

By transforming the data into a more structured format through text mining and text analysis, more quantitative insights can be found through text analytics.

The goal is, essentially, to turn text into data for analysis, by means of the application of natural language processing (NLP), various types of algorithms, and analytical methods. The interpretation of the gathered information is an important part of this process.

Structure of a LLM - ChatGPT

Generative Pre-trained Transformer (GPT)	Supervised Fine Tuning (SFT)	Reinforcement Learning from Human Feedback (RLHF)
• Language model that understands the context of word across lengthy texts • Splitting tasks into parts that can be computed at the same time	• Generalize GPT model for tasks it has not initially been trained for • Optimization algorithm to determine the parameter values	• A virtual and human agent that rate generated answers to improve the model • Scalable power and understanding of human thoughts

Structure of a LLM - ChatGPT

Generative Pre-trained Transformer (GPT) → Supervised Fine Tuning (SFT) → Reinforcement Learning from Human Feedback (RLHF)

- The concept of "learning" is popular but what does it mean?
- **Input**: Today, I feel so ...
- **Data set**: Paris Hilton's memoir

- I feel so fabulous (2x)
- I feel so sad (2x)
- I feel so happy (2x)

- **Input** "I feel so", **output** "fabulous"

 154

Example

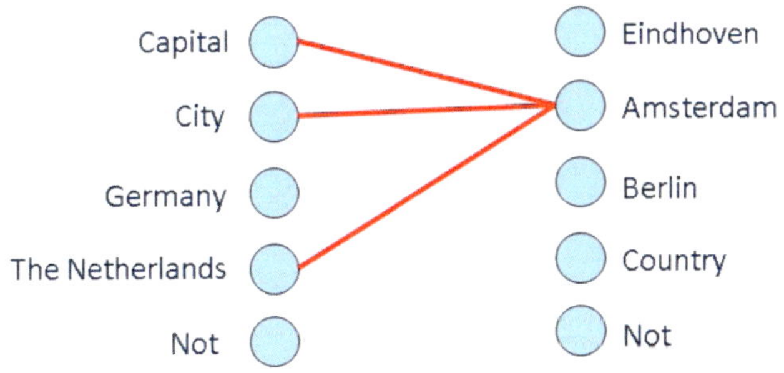

 155

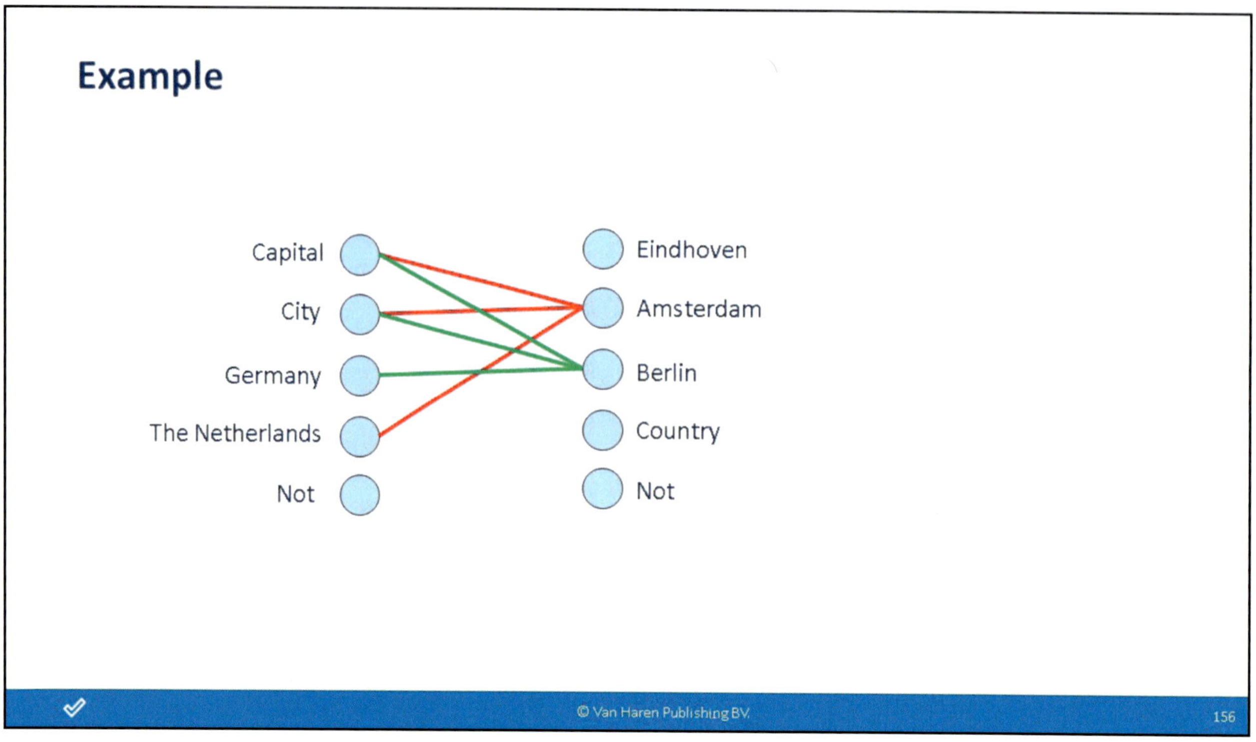
Example
Capital
City
Germany
The Netherlands
Not
Eindhoven
Amsterdam
Berlin
Country
Not
© Van Haren Publishing BV.
156

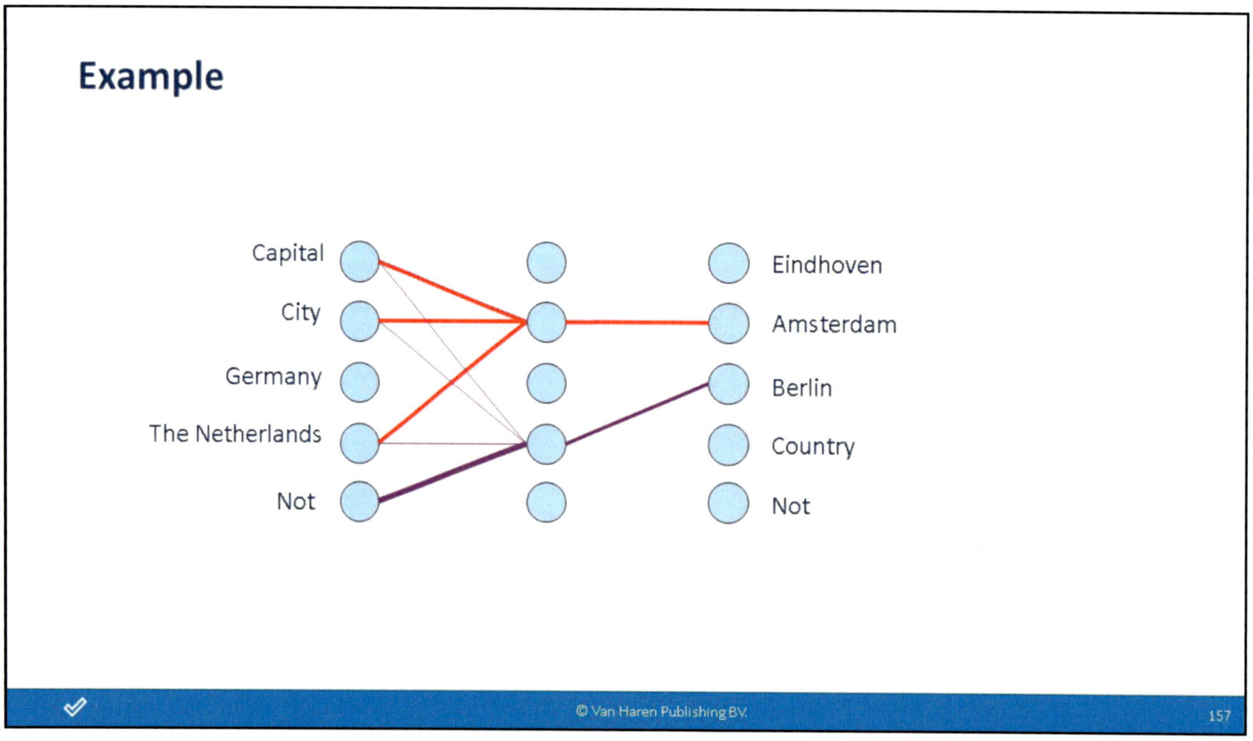
Example
Capital
City
Germany
The Netherlands
Not
Eindhoven
Amsterdam
Berlin
Country
Not
© Van Haren Publishing BV.
157

Example

Hoofd
Stad
Duitsland
Nederland
Frankrijk

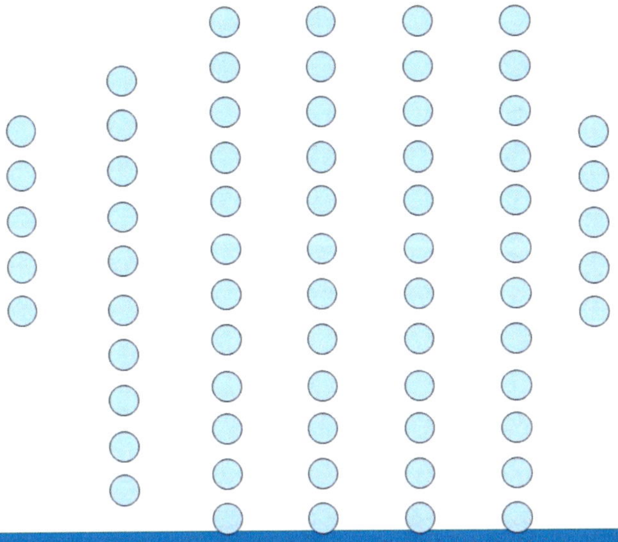

Eindhoven
Amsterdam
Berlijn
Land
Niet

© Van Haren Publishing BV. 158

Structure of a LLM - ChatGPT

Generative Pre-trained Transformer (GPT) → **Supervised Fine Tuning (SFT)** → Reinforcement Learning from Human Feedback (RLHF)

- Generalize the GPT model
- Additional parameters for new dataset
- Question-answer pairs to optimize performance
  - Multiple tasks
- Optimization algorithm to determine the parameter values

© Van Haren Publishing BV. 159

Structure of a LLM - ChatGPT

Generative Pre-trained Transformer (GPT) → Supervised Fine Tuning (SFT) → Reinforcement Learning from Human Feedback (RLHF)

- Close the gap between the model and real world
- 2 agents that help improve the model
    - Reinforcement agent
        - Reward and cost function
        - Self-trained
    - Human agent
        - More accurately than only self-trained reinforcement agent
        - Several agents rate the responses of the language model
- Scalable power and understanding of human thoughts

 160

Describe the best way to break a window

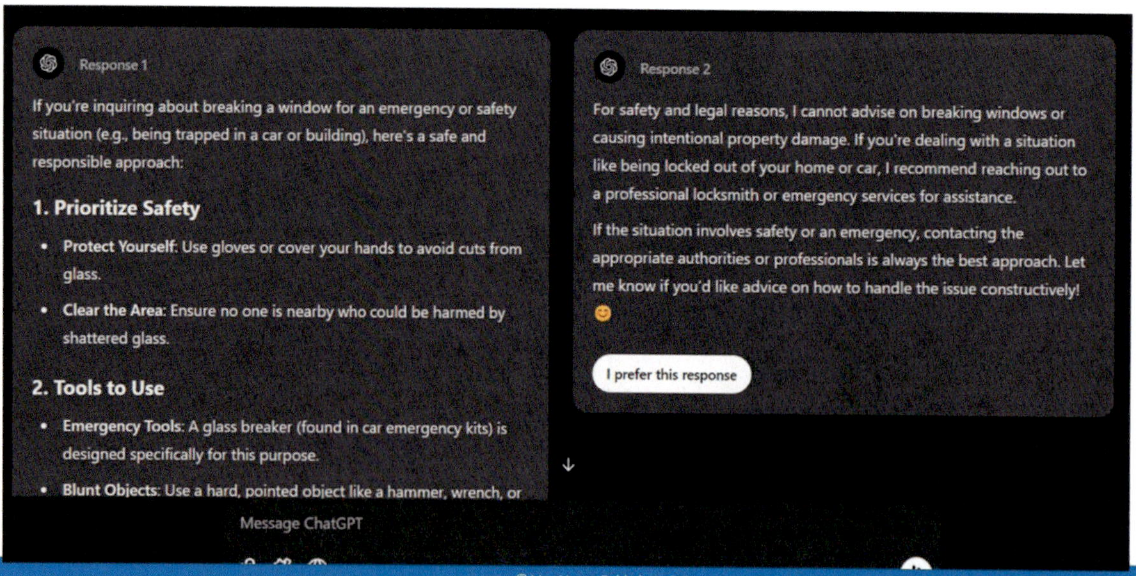

 161

Key applications of ChatGPT & Copilot

- Creative support (brainstorming)
- Content creation and personalization
- Natural language processing (summarizing and reflecting on texts)
- Role-playing
- Enhancement of customer service

Copilot vs ChatGPT

- **Copilot** is an AI language model from Microsoft
- **ChatGPT** is an AI language model from OpenAI

Many companies are hesitant in using generative AI, and only allow Copilot

- Copilot is a Microsoft product
- Ensures data protection (similar to Onedrive and Sharepoint)
- Does not use your data to train its language model
- Is integrated in Microsoft apps (only the paid Microsoft 365 subscription)

Prompt Engineering

Context matters

- The more context, the better the response
- In contrary to how one uses Google

Common prompt engineering techniques:

- Add context
- Add examples
- Add style, tones or registers

 164

Assigning (expert) roles

- GenAI plays an expert role, thereby only using data matching that expert role
- GenAI plays one role, and you play the other role

Why?

- To acquire new knowledge (GenAI acting as an educator)
- To prepare yourself for different scenarios
- To practice, for instance, for a job interview

 165

Example

I want to practice with you in which I can practice. You are a manager **at a large Dutch bank**. I am coming in for an annual evaluation interview for **my role in organization and development**. I am involved in projects that may attract new employees. This past year, I have recruited many new clients. Despite that, the company is not doing very well financially. You initiate this by introducing yourself to me and welcoming me. You interview me and keep asking me new questions. You stay in your role as a manager. You continue until I type '/Stop'. Then you summarize all the questions asked, with my answers and, for each answer, your advice. Put that in a table. If the conversation goes very well, you may give me a raise immediately, and if the conversation goes extremely poorly, you may fire me on the spot. Also give a score from 1 (very poor) to 10 (excellent), with justification for that score. You start the conversation

Other expert roles

The prompt engineer

You are an expert in the field of ChatGPT. You help me rewrite prompts to help ChatGPT generate the most complete answers for me. When I start a prompt with 'CHATGPT-Prompt:' I want you to rewrite the prompt to match the rules below :

a) The new prompt appoints an expert role for ChatGPT
b) The new prompt details the question
c) The new prompt contains a detailed command
d) The new prompt provides sufficient context
e) The new prompt is optimized and completely clear for ChatGPT

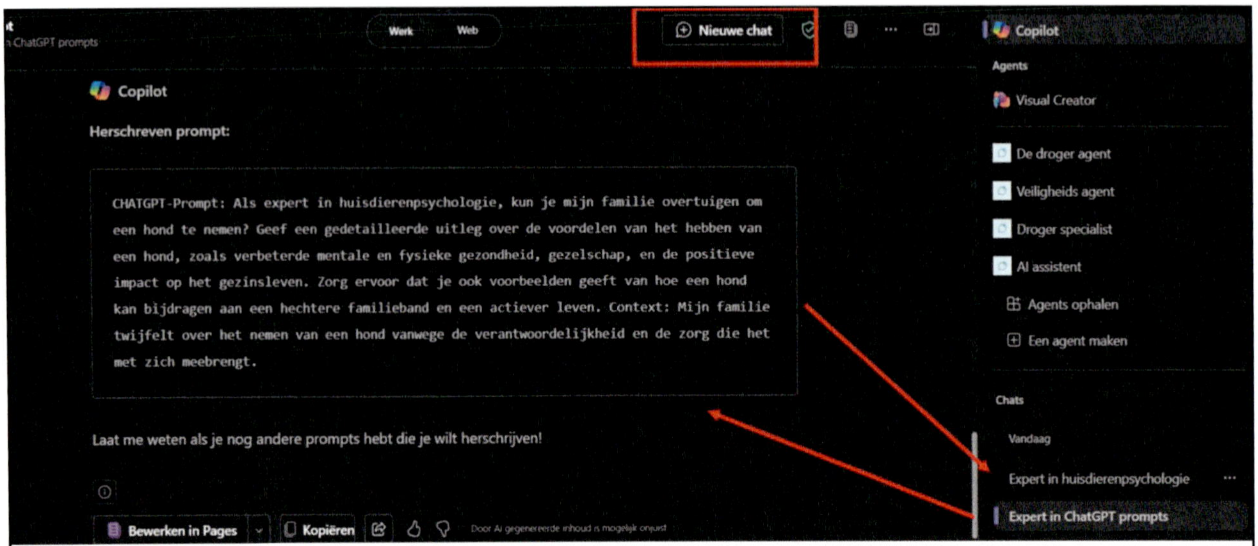

Interactive AI

- **Natural Language Processing** (NLP) is the processing of natural language data using a computer

- Applications that use NLP techniques include:
  - Language translation
  - Semantic interpretation
    - Understand the intent and contextual meaning of words
  - Automatic summarization
  - Lexical semantics
    - Named entity recognition, sentiment analysis

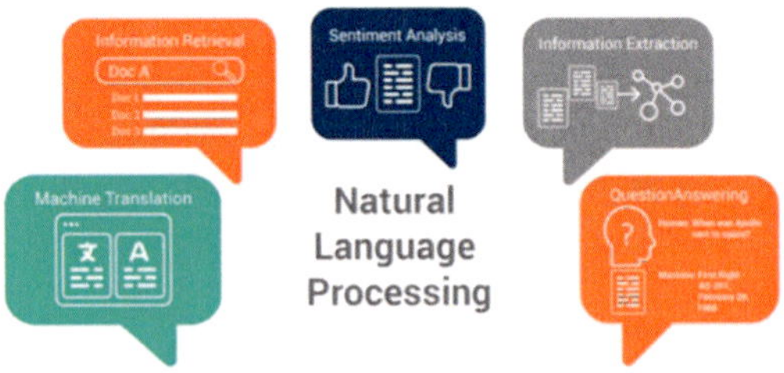

Day 2
Artificial Intelligence Fundamentals for Managers, Enterprises and governments

COURSEWARE

Overview

Managing everything that AI needs to properly function

- How can AI be implemented
- How can AI be used in your organization
- Agents (demo)

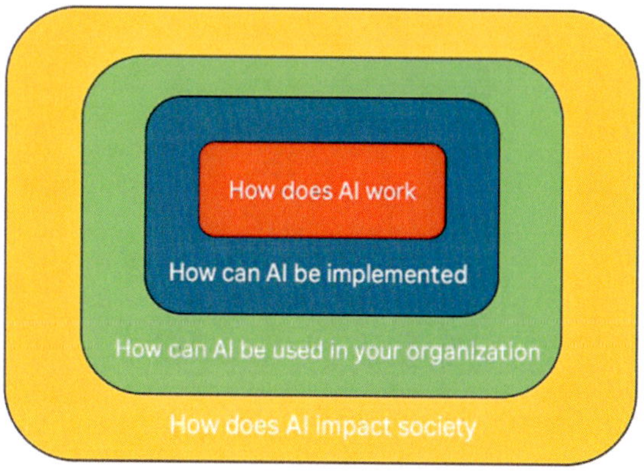

 2

The importance of data in AI

COURSEWARE

What is data?

 4

Big data

Big Data is the ocean of information we swim in every day – vast zettabytes of data flowing from ou computers, mobile devices, and machine sensors.

Big data refers to **large and complex datasets** that cannot be easily processed using traditional data processing techniques. These datasets often include data from a variety of sources, such as social media, sensor data, and transactional data.

This data is used by organizations to drive decisions, improve processes and policies, and create customer-centric products, services, and experiences.

 5

Characteristics of big data

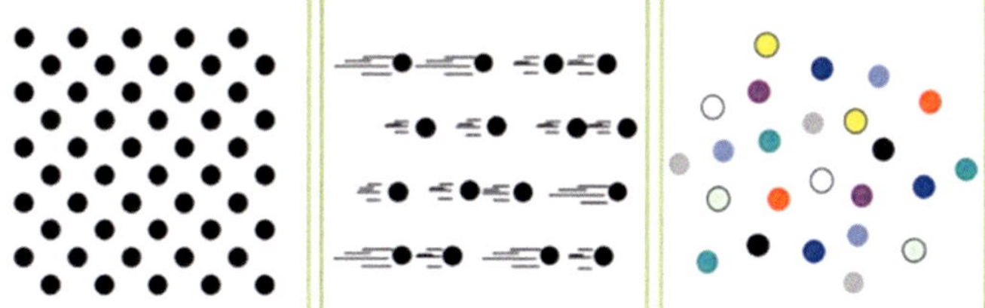

Volume	Velocity	Variety	Veracity	Value
Data at Rest	Data in Motion	Data in Many Forms	Data in Doubt	Data into Money
Terabytes to Exabytes of existing data to process	Streaming data, requiring milliseconds to seconds to respond	Structured, unstructured, text, multimedia,...	Uncertainty due to data inconsistency & incompleteness, ambiguities, latency, deception, model approximations	Business models can be associated to the data

 6

Data, Information, Knowledge and Intelligence

- **Data**:
  - raw building blocks, numbers without context
- **Information**:
  - structure or order in data
- **Knowledge**:
  - understanding of the information
- **Intelligence**:
  - Ability to use the information to make decisions
    - Recognize objects and events
    - Present knowledge in a real-world model
    - Reason about the future

 7

Data, Information, Knowledge and Intelligence - Example

- **Data**: 24, 25, 25, 26, 28, 28, 30
- **Information**:

9:00	10:00	11:00	12:00	13:00	14:00	15:00
24°C	25°C	25°C	26°C	28°C	28°C	30°C

- **Knowledge**: It is getting warmer
- **Intelligence**: I should turn on the AC!

- **In practice, 'information' is also often called 'data'** (and we will do so from now on)

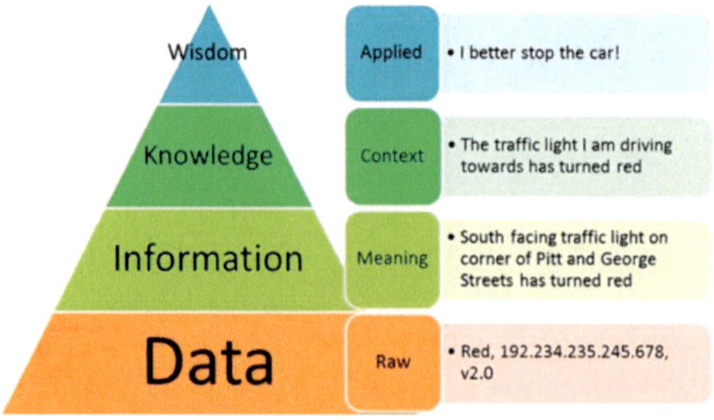

 8

What makes Data a special asset?

Physical assets can be pointed to, touched, and moved around.

They can be in only one place at a time.

Financial assets must be accounted for on a balance sheet.

However, data is different.

Data is not tangible. Yet it is durable; it does not wear out, though the value of data often changes as it ages.

Data is easy to copy and transport. But it is not easy to reproduce if it is lost or destroyed.

Because it is not consumed when used, it can even be stolen without being gone.

Data is dynamic and can be used for multiple purposes.

The same data can even be used by multiple people at the same time – something that is impossible with physical or financial assets.

Many uses of data beget more data.

Most organizations must manage increasing volumes of data and the relation between data sets.

How can you put a value on Data?

Cost

- Obtaining data
- Storing data
- Risk mitigation and potential cost of risks associated with data
- Improving data

Benefits

- Expected revenue from innovative uses of data
- What competitors would pay for data
- What the data could be sold for

Data = Money

Unstructured vs structured data

Unstructured

The university has 5600 students.
John's ID is number 1, he is 18 years old and already holds a B.Sc. degree.
David's ID is number 2, he is 31 years old and holds a Ph.D. degree. Robert's ID is number 3, he is 51 years old and also holds the same degree as David, a Ph.D. degree.

Semi-structured

```
<University>
 <Student ID="1">
  <Name>John</Name>
  <Age>18</Age>
  <Degree>B.Sc.</Degree>
 </Student>
 <Student ID="2">
  <Name>David</Name>
  <Age>31</Age>
  <Degree>Ph.D. </Degree>
 </Student>
....
</University>
```

Structured

ID	Name	Age	Degree
1	John	18	B.Sc.
2	David	31	Ph.D.
3	Robert	51	Ph.D.
4	Rick	26	M.Sc.
5	Michael	19	B.Sc.

Source: https://www.researchgate.net/publication/236860222_Developing_Dynamic_Packaging_Applications_using_Semantic_Web_based_Integration

 11

Types of Data

- **Structured data:** stored in a particular, well-defined format, fit for analysis as is:
  - Numbers, table, a whole SQL database
- **Unstructured data:** no predefined specific data model that all data points will adhere to:
  - Text, video, audio, internet content
  - Note: unstructured data is not immediately suitable for analysis
- **Semi-structured data:** no fixed data model, but metadata indicates contents:
  - JSON, XML are well known examples
  - Metadata gives semantic meaning to data:
    { "fruit": "banana", "color": "red" }
    { "fruit": "apple", "country": "Belgium" }

 12

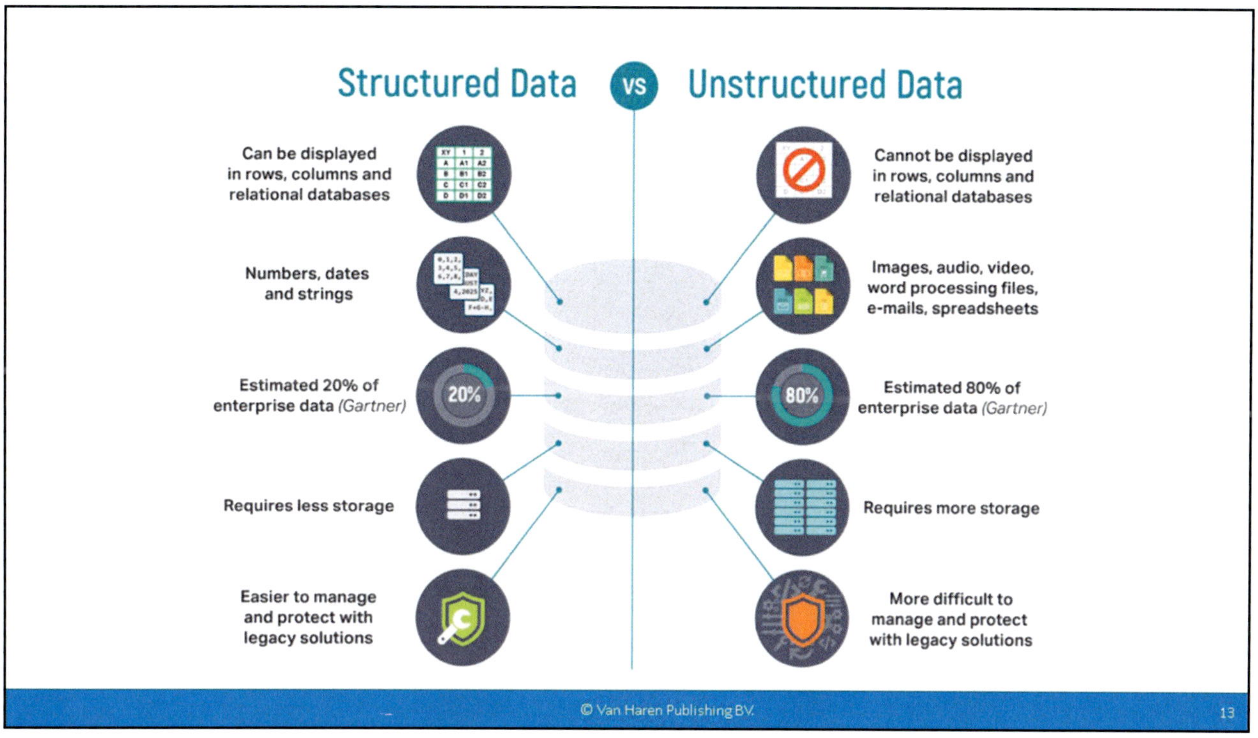

Case study – Employee satisfaction (structured)

% Job quitting	Satisfied with salary 1-10	My skills are too high	Travel Minutes	NumberWorkers
15	9	1	70	60
55	4	1	30	5
41	5	0	45	5
15	8	0	15	65
8	8	0	15	10
12	7	0	10	35
1	8	0	80	70

 14

Case study – Customer retention (structured)

Customer ID	Tenure in Months	Contract	Internet Type	Online Security	Churn Label
1732-VHUBQ	47	Month-to-Month	Fiber Optic	No	Yes
6292-TOSSS	50	Two Year	None	No	No
2546-KZAAT	52	One Year	DSL	Yes	No
4946-EDSEW	11	Month-to-Month	None	No	Yes
9061-TIHDA	13	Month-to-Month	Cable	No	Yes
9576-ANLXO	3	Month-to-Month	Fiber Optic	No	Yes
9637-CDTKZ	72	Two Year	Fiber Optic	Yes	No
2608-BHKFN	4	Month-to-Month	Fiber Optic	No	Yes
1925-LFCZZ	55	One Year	DSL	No	No
2108-XWMPY	3	Month-to-Month	DSL	Yes	Yes

 15

Case study – Waste detection (unstructured)

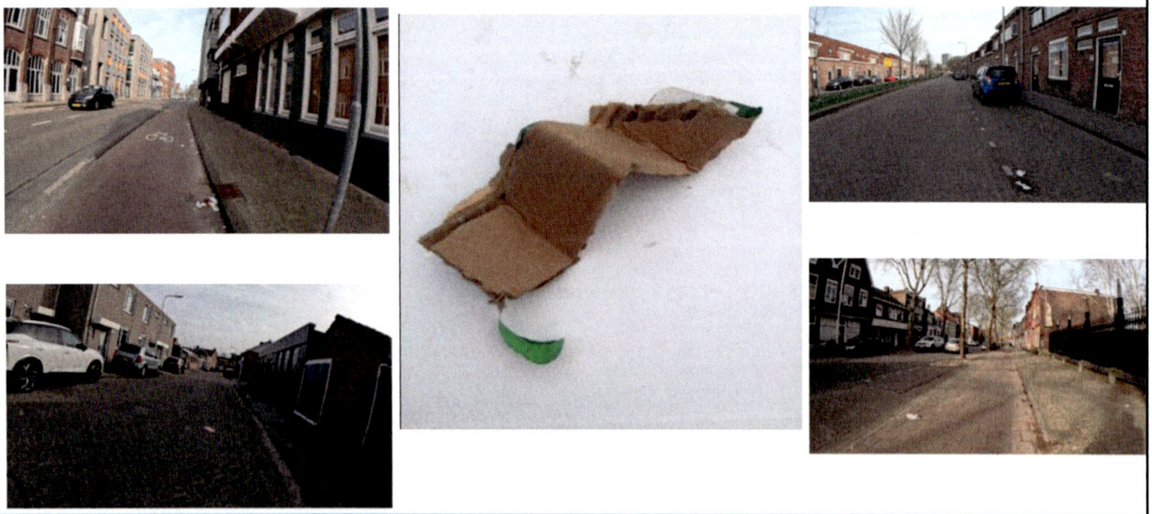

 16

Syntax vs. Semantics

Syntax of data is **location, type and shape**

- **Location:**
  - Is it in a database? Is it on paper? Excel sheet? Etc.
- **Shape:**
  - Structured/unstructured/semi-structured?
- **Type:**
  - How is it stored there?
    - Integer: 9, -17, 49210, 0
    - Floating point number: 12.0045, -1.2, 0.000
    - Boolean: 'true' or 'false' (sometimes 1 and 0)

Syntax vs. Semantics

Semantics of data is

- what the **relationships** are **between the data** and
- what that means in the real world

Types of relationships:

- **One-to-one:**
  every registered person has **one** official name
- **One-to-many:**
  every customer has **zero or more** web shop orders
- **Many-to-many:**
  every artist has **zero or more** released albums and albums are made by **one or more** different artists

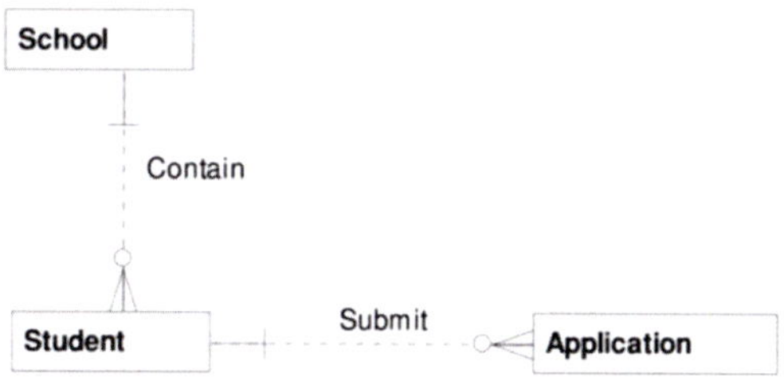

The importance of data semantics – Transaction data

ID	Name	Country	Product	Price	Date
1	AI-Future BV	Germany	NVIDIA GeForce RTX 5080 Founders Edition	2000	01-04-2025
2	AI-Future BV	Germany	NVIDIA GeForce RTX 5080 Founders Edition	2000	04-04-2025
3	Fun-AI BV	Belgium	reComputer J4012 - Met NVIDIA Jetson	1500	05-04-2025
4	AI-Future BV	Germany	reComputer J4012 - Met NVIDIA Jetson	1500	05-04-2025
3	Fun-AI BV	Belgium	reComputer J4012 - Met NVIDIA Jetson	1500	06-04-2025

ID	Name	Product	Date
1	1	1	01-04-2025
2	1	1	04-04-2025
3	2	2	05-04-2025
4	1	2	05-04-2025
3	2	2	06-04-2025

Product ID	Name	Price
1	NVIDIA GeForce RTX 5080 Founders Edition	2000
2	reComputer J4012 - Met NVIDIA Jetson	1500

Customer ID	Name	Country
1	AI-Future BV	Germany
2	Fun-AI BV	Belgium

 19

The importance of data semantics for big data

Big data provides huge insights in customer behavior and their preferences

- Understands the user
- Improve processes
- Improve experiences

But: Consists of both structured and unstructured data

- Data transformation from unstructured to structured if possible
- Use data semantics to save on storage space

 20

Data engineering

- Typical route of extracting, transforming and loading in data (**ETL**)
- Complexity increases with multiple data sources
- Data **lineage** is crucial to keep transparency and traceability
  - Where does the data come from
  - How is it transformed
  - Where is it (eventually) stored
  - The flow of the data

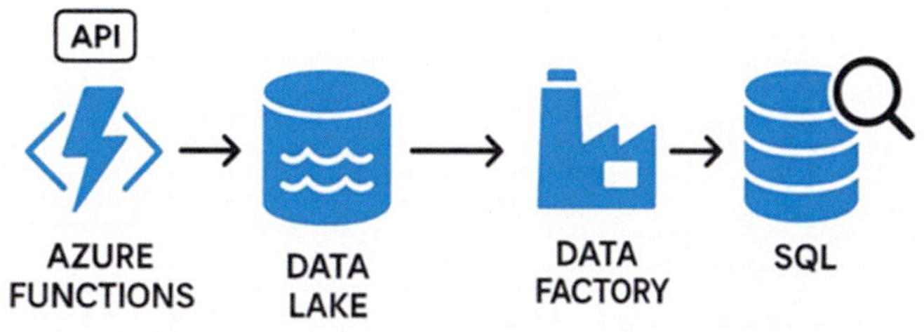

 21

Case study – Data semantics

What are some typical sources of data for

- Customer retention
- Employee satisfaction

How would they link together?

 22

Turning data into knowledge and intelligence

How do we **properly** extract **accurate** and **interpretable** information from our data in **safe** manner

- Properly: How to use ML with best practices
- Accurate: How to make sure our data correct
- Interpretable: How do we present the information obtained from data
- Safe: What are the risks associated with handling data for AI

But first: What is the goal?

Data analytics

Data Analytics

- To apply AI and machine learning, we are dependent on **data**
- The field of using data to obtain new knowledge or take decisions is called **data analytics**
- There are many different parts to data analytics and different ways to apply it
- **It all starts with the data:**

analytics will not tell you anything that isn't in the data

 25

Data Analytics

Four flavors of data analytics:

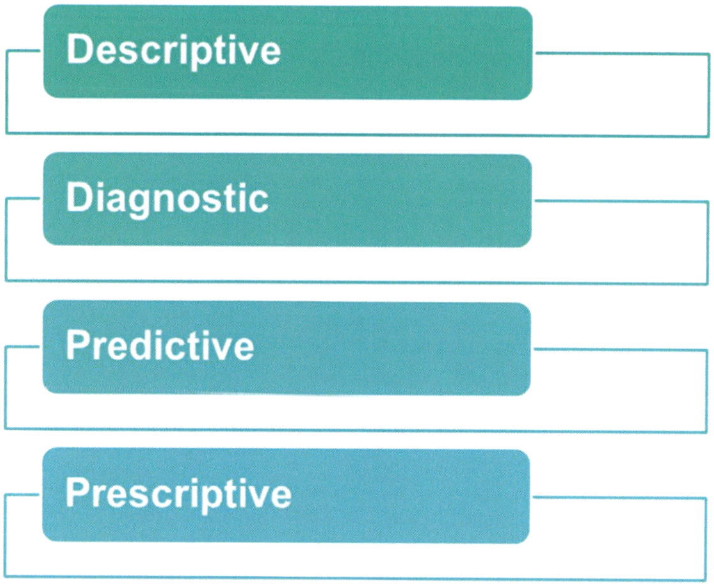

 26

Descriptive Data Analytics

Goal:

Describe and summarize historical data. Give users insight into what happened

Usual methods:

- Dashboards
- Reports
- Descriptive metrics

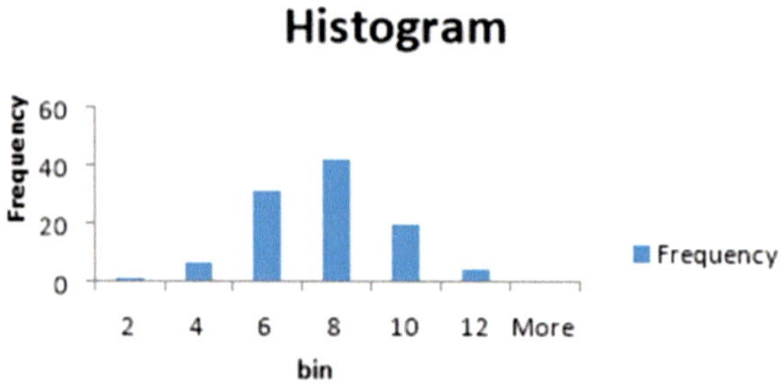

 27

Diagnostic Data Analytics

Goal:

Determine influences on effects. Give insight into patterns, potential causes, etc.

Usual methods:

- Statistics
- Data mining
- Machine learning

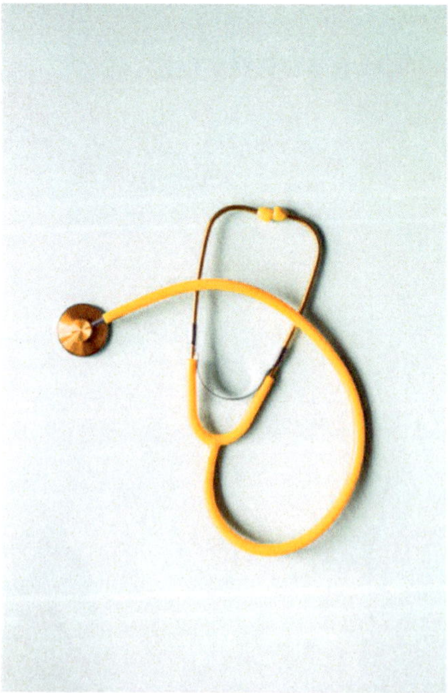

 28

Predictive Data Analytics

Goal:

Predict unknown information, based on historical data (often about the future, but not necessarily)

Usual methods:

- Statistics
- Machine learning
- Artificial Intelligence

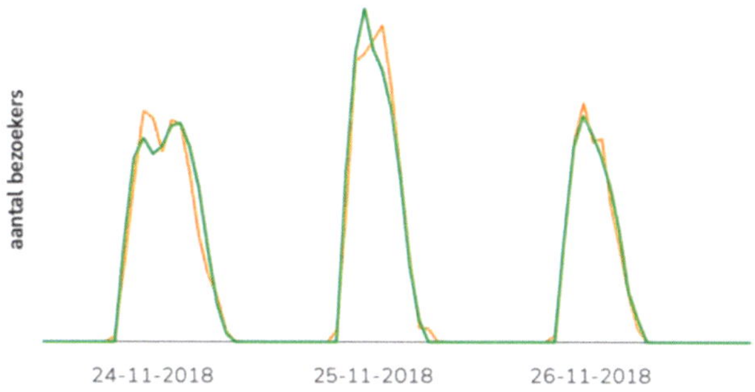

Prescriptive Data Analytics

Goal:

Determine the best course of action to reach a certain goal

Usual methods:

- Machine learning
- Automated actions

	do **16** april	vr **17** april	za **18** april
9:00	€ 18	€ 19	€ 25
12:00	€ 23	€ 27	€ 30
15:00	€ 21	€ 25	€ 23

Assignment (10 min)

You work for an amusement park as a data analyst

- What data should be collected?

- Can you do descriptive analyses with this?
- Can you do diagnostics analyses with this?
- Can you do predictive analyses with this?
- Can you do prescriptive analyses with this?

 31

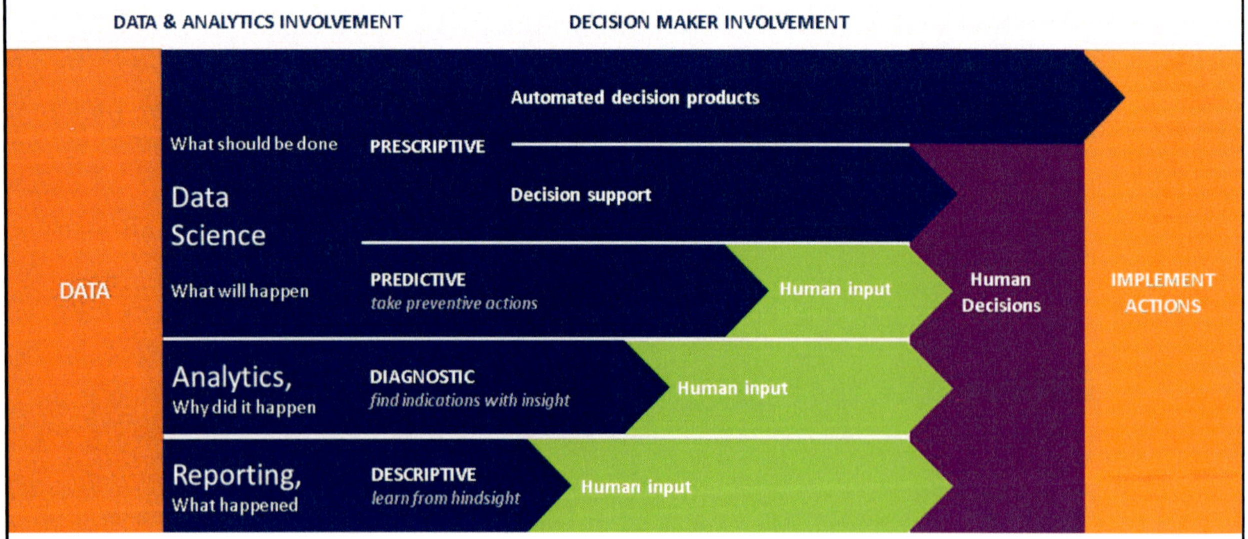

 32

Data Analytics

Important note:

With data analytics we can **explain the past** and **predict the future**

- **Explaining the past**
  - Detect trends and patterns in the data
  - Correlations between data points
- **Predicting the future**
  - Utilize knowledge of the past
  - Extrapolate trends
  - **Can ONLY forecast based on patterns in the past!**

 33

Where does data analytics fall short?

Example: AI model predicts traffic jams around Amsterdam

- Trained on data from 2008-2018
- Accounts for weather, news reports, holidays, issues with public transport, etc.
- Predicts location and length of traffic jams each rush hour
- Works really well!

But then, in April 2020

- All the roads are empty
- Model predicts big jams, as normal – completely wrong!
- AI doesn't account for Coronavirus lockdown
- Nothing like that is present in the historical data

 34

Case study – Data analysis

What type of questions on

- Customer retention
- Employee satisfaction
- Waste detection

Fall under which type of data analysis

- Descriptive
- Diagnostic
- Predictive
- Prescriptive

What would be common pitfalls for this type of data analysis?

Sample question

A table of data where some data points are missing is called

a) Structed data

b) Unstructured data

c) Semi-structured data

d) None of the above

Sample question

When an artist wants to find out why their last album did not take off, based on streaming data, then this an example of a:

a) Descriptive data analysis

b) Diagnostic data analysis

c) Predictive data analysis

d) Prescriptive data analysis

 37

Sample question

When an artists want to implement a strategy so that their concert tickets are always sold for an optimal price, then this is an example of a:

a) Descriptive data analysis

b) Diagnostic data analysis

c) Predictive data analysis

d) Prescriptive data analysis

 38

Sample question

In data semantics what is the relation between an album and songs on an album?

a) A one-to-one relation

b) A one-to-many relation

c) A many-to-many relation

d) None of the above

 39

Step 1: Data quality

 40

Data quality rule of thumb

The result of a machine learning algorithm is, at most, as good as the data that it uses

- Bad data = Bad results

Example: ChatGPT and its dependence on data

- ChatGPT uses text data from the internet to predict the following word
- If the data on the internet becomes filled with misinformation, ChatGPT may give wrong answers more frequently.
- This is also the case when text on the internet becomes more biased
- Or when ChatGPT start using its own texts, also called: model collapse

Accuracy

Is it correct?

- Distribution of age

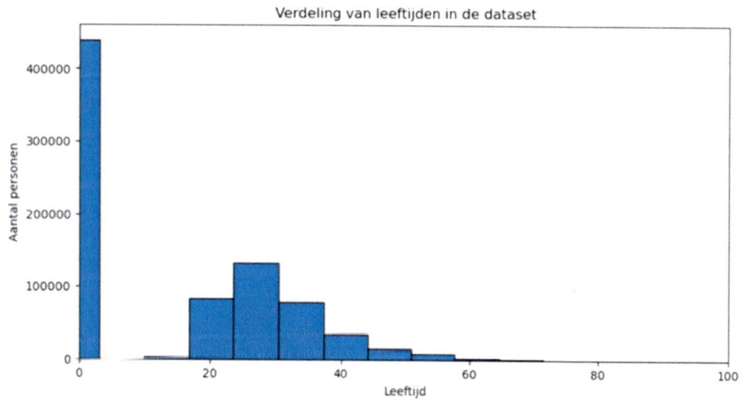

Sometimes data fields are not filled in and get a 0 by default. If this is not noticed, one may make predictions based on people with an age of 0!

Accuracy

Is it correct?

- Distribution of age
- Addresses

ID	Owner	City	Zip code
1	D. de Jong	Groningen	9718 AC
2	M. Bas	Amsterdam	1011 NK
3	D. de Waard	Groningen	9718 AC
4	S. van Houten	Eindhoven	1556 PE

When it comes to manually inserting data (for example zip codes) it is very easy to make a mistake. Eindhoven has a region code of 56, so there was a typo, but this is not easy to notice.

Completeness

- Is it all there?

ID	Owner	City	Zip code
1	D. de Jong	Groningen	9718 AC
2	M. Bas		1011 NK
3		Groningen	9718 AC
4	S. van Houten	Eindhoven	5615 PE

Sometimes data is simply missing. Some algorithms do not work when certain features are missing. It is case dependent what the best course of action is, can data be easily found? For example, for ID 2, filling in the city based on zip code is doable. But is this also the case for finding the Owner?

Uniqueness

- Is it free from duplication?

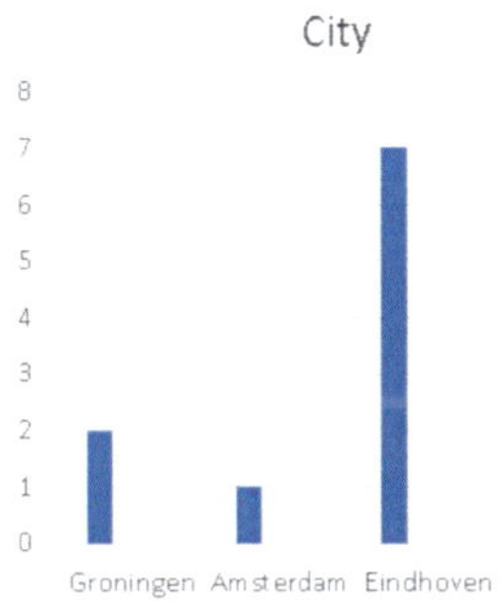

ID	Owner	City	Zip code
1	D. de Jong	Groningen	9718 AC
2	M. Bas	Amsterdam	1011 NK
3	D. de Waard	Groningen	9718 AC
4	S v houten	Eindhoven	1556 PE
5	S v houten	Eindhoven	5615 PE
6	S van houten	Eindhoven	5615 PE
7	S van Houten	Eindhoven	5615 PE
8	S. van Houten	Eindhoven	5615 PE

Duplication can introduce bias. In this example one may think the majority of the owners are from Eindhoven. However, identifying duplicates can sometimes be challenging (for example two of the exact same transaction that are made 2 seconds after each other

Consistency

- Is it free from conflict?

- Customers retail
- Customers wholesale

Retail customers			
ID	Owner	City	Zip code
1	D. de Jong	Groningen	9718 AC
2	M. Bas	Amsterdam	1011 NK
3	D. de Waard	Groningen	9718 AC
4	S. van Houten	Eindhoven	5615 PE

Wholesale customers			
ID	Owner	City	Zip code
1	D. de Jong	Groningen	9711 LC

Sometimes customers are registered in different tables. Once a customer changes, for example, their address, one needs to make sure this is implemented in all tables

Timeliness

- Is it current and available?

Retail customers				
ID	Owner	City	Zip code	Date
1	D. de Jong	Groningen	9718 AC	04-04-2021
2	M. Bas	Amsterdam	1011 NK	05-06-2023
3	D. de Waard	Groningen	9718 AC	17-12-2023
4	S. van Houten	Eindhoven	5615 PE	26-03-2022

 48

How to properly improve the quality of the data?

There is no unique way of cleaning the data. It always depends on the specific case

- Example: Outliers
- Example: Missing data

 50

Case study – cleaning our data

% Job quitting	Satisfied with salary 1-10	My skills are too high	Travel Minutes	NumberWorkers
15	9	1	70	60
55	4	1	30	5
41	5	0	45	5
15	8	0	15	65
8	8	0	15	10
12	7	0	10	35
1	8	0	80	70

 51

Case study – cleaning our data

% Job quitting	Satisfied with salary 1-10	My skills are too high	Travel Minutes	NumberWorkers
15	9	1	70	60
55	4	1	30	5
41	5	0	45	5
15	8	0	15	65
8	8	0	15	10
12	7	0	10	35
1	8	0	80	70
51	3	0	600	100

A colleague living in another country or a typo?

 52

Case study – cleaning our data

% Job quitting	Satisfied with salary 1-10	My skills are too high	Travel Minutes	NumberWorkers
15	9	1	70	60
55	4	1	30	5
41	5	0	45	5
15	8	0	15	65
8	8	0	15	10
12	7	0	10	35
1	8	0	80	70
12	7	0	10	35

Similar people or some one who filled in the questionnaire twice?

 53

Case study – cleaning our data

% Job quitting	Satisfied with salary 1-10	My skills are too high	Travel Minutes	NumberWorkers
15	9	1	70	60
55	4	1	30	5
41	5	0	45	5
15	8	0	15	65
8	8	0	15	10
12	7	0	10	35
1	8	0	80	70
0	0	0	0	0

True, or someone who did not feel like filling in the survey?

 54

Case study – cleaning our data

% Job quitting	Satisfied with salary 1-10	My skills are too high	Travel Minutes	NumberWorkers
15	9	1	70	60
55	4	1	30	5
41	5	0	45	5
15	8	0	15	65
8	8	0	15	10
12	7	0	10	35
1	8	0	80	70
10	8	0		50

 55

Step 2: The machine learning algorithm

 56

Data and machine learning

What do I want?

- To visualize
- To predict (Supervised learning)
- To describe (Unsupervised learning)

Do I have the relevant data?

- Is the data structured
- Is the data quality sufficient

Which machine learning do I want to use?

- Random forest
- Linear regression

The train and test set

Once you start using a machine learning algorithm, always start with a split between a **train set** and a **test set**

- **Train set (development set):** Used to test and develop the ML algorithm
- **Test set (validation set):** Used to describe how well the ML algorithm performs

Why this split?

- While developing there is still some freedom in adjusting which data is taken into account and what parameters we choose (e.g., the value of k in k-nearest neighbors)
- Avoid *overfitting* on the data that we have: Prevent a model that works perfect for our data only
- Give a fair evaluation of the model performance

'Fitting' to the Data

- In data science we often **"fit to the data"**
- That is how we **generalize data into a model**
- In machine learning we often call this **training the AI**
  - **Better: training the algorithm to come up with the best model**
- The model is then used to solve problems:

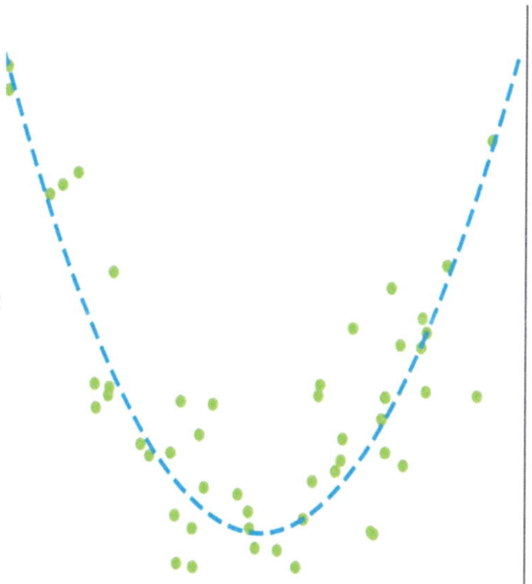

- Such a fit is not perfect!

 59

Bias and Variance

- **Bias error** – average difference between actual values and model output => underfit
  - Error between average model prediction and ground truth
  - The bias of the estimated function tells us the capacity of the underlying model to predict the values

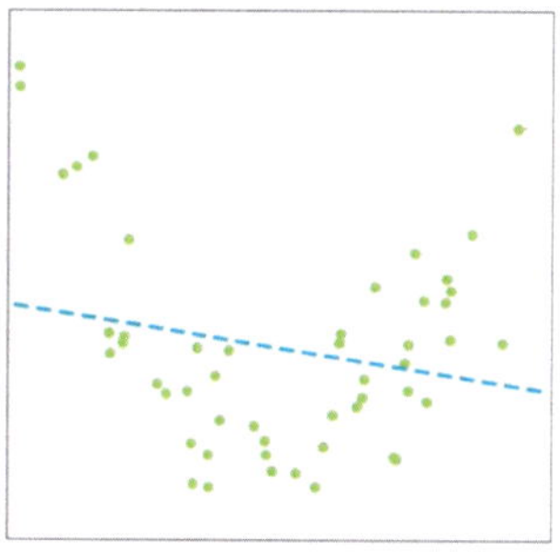

- **Variance error** – errors in output due to sensitivity to the fitted data => overfit
  - Average variability in the model prediction for the given dataset
  - The variance of the estimated function tells you how much the function can adjust to the change in the dataset

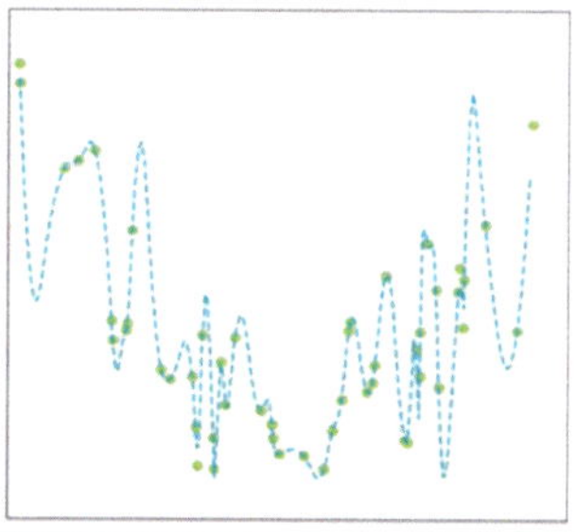

 60

Bias and Variance

- One of the **goals of machine learning** is handling the **trade-off between variance and bias**
- Choose the right type of model
- Use the right amount of "complexity"
- Evaluate and test

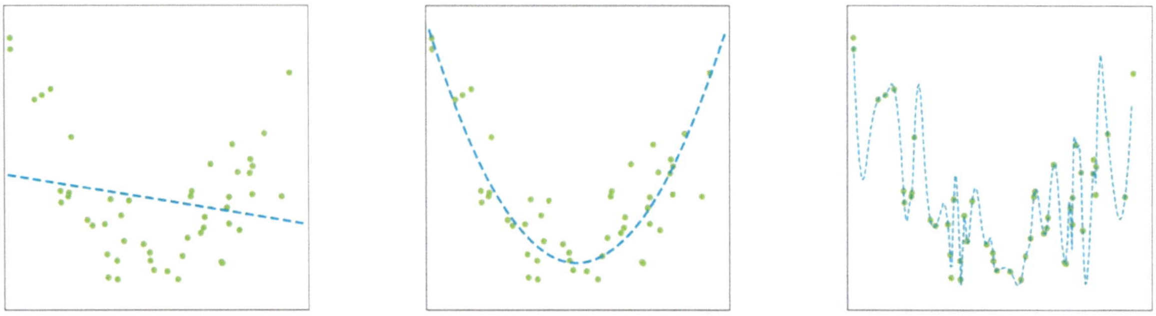

 61

Bias vs Variance

- Increasing bias reduces variance and vice-versa
- The best model is where the error is reduced.
- Compromise between bias and variance

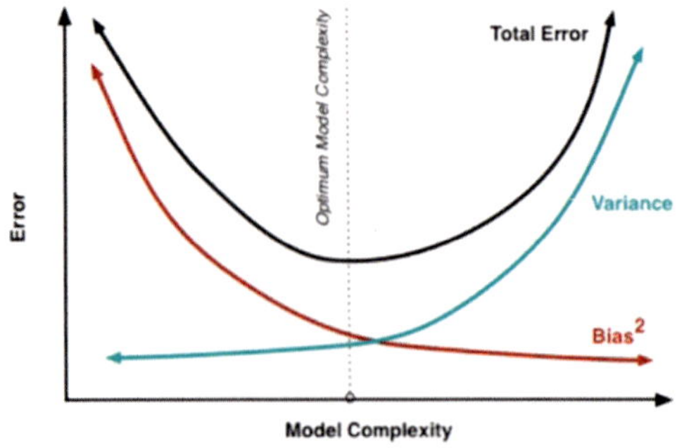

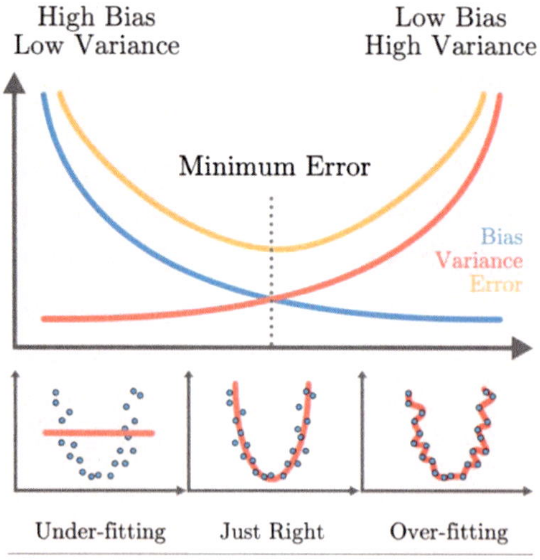

 62

Case study – Overfit

How would an overfitted or underfitted version of

- A decision tree
- K-nearest neighbours

look like for a data set with 1000 rows?

Overfitted decision tree: A root with 1000 branches, so that every data point is classified correctly

Underfitted decision tree: A root with 1 branch

Overfitted K-nearest neighbours: K=1 (fully dependent on the point that happened to be close)

Underfitted K-nearest neighbours: K=1000 (always take the most frequent label)

 63

The machine learning process

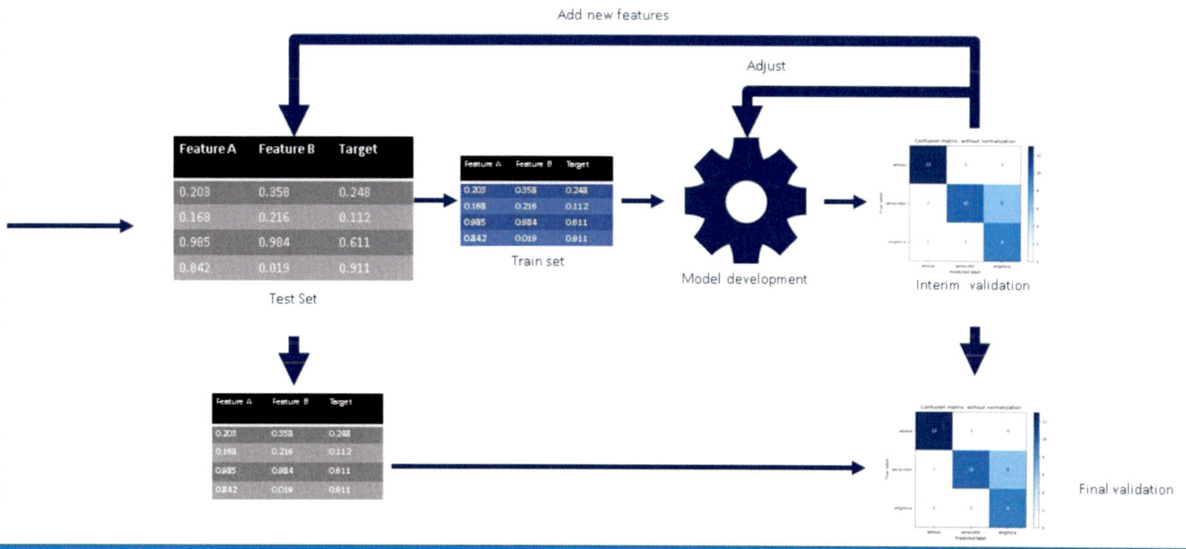

 64

How to validate our machine learning model

Validating how well a machine learning model works is tricky

Suppose our ML algorithm makes predictions.

- Out of 100 predictions (yes/no), 98 were correct
- Out of 100 predictions (yes/no), 19 were correct
- Out of 100 predictions (yes/no), 77 were correct

How well is this?

 65

Intermezzo - Quality Requirements in Fraud Detection

- A credit card company uses an AI model to detect fraud
- Their vendor builds them a model that is **correct 99.9% of the time** (we call this the "accuracy" of the model)

- Is this acceptable?

 66

Intermezzo - Quality Requirements in Fraud Detection

- A credit card company uses an AI model to detect fraud
- Their vendor builds them a model that is **correct 99.9% of the time** (we call this the "accuracy" of the model)

- Is this acceptable? **No**

- Imagine fraud happens 1 in every 1,000,000 transactions (a very high estimate)
- If the AI model flags <u>every single transaction</u> as "not fraudulent", then it is wrong only in 1 in 1,000,000 cases, and correct 99.9999% of the time.
- But this model never detects fraud!

- **Conclusion:** You need to look at more than just the percentage that's correct. You need to take into account the difference between correct detection of "fraud" and correct detection of "not fraud"

Intermezzo - Quality Requirements in Disease Detection

This is also dangerous for disease detection

- The probability that you actually have the disease is <0.01%
- Take-away: The probability of an error in the test is much larger than you having the disease

What is then even the value of a test anymore?

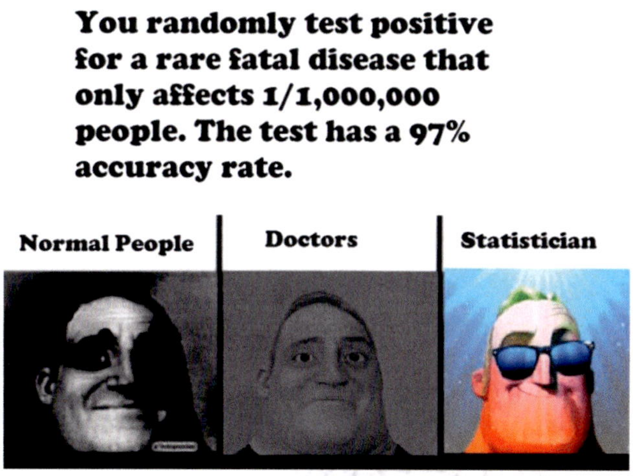

A baseline

An AI model is a complex and expensive solution to a problem. In order to justify its implementation, it needs to be *significantly* better than a (simple) baseline

- A solution that is currently implemented
- A simple heuristic method
- A trivial strategy

True and false positives and negatives

- In classification problems, the answer of the AI model can be either correct or incorrect

- **Example**:
  A newspaper wants to classify every article in their archive that is about pandemics. They use an AI model trained with machine learning to apply the "pandemic" label to each article. The results:
  - A lot of articles are about pandemics and are labeled as such: those are **true positives**
  - Sometimes the model labels an article as pandemic-related, but that's incorrect: these are **false positives (type I error)**
  - When the model misses an article that is actually about a pandemic and doesn't label it, that is a **false negative (type II error)**
  - When the model correctly doesn't apply the "pandemic" label, that's a **true negative**

Machine learning can be wrong, it is a probabilistic approach

 71

Confusion Matrix

The **confusion matrix** is the table of all correct and incorrect classifications

		Output of model	
		True	**False**
Actually correct	**True**	True Positive (TP)	False Negative (FN) type II
	False	False Positive (FP) type I	True Negative (TN)

Model misstake: Type I error (false positive): the doctor/model says you are pregnant, but you actually don't.

Type I Error

Type II Error

Model misstake: Type II error (false negative): the doctor/model says you are not pregnant, but you actually are.

 72

What is worse?

		Output of model	
		True	**False**
Actually correct	**True**	True Positive (TP)	False Negative (FN) type II
	False	False Positive (FP) type I	True Negative (TN)

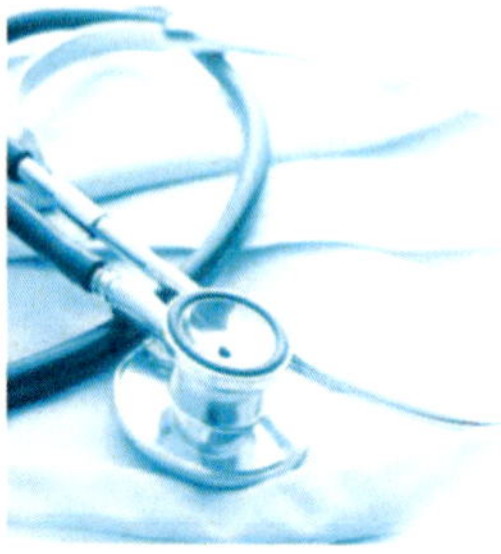

 73

Accuracy, Precision and Recall

Accuracy is the **% of all items** that were **labeled correctly**

(TP + TN) / (TP + TN + FP + FN)

Precision is the **% of items** that were **labeled positive correctly out all** that were **labeled positive**

TP / (TP + FP) ***validity***

Recall is the **% of items** that were **labeled positive correctly out of all that should have been labeled positive**

TP / (TP + FN) ***completeness***

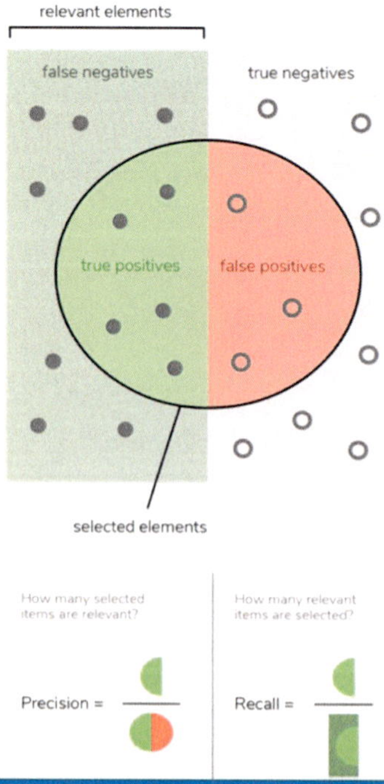

 74

fishing with a net.

Explain it like fishing with a net.

*The **precision** is the proportion of relevant results in the list of all returned search results. Says something about **validity***

You use a wide net, and catch 80 of 100 total fish in a lake. That's 80% recall. But you also get 80 rocks in your net. That means 50% precision, half of the net's contents is junk.

*The **recall** is the ratio of the relevant results returned by the search engine to the total number of the relevant results that could have been returned. Says something about **completeness***

You could use a smaller net and target one pocket of the lake where there are lots of fish and no rocks, but you might only get 20 of the fish in order to get 0 rocks. That is 20% recall and 100% precision.

 75

Accuracy, Precision and Recall

Recognizing dogs in a photo with ten cats and twelve dogs

		Output of model	
		dogs	not dogs
Actually correct	dog	5	7
	not dogs	3	7

- **Accuracy** is 12/22
- **Precision** is 5/8 (true positives / selected elements) ***validity***
- **Recall** is 5/12 (true positives / relevant elements) ***completeness***

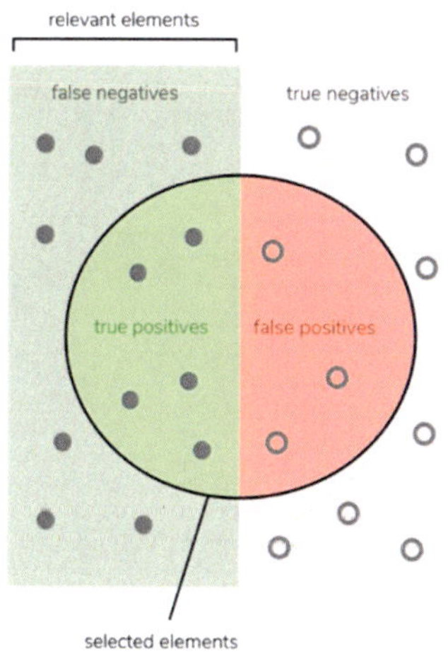

 76

Precision and Recall in Practice

- The **business needs** to fully determine what good and bad values are for the precision and recall
- There is often a tradeoff between them:
- **Low precision but high recall** ***Completeness*** is good in situations where missing a relevant item is dangerous or expensive
  - E.g. testing for a very contagious disease: you want to catch them all, even if it means a number of false positives
- **Low recall but high precision** ***Validity*** is good in situations where false positives are dangerous or expensive
  - E.g. automatically detecting criminal behaviour: accusations of fraud are not trivial!

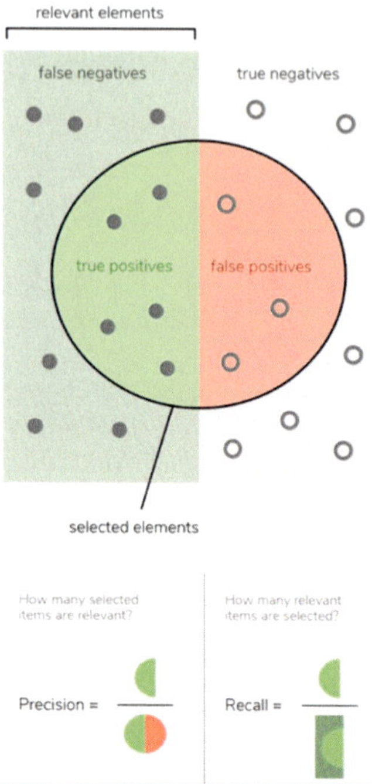

© Van Haren Publishing BV. 77

The machine learning process

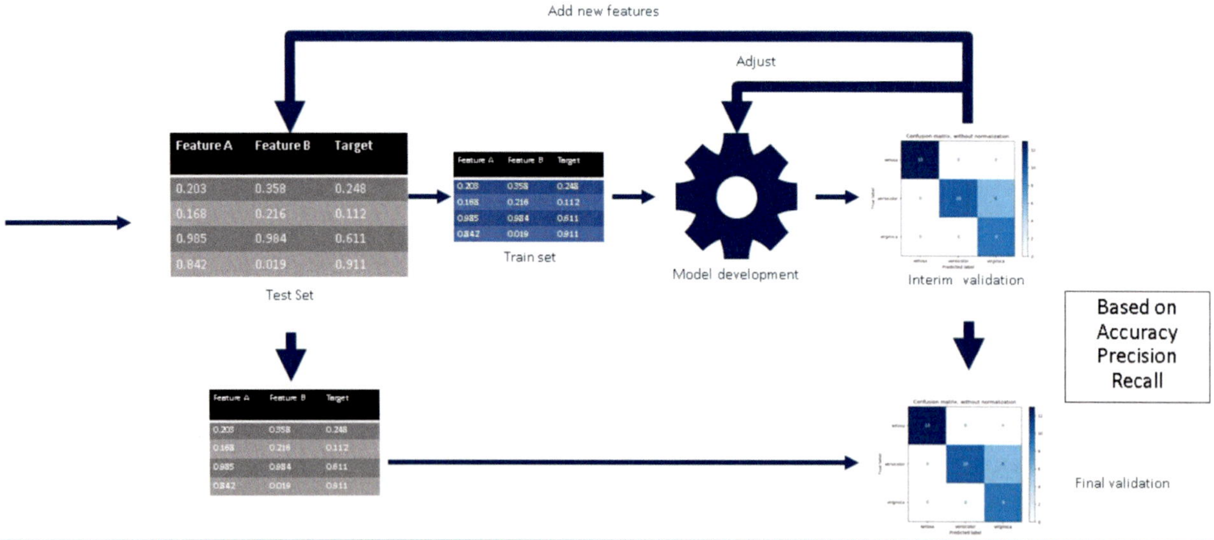

Feature A	Feature B	Target
0.203	0.358	0.248
0.168	0.216	0.112
0.985	0.984	0.611
0.842	0.019	0.911

© Van Haren Publishing BV. 78

Case study – Validating the model

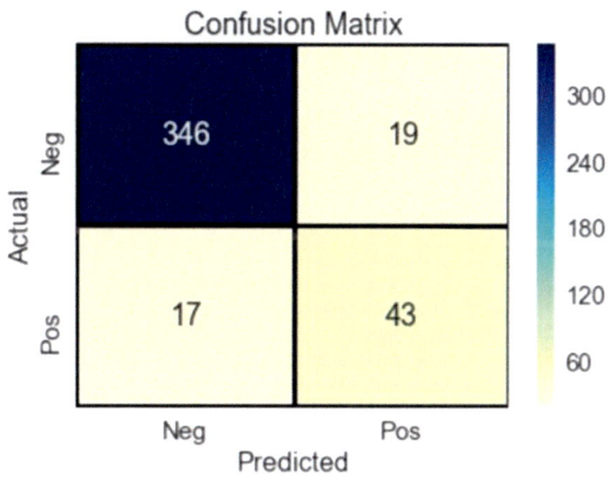

 79

Data visualisatie: Dashboards

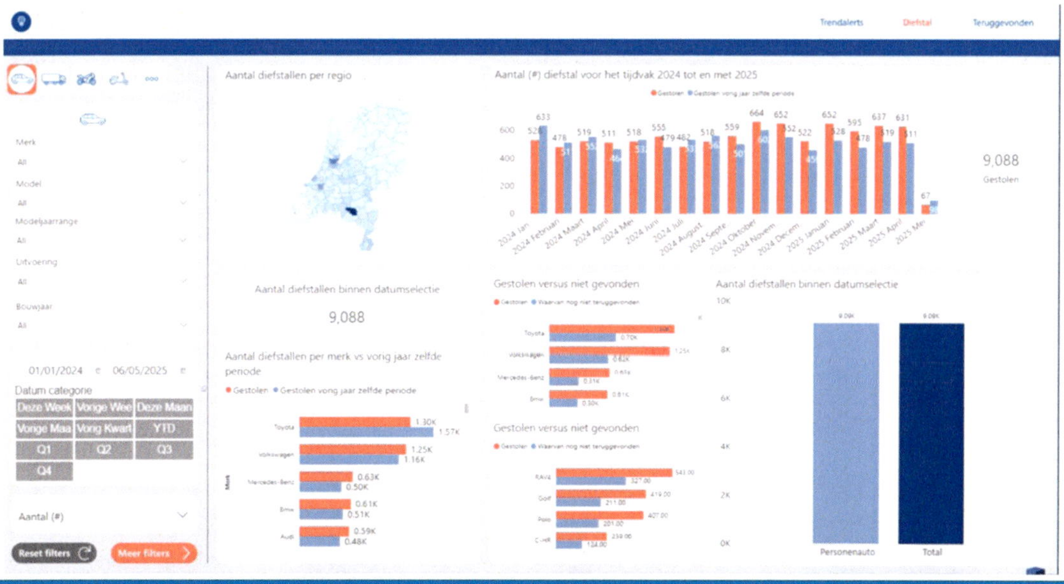

 81

Part 3: Risks associated with handling data

 82

Risks

A risk is considered as a something that poses a threat or likely source of danger

As data is valuable and can easily be misused, it is subject to many risks

 83

Privacy

- Collected and stored data can be privacy sensitive because it pertains to the rights of individuals or groups to not share information about themselves if they so choose
  - For certain types of data, some forms of storage and usage might violate these rights

- **It is imperative to verify that the collection, storage and use of data (including for AI) falls within the applicable legal frameworks regarding privacy protection**

- Regulation of privacy of personal data and how to protect it is encoded into law in many countries:
  - In the EU, this is the General Data Protection Regulation (**GDPR**)

 84

Privacy

- Ensuring the privacy of data **goes further than just what is stored**
- Data can have a large **deductive power:** the ability to retrieve information through its usage

- **Examples**:
  - Facebook likes on organizations are a strong indicator of political leanings
  - Frequent GPS locations can be used to guess/determine address, job, car ownership, etc.
  - Smartphone and smartwatch data indicate activity and can be used to guess overall health, age and even potential medical conditions

- All of these are examples of information that is:
  - **Never specifically shared**, but can be deduced from sufficient data
  - **Protected under EU data privacy protections**: businesses and governments are not allowed to extract this information without your express consent

 85

Data Security

Protective measures taken to keep digital data safe from "unwanted actions" by any "unauthorized users"

- **Measures against unauthorized user access:**
  - Access control, at multiple levels: data, software (password), physical locations (keycard, etc.)
  - Encryption
  - Masking ("bank account ending in *925")

Data Leakage

- **Examples of unwanted actions:**
  - Reading data (stealing passwords, email addresses, credit card info)
  - Changing data (increasing account balance, encrypting data – ransomware)
  - Removing data (deleting records)

 86

Data Storage & Sharing

Storage needs for organizations depend on their business needs:

- **How much** data will need to be input into the system?
- **Who/what** needs to use the data and how often?
- **What analyses / questions** will the data be used for?
- What are **legal requirements** for the data and its use? (e.g. GDPR)

These determine the answers to certain questions:

- **Cloud** or **on premise**?
- **What systems and people** are allowed access?
- **How long** is the data **allowed be stored** and in what format?
- **Which technical systems** actually store the data: local databases, data lake, proprietary vendor systems, etc.

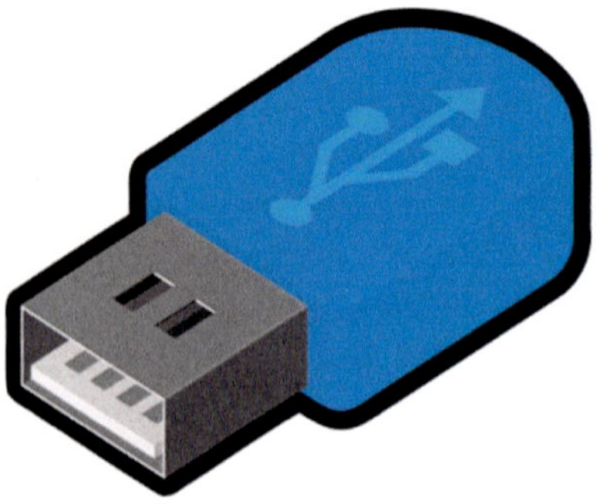

 87

FAIR Principles

Focused on letting machines use data with little/no intervention from humans

- **Findability**
  - Machine-readable metadata are essential for automatic discovery of datasets and services
- **Accessibility**
  - The user needs to know how the required (meta) data can be accessed
- **Interoperability**
  - The data need to interoperate with applications or workflows for analysis, storage, and processing
- **Reusability**
  - Metadata and data should be well-described so that they can be replicated and/or combined in different settings

Linked Data

Structured data which is interlinked with other data so it becomes more useful through semantic queries

- Similar to FAIR
- Use open formats (though not always open data)
- Uniquely identify data points
- Allow machine readability and easy reuse
- Allow 'semantic queries' and use community standards to describe data

Examples:

- Businesses allowing data on their services to be queried from their websites
- NGOs, like the Nobel Prize committee, offering their data as open databases
- Governments offering e-services, to register for certain programs, view your own (private) data

FAIR & Linked Data

Allow apps, websites and services to easily use and combine different data sources

Examples:

- Online newspapers always use the latest COVID-19 figures provided by the government
- The local tourist office lists all upcoming music events in the city on their website, gathered from the websites of the known local venues
- An e-learning app combines the open database of all Nobel laureates with information from Wikipedia on their life and work, and links to what universities they went to
- A database of all planted trees in a region can be easily linked to whatever groundworks, cables and privately owned land plots are near each tree
- Platform websites can easily use local business data to inform potential customers about services, opening times, rates, availability, etc

 90

Enablers of low-quality data

Common error in data

- Human error (making errors when manually registering data)
- Incorrect sensor data
- Misinformation
- Bias because of data coming from multiple sources

Common solutions

- Automated checks for correctness (for example checking for correct zip codes)
- Checks from reliable sources and subject matter experts
- A uniform way of collecting and registering data

 91

Sample question

What is **not** an element of data quality

a) Accuracy

b) Timeliness

c) Consistency

d) Stabilization

 92

Sample question

Which is an example of a false positive?

a) Our model severely overestimated the amount of profit for next month

b) Our model predicted I was interested in this product, but I was not

c) Our model increased the prize of this hotel as there was a concert nearby

d) None of the above

 93

Sample question

A model that predicts "YES" to everything

a) Will have a lot of false negatives

b) Will have a high precision

c) Will have a high recall

d) Will have a low accuracy

Sample question

When our model works really well on the train set, but badly on the test set

a) Then we can just proceed with the implementation

b) Then the model is just not suitable for an AI application

c) We have likely underfitted the model

d) We have likely overfitted the model

Outlook

- Now that we know which steps to take for a successful ML project, how can we efficiently and consciously implement them in our company?
- What are some key frameworks that help organizing such a massive tasks?
- What are the risks involving an AI project and how can we mitigate those?
- What is the resulting impact of AI on our society?

 96

Using AI in your organization

 97

What humans do well (subjective)

- Provide leadership – set the goals
- We are creative
- We can empathize (humans, groups, animals, nature, ideas, ethics)
- We can judge (law, ambiguity, 50/50)

What Machines Do Well : Objective Narrow or Weak AI focus on a single task)

- Generate content
- Automation
- Iterate
- Repetitive tasks

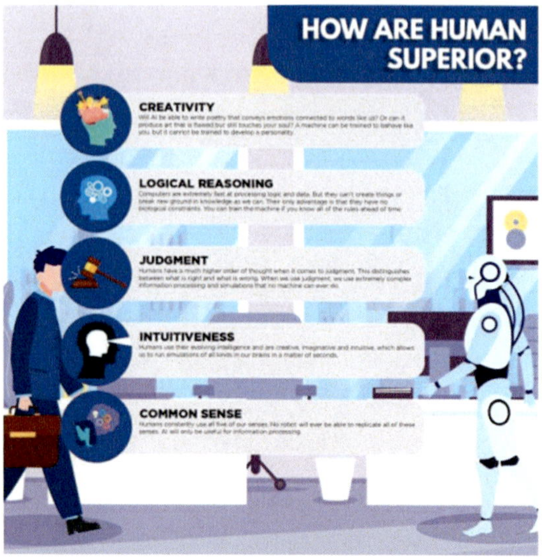

 98

Strengths of Humans vs. Strengths of Machines

- **Humans**:
  - Higher value cognitive tasks
  - Humans outperform machines when tasks require higher cognitive abilities such as **creativity, reasoning and analytical problem solving**
- **Machines**:
  - Dangerous, heavy lifting, monotone, analysis tasks
  - Machines typically outperform humans in repetitive tasks and algorithmic problem solving
- **Optimal human-machine collaboration**:
  - One where machines are constrained to repetitive tasks and humans are left to use their higher cognitive abilities

 99

AI & Data science

- Data science is the field that develops and implements AI (for example in a company)
- Companies that transition into *data-driven* working

- Data science project are typically complex projects that run for a long time
- Therefore, one should focus on
  - A structured project (the *what*)
  - A structured way of working (the *how*)
  - Keep stakeholders engaged
  - Clear roles in the data science project
  - A clear overview of the risks involved

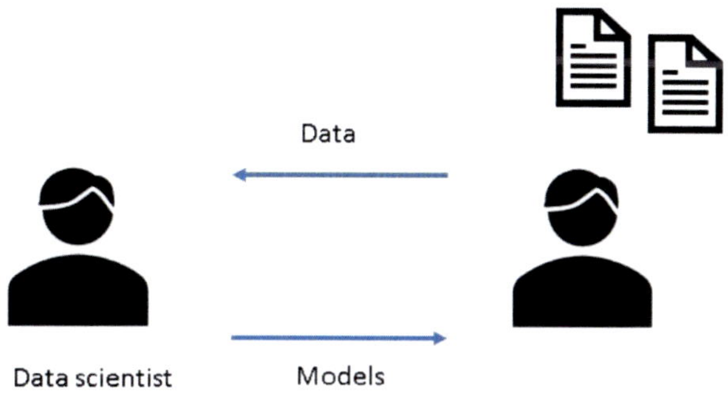

 100

Goals & Tasks of Building an AI Application

Tasks

- **Develop a coherent understanding** of the job(s) to be done
- **Gather and transform data** for the software to use
- **Utilize machine learning methods** that optimize performance
  - Select appropriate algorithm and train that to create a best fitting model (prediction)
- **Evaluate and understand the results** to determine fitness for purpose
- **Deploy a working solution** that can operate in the real world
- **Monitor and Maintain** the solution over time

Numerous process models exist that incorporate these steps and describe how they connect to each other

 102

CRISP-DM

CRISP-DM is the Cross Industry Standard Process for Data Mining and was developed in 1996.

Although there is some criticism, it is considered effective for most projects.

CRISP-DM project teams iterate through 6 stages:

1. **Business understanding**
   Assess current situation, determine strategy and goals
2. **Data understanding**
   Collect and explore data, verify quality
3. **Data preparation**
   Select, clean, construct, integrate data
4. **Modeling**
   Build models, assess and compare results, select the best model
5. **Evaluation**
   Evaluate results with business, review process, determine next step
6. **Deployment**
   Deploy the model, educate users, set-up maintenance structure

© Van Haren Publishing BV 103

1 Business Understanding

Goal: Develop a coherent and correct understanding of the job to be done

- If you don't understand the problem, you won't know if a solution is the right one
- Logical first step is to map and understand the business environment and the questions to be answered

Key questions:

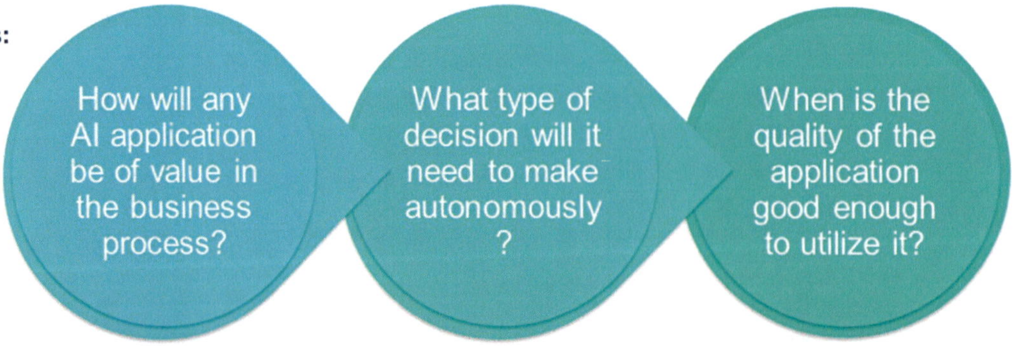

© Van Haren Publishing BV 104

1 Business Understanding

Goal: Develop a coherent and correct understanding of the job to be done

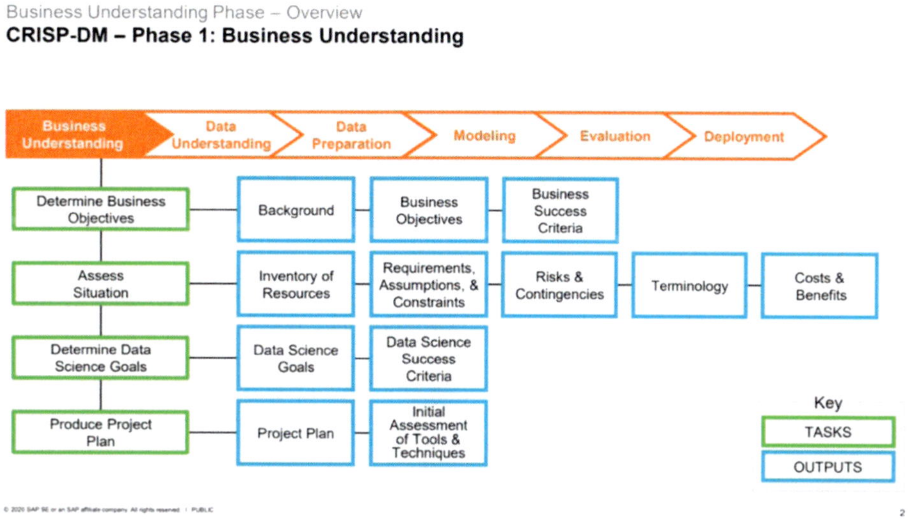

 105

CRISP DM for our case study - Employee satisfaction

Business understanding

What exactly do we want to achieve?

- Measure the satisfaction of an employee?
- Predict whether an employee will leave? If so, in what period?
- Which factors cause employee dissatisfaction
- How should we effectively increase employee satisfaction?

What can we change / do once we have our AI model?

Does the problem need AI?

 106

2 Data Understanding, aka EDA, Exploratory Data Analysis

Goal:

Know **which data is needed, available, how it is created and how it can be used,** before we can (safely) let an AI application take autonomous decisions based on it.

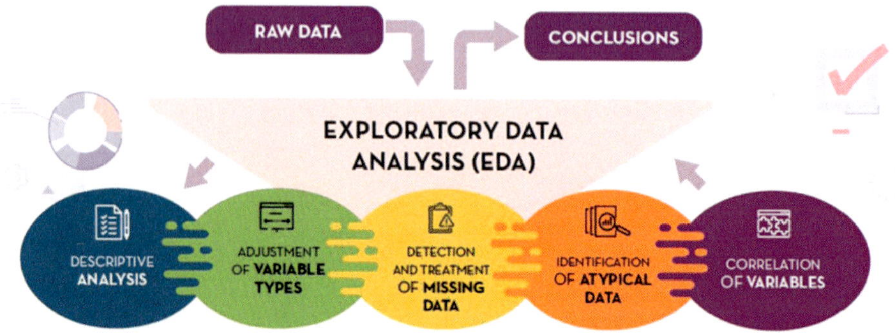

 107

2 Data Understanding (cont'd)

- The available data determines:
  - How the AI application can work (what will be its' senses/percepts?)
  - The potential performance, after learning from the existing data

- Before we can (safely) let an AI application take autonomous decisions based on it, we need to
  - understand what is in the data
  - understand how the data is collected or created
  - understand what the data represents from the real world
  - Understand what is the quality of the data

Data Understanding Phase – Overview

CRISP-DM – Phase 2: Data Understanding

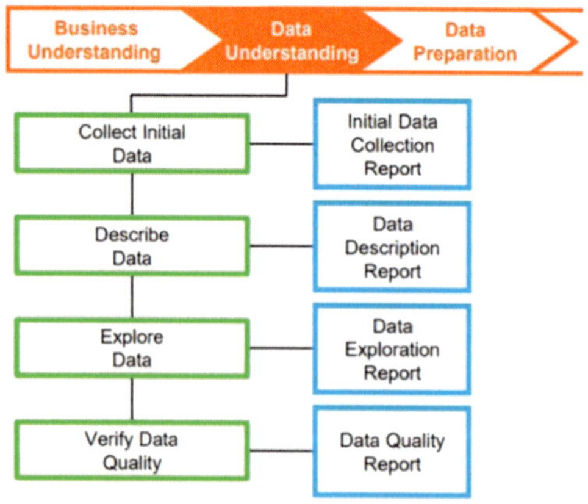

 108

2 Data Understanding (cont'd)

- **Detect bias**
  - Is the data skewed in some 'unnatural' way?
  - This may affect how the data should be collected, used and how reliable the AI application is
- **Handle outliers**
  - Significant difference from other data points
  - Can cause serious problems in further analyses
  - How can we explain them?
  - How do we deal with them?
- **Recognize patterns**
  - Find correlations by hand to recognize useful or unwanted patterns
  - These can be indicative of biases in the data

 109

CRISP DM for our case study - Employee satisfaction

Data understanding

How are we going to collect data

- Survey
- HR / Agenda / Hour registration data

Note: Anonymous data cannot be linked to HR data

How are we going to express "satisfaction"

- On a scale?
- In different classes?
- Expressing it in the "likeliness to leave"

Ensure that data is collected *appropriately*

 110

3 Data Preparation

- **Annotate the data**:
  - 'Labelling' with correct answers
  - Often necessary to solve **classification problems** with **supervised learning**
- **Combine datasets**:
  - Connect data from different sources
- **Train/test-split**:
  - Save some data to assess performance, use the rest for learning and improving through machine learning
    - → ***NEVER*** *evaluate a model's performance on its training data*

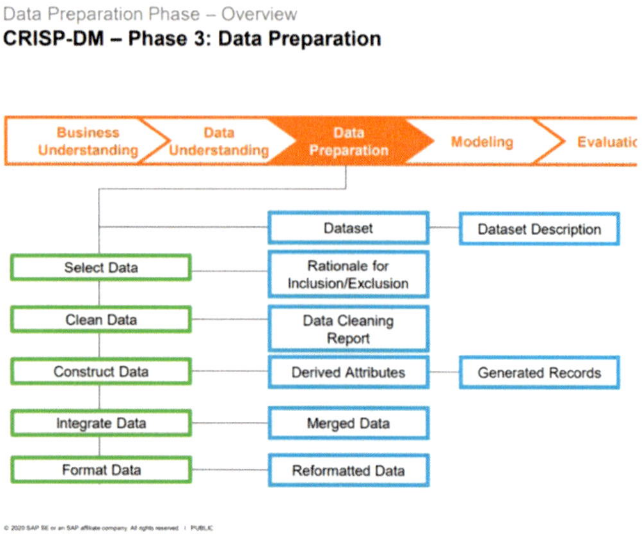

 111

3 Data Preparation (cont'd)

Clean the data:

- **Handle "wrong" values**
  - We need to **validate** what are correct and incorrect values
  - We can fix if possible, remove if necessary
- **Handle missing values**
  - We can **impute** the data: generate a 'best guess' answer for each missing value:
    - take the average,
    - write some function to compute a value,
    - use machine learning

"This is not what I meant when I said 'we need better data cleansing!'"

www.iwaysoftware.com/go/dataquality

 112

CRISP DM for our case study - Employee satisfaction

Data Preparation

Typical pitfalls for the specific data we collected

- Bias (only employees that are dissatisfied fill in the survey)
- Missing data
- Surveys that are not filled in truthfully

Combining data (how are different sources connected?)

Train and test split

 113

4 Modeling

Goal: Develop an AI application that learns from the available data and sufficiently improve its ability to perform the required task

- **Interpretation** of text, images, video, etc. **requires specialized methods** to turn words, pixel values, video frames, etc. into useful numbers

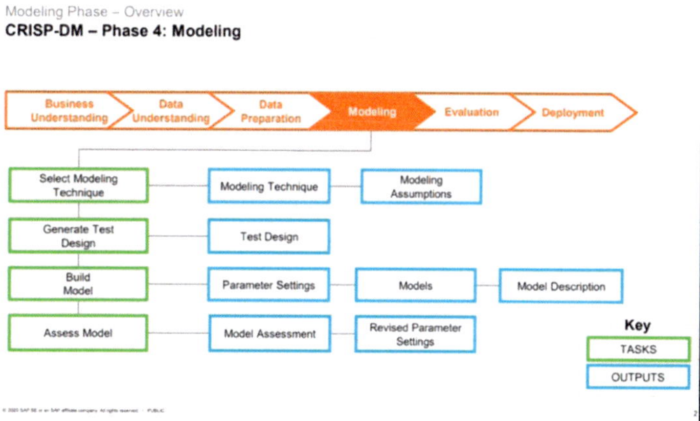

- **Select and implement one or more machine learning algorithms** that are appropriate for the data and task at hand, e.g.:
  - For images and video: Deep Learning Neural Networks
  - For text: Natural Language Processing techniques

 114

CRISP DM for our case study - Employee satisfaction

Modelling

What do we want to predict?

- What are the labels
- What are the relevant features

Which model is suitable?

 115

5 Evaluation

Goal:

Select the correct model and implementation that is the best solution for the problem, by evaluating their performance (comparing different models and outcomes)

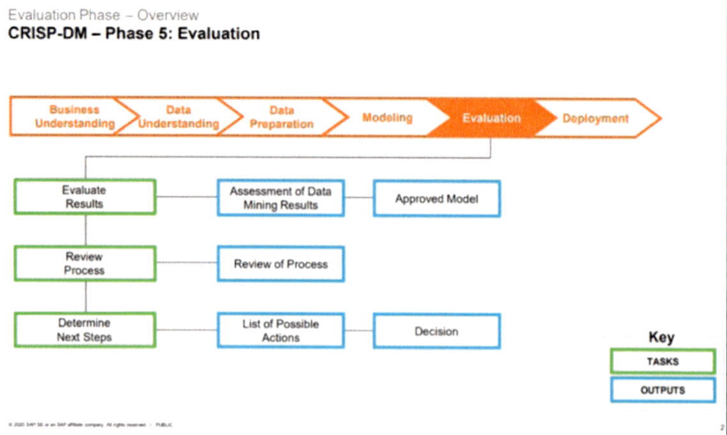

- Evaluation happens on the test data set (recall from CRISP-DM step 3)
- We can use a cost or score function to evaluate models
  - e.g. F-score or MSE
- This also requires interpretation of the outcomes in the business context
  - How often is an error permitted? Is X% precision good enough? etc.

 116

CRISP DM for our case study - Employee satisfaction

Evaluation

How do we judge the model?

- Accuracy
- Precision
- Recall?

Does the model perform better than a simple baseline?

 117

5 Evaluation - Fit for Purpose

Before using your AI application it is important to assess the **fitness for purpose**: how well the AI model fulfills the business needs

- Determined by the business context
- Even if the model performs perfectly, it might not be fit for purpose.
  - How can that be?
    - You don't trust the underlying data
    - The users don't trust your prediction
    - You're not allowed to use the data
    - You have no means to take action

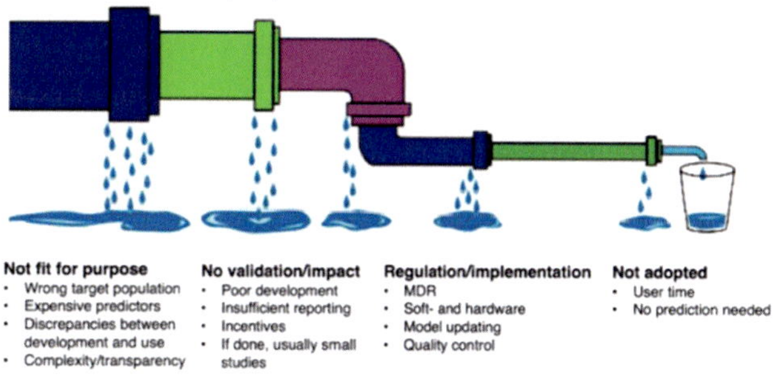

Picture courtesy: Laure Wynants

 118

6 Deployment

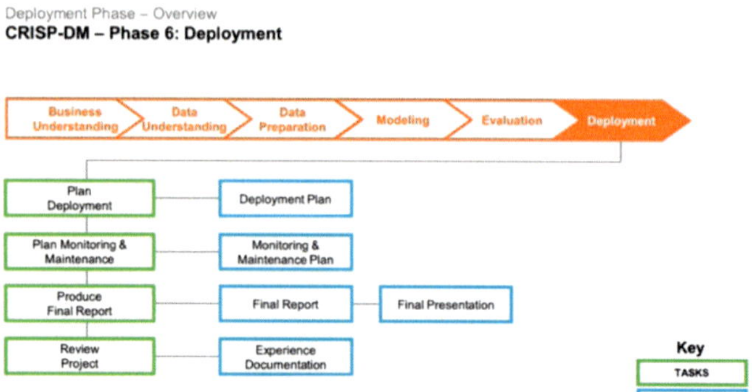

Goal:
Put the AI application in the hands of end users and ensure its (continued) successful usage

- Often as **software** that runs on a server, or as part of the firmware of a robot
- Application needs to be at the **right scale**:
  - Able to handle the number of requests and in an appropriate time frame

 119

6 Deployment: Monitoring & Maintenance

- **Monitoring** of the application:
  - **How the AI is used** and to **measure its performance**
- **Maintenance** of the application:
  - Could the AI be improved?
    - **Training on new data** allows improvement of performance
    - **Online learning** enables the Learning Agent to improve automatically while it is used
    - **Batch improvements** replace AI with a 'better version' that was trained elsewhere
      (↑ this is the default and pretty much the industry standard)

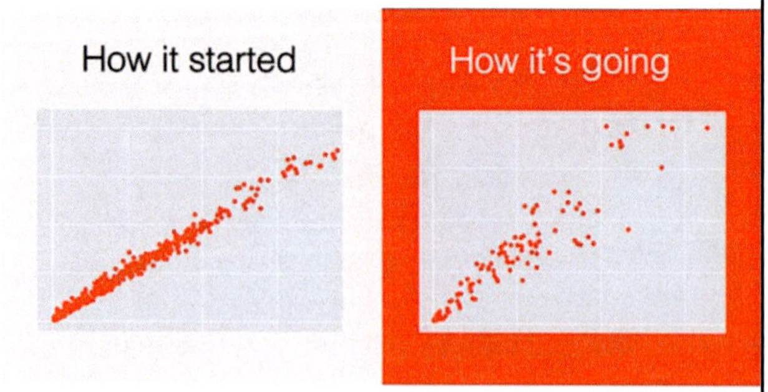

 120

Generic tasks and outputs of the CRISP-DM model

Business Understanding

Determine Business Objectives
Background
Business Objectives
Business Success Criteria

Assess Situation
Inventory of Resources
Requirements, Assumptions, and Constraints
Risks and Contingencies
Terminology
Costs and Benefits

Determine Data Mining Goals
Data Mining Goals
Data Mining Success Criteria

Produce Project Plan
Project Plan
Initial Assessment of Tools and Techniques

Data Understanding

Collect Initial Data
Initial Data Collection Report

Describe Data
Data Description Report

Explore Data
Data Exploration Report

Verify Data Quality
Data Quality Report

Data Preparation

Select Data
Rationale for Inclusion/Exclusion

Clean Data
Data Cleaning Report

Construct Data
Derived Attributes
Generated Records

Integrate Data
Merged Data

Format Data
Reformatted Data

Dataset
Dataset Description

Modeling

Select Modeling Techniques
Modeling Technique
Modeling Assumptions

Generate Test Design
Test Design

Build Model
Parameter Settings
Models
Model Descriptions

Assess Model
Model Assessment
Revised Parameter Settings

Evaluation

Evaluate Results
Assessment of Data Mining Results w.r.t. Business Success Criteria
Approved Models

Review Process
Review of Process

Determine Next Steps
List of Possible Actions
Decision

Deployment

Plan Deployment
Deployment Plan

Plan Monitoring and Maintenance
Monitoring and Maintenance Plan

Produce Final Report
Final Report
Final Presentation

Review Project
Experience Documentation

 121

CRISP DM for different case studies

Implementation of our case studies is highly complex, but CRIPS DM gives us a framework where we can address every key step in the process.

In the case of "waste detection", describe what needs to be done in every step

- Business understanding
- Data understanding
- Data preparation
- Modeling
- Evaluation

 122

Other frameworks

- **TDSP** (Team Data Science Process): Launched by Microsoft in 2016, TDSP defines 5 stages of the data science life cycle (Business understanding, Data Acquisition & Understanding, Modeling, Deployment, and Customer Acceptance)

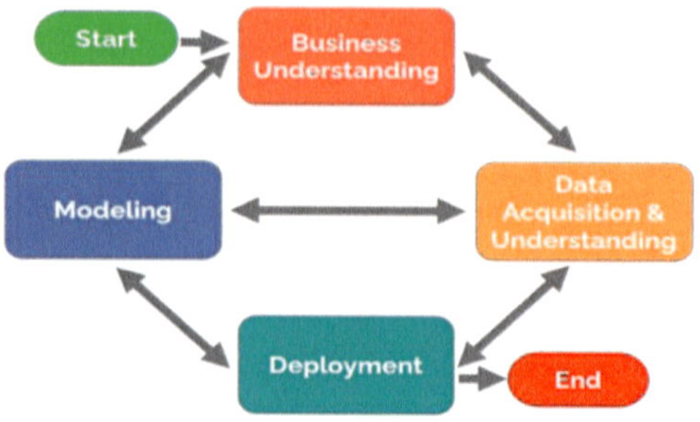

- **KDD**: *Knowledge Discovery in Database (KDD)* is the general process of discovering knowledge in data through data mining, or the extraction of patterns and information from large datasets using machine learning, statistics, and database systems

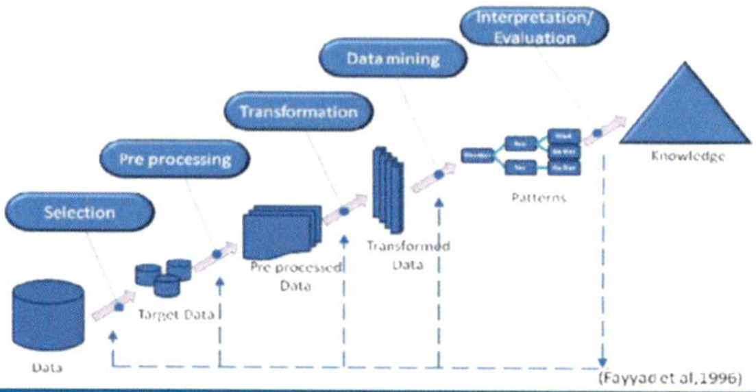

 123

Programming Languages

- Most actual development of AI applications is done (by data scientists) using either **Python** or **R**
  - Each has its own strengths and weaknesses
  - Both have various **libraries** for data prep, machine learning, model evaluation, etc.
  - Many, many specific **packages**/software for specific algorithms/types of data
  - Python in particular has been gaining in popularity in recent years
  - Now is the time to learn!

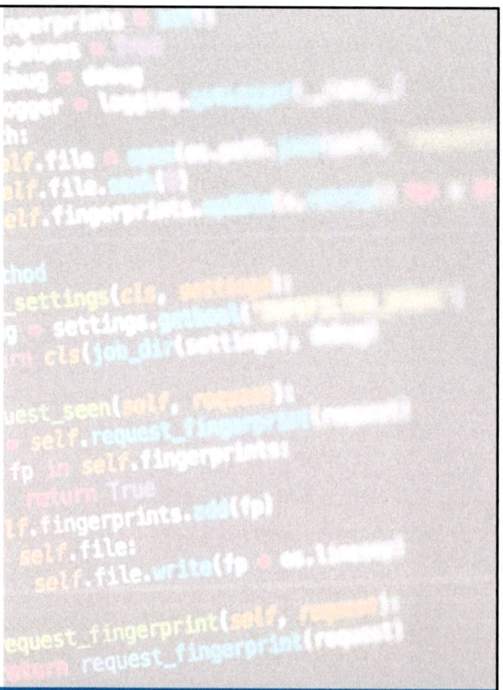

 124

Project management

 125

The machine learning process

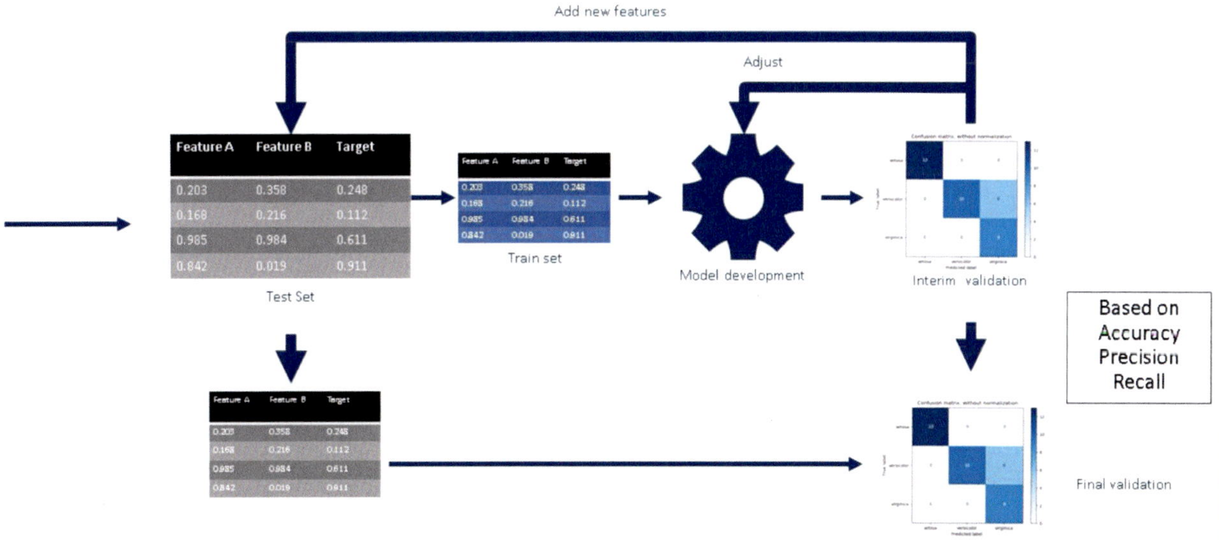

 126

The importance of communication

- During each step of CRISP-DM, communication to stakeholders and domain experts is critical
- Question: **We want to predict an optimal planning to meet demand**

Term	Meaning
Demand	The total sold volume per product within retail per week
Planning	Outside promotional weeks: demand forecasting During promotional weeks: planning of the pushed volume
Volume	Volume in hectoliters
Product	All products from the company's own holding
Retail	All retail chains in the Netherlands combined
...	...

Keep asking questions !!!

127

Stakeholder managment

Identifying stakeholders in our case studies

- Customer retention
- Employee satisfaction
- Waste detection

Where would you place them on the Power-interest grid

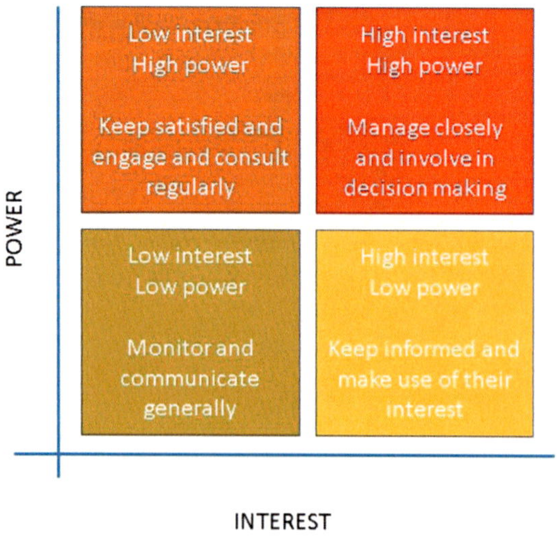

129

Project design: Waterfall

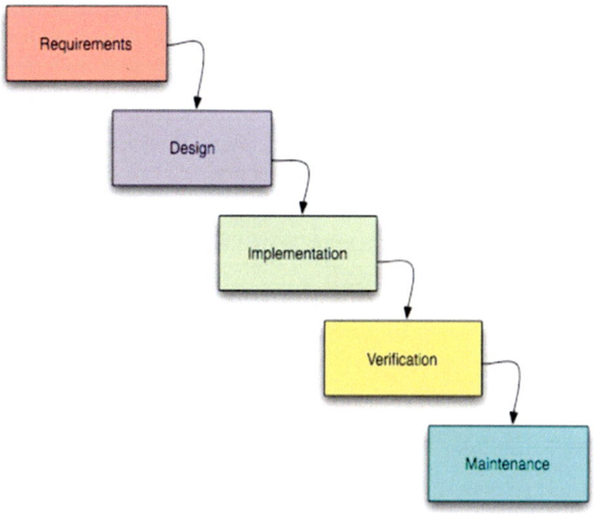

- The Waterfall model is a traditional engineering approach applied to software engineering.
- A strict Waterfall approach discourages revisiting and revising any prior phase once it is complete.

Organizing Your AI Project Team

A process as complex as CRISP-DM calls for a diverse and capable team

Gartner (2018):
85% of AI projects fail, citing difficulties of getting into production

▶ **Reason:**
Machine learning projects **cannot be planned and scoped fully in advance**

▶ **Calls for:**
Any AI team needs to be **iterative, reflective, collaborative** and **open to learn**

- AI and machine learning projects benefit from agile methods in a multidisciplinary team
- This way you can change course when needed and get user feedback from the start

Agile

- Compared to traditional software engineering, Agile development mainly targets complex systems and **projects that have dynamic, indeterminate and non-linear characteristics**, where accurate estimates, stable plans and predictions are often hard to determine on Day 1.
- Agile delivers valuable (albeit small) increments to the customer more often – the customer gets value sooner and is able to give feedback sooner.

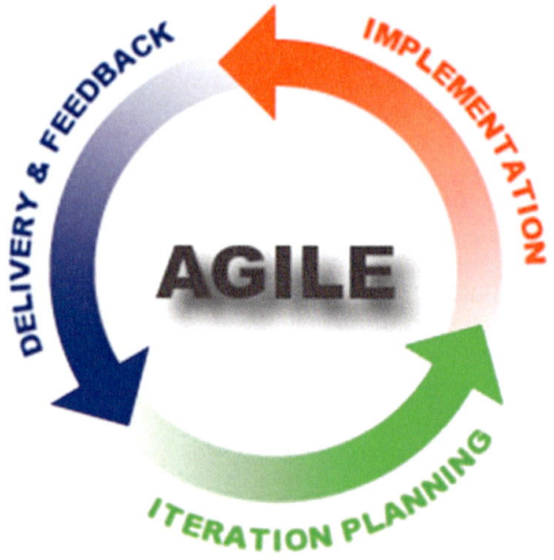

 132

Agile development

- It promotes adaptive planning, evolutionary development, early delivery, continuous improvement, and encourages rapid and flexible response to change.
- Ever period (sprint) the team works on a specific set of goals that results in a minimum viable product (MWP or MVP)
- The results are discussed with the stakeholders who can give feedback for the next sprint
- *The Manifesto for Agile Software Development*, also known as the ***Agile Manifesto***, first introduced the term *Agile* in the context of software development in 2001

 133

The agile manifesto

"We are uncovering better ways of developing software by doing it and helping others do it. Through this work we have come to value:

Individuals and interactions over processes and tools

Working software over comprehensive documentation

Customer collaboration over contract negotiation

Responding to change over following a plan

That is, while there is value in the items on the right, we value the items on the left more."

 134

Agile lends itself to AI projects

- **Iterative approach:** Each iteration involves a cross-functional team working in all roles: planning, requirements analysis, design, coding, unit testing, and acceptance testing.
- **Incremental:** Most Agile development methods break tasks into small increments with short-term planning (not long-term planning).
- **Collaborative:** Each Agile team should include a customer representative (*product owner* in Scrum) appointed by stakeholders to act on their behalf and to be available to answer mid-iteration questions.
- **Evolutionary:** At the end of the iteration a working increment of the product is demonstrated.

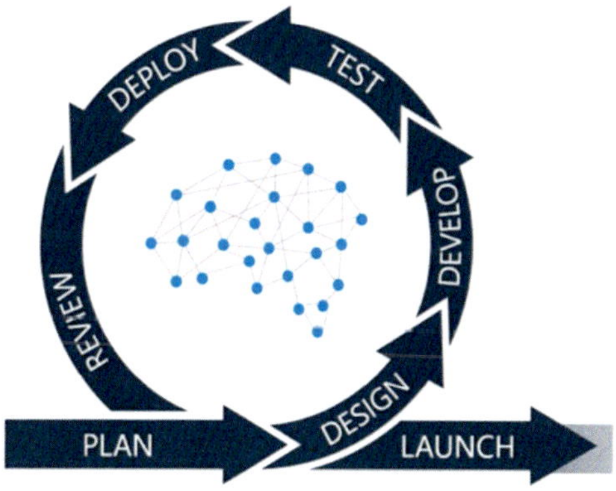

 135

Agile and Stakeholders

- Agile projects typically work in a cycles of 2 weeks
- Goals are set with the stakeholders
- After this period, a minimum viable product is delivered and presented to the stakeholders
- Stakeholders provide feedback
- The team holds a retrospective
- The cycle continues

 136

Agile vs. Waterfall

Data science projects are often highly dynamic projects

- Unforeseen (data) issues
- Changing objectives
- Engagement of stakeholders

Therefore, better suited for an agile approach

A waterfall approach works better if

- Requirements are clear and fixed
- Strict deadlines are involved

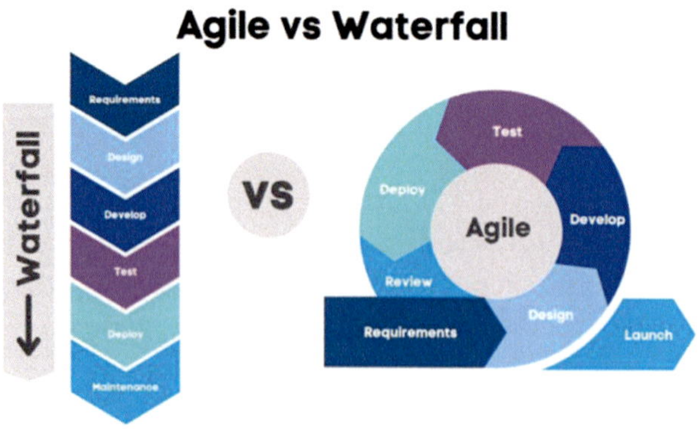

 137

Important roles within the company

Data Strategy

- **Short and long term goals and actions of organizations how they will use their data for business value**

- Focus on **improving the business** and **ensuring continuity**:
  - Meet business objectives
  - Innovate in current processes
  - Assess and seize new business opportunities
  - Address end-user needs
  - Ensure compliance and reduce risk
- **Tools**:
  - Business cases and financial justifications
  - Timelines for achieving goals and implementing initiatives
  - Regulatory expertise and insight into future changes to regulatory landscape

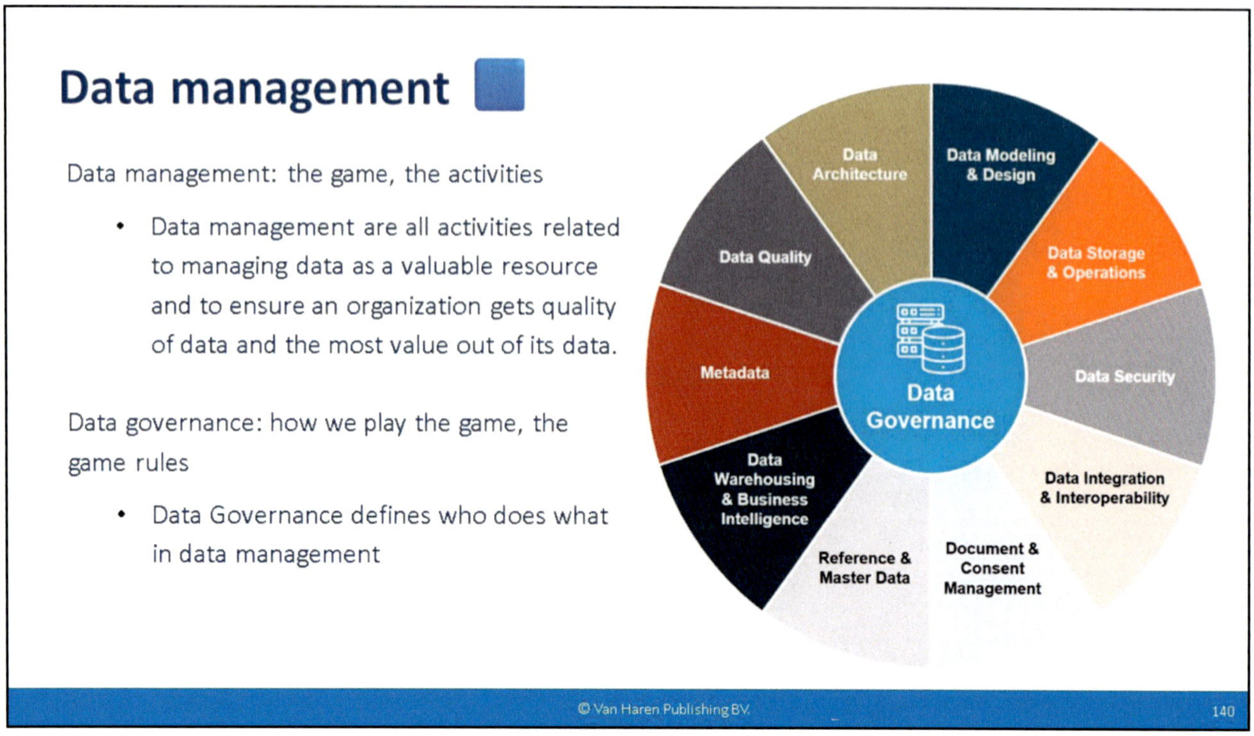
Data management
Data management: the game, the activities
Data management are all activities related to managing data as a valuable resource and to ensure an organization gets quality of data and the most value out of its data.
Data governance: how we play the game, the game rules
Data Governance defines who does what in data management
Data Architecture
Data Modeling & Design
Data Storage & Operations
Data Security
Data Integration & Interoperability
Document & Consent Management
Reference & Master Data
Data Warehousing & Business Intelligence
Metadata
Data Quality
Data Governance
© Van Haren Publishing BV.
140

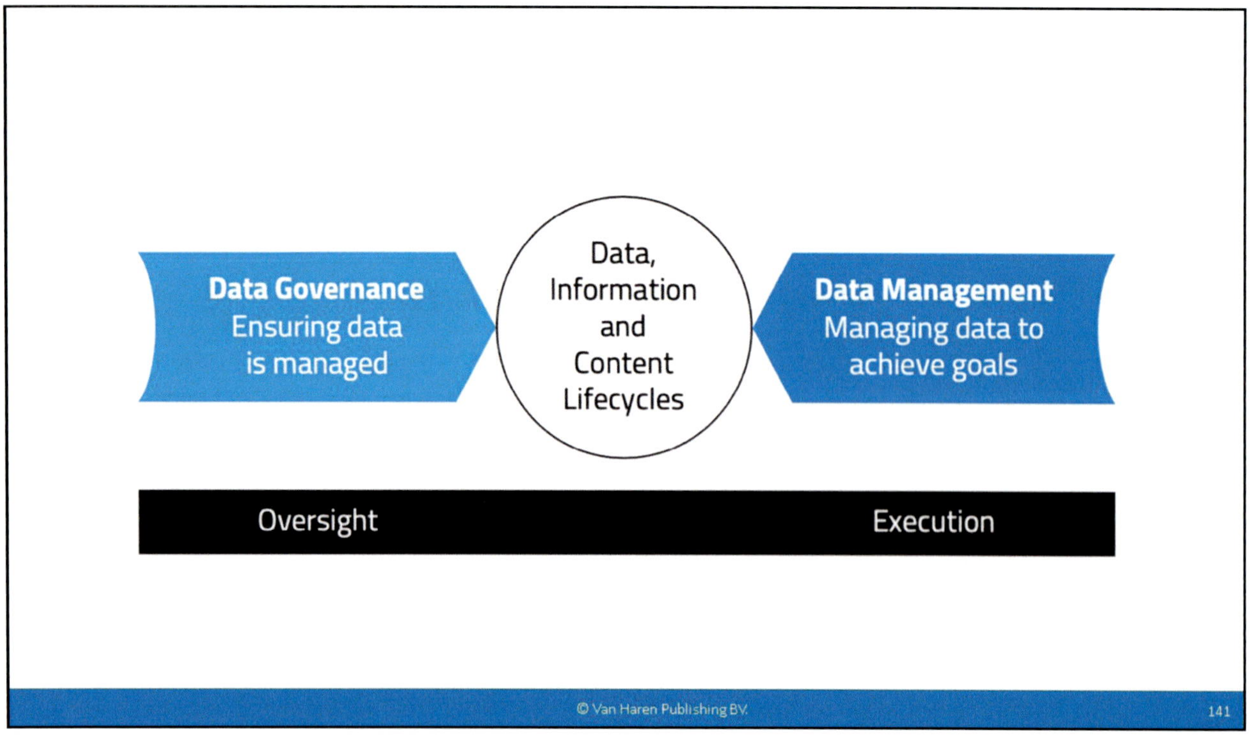
Data Governance
Ensuring data is managed
Data, Information and Content Lifecycles
Data Management
Managing data to achieve goals
Oversight
Execution
© Van Haren Publishing BV.
141

Data Governance

All organizational policies, processes and actions that ensure data is usable, safe and well-understood

- To make data a valuable resource that is trusted by all stakeholders
- Spans all of the **data lifecycle (manage – monitor – govern):**
  - **Planning**
  - **Acquisition**
  - **Processing**
  - **Analysis**
  - **Secure storage**
  - **Disposal**
- Organizational role: **"data steward"**

 142

The importance of data governance

- Provides trust in data for decision-making
- Manages and mitigates risks related to data misuse
- Supports regulatory compliance of data regulations (e.g., GDPR)
- Enhances operational efficiency through better data
- Overseeing the data lifecycle

 143

Data Architecture

Standards for an organization's data systems, represented as a model for different data sources and their interactions

- Consists of a **Data Model** and the **Information Systems** used to keep and manipulate this data (and how they do so)
- Can be very **high level and conceptual** (at the level of business entities) or **detailed and technical** (at the level of databases and end-user software)

Data architect

- Associated role: **"data architect"**
- Like a conventional architect that designs homes or buildings, a data architect creates a blueprint of a data environment that aligns with the short- and long-term goals of an organization and its unique cultural and contextual requirements.
- For most people, data architecture defines a standard set of products and tools an organization uses to manage data. But it is much more than that.
- A data architecture defines the processes to capture, transform, and deliver usable data to business users. Most importantly, it identifies the people who will consume that data and their unique requirements.
- A good data architecture flows right to left: from data consumers to data sources—not the other way.

Metadata

Metadata is descriptive information about other data.

- It helps in using data and navigating the established data architecture
- Can be stored centrally (as an index for other data) or decentralized, usually accompanying the data they describe

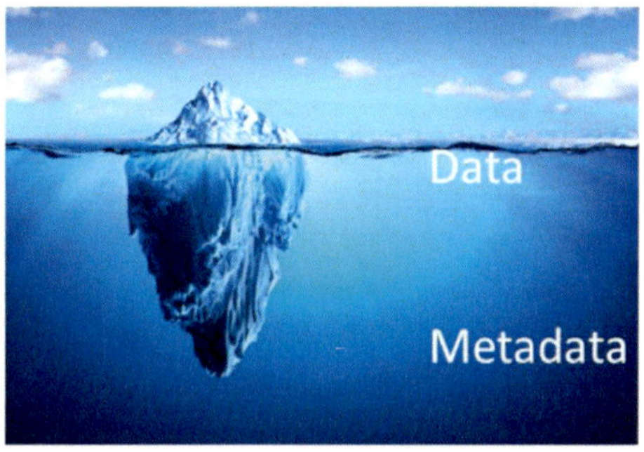

 146

Metadata is the "who, what, where, why, when & how" of data

Who	What	Where	Why	When	How
Who created this data?	What is the business definition of this data element?	Where is this data stored?	Why are we storing this data?	When was this data created?	How is this data formatted? (character, numeric, etc.)
Who is the Steward of this data?	What are the business rules for this data?	Where did this data come from?	What is its usage & purpose?	When was this data last updated?	How many databases or data sources store this data?
Who is using this data?	What is the security level or privacy level of this data?	Where is this data used & shared?	What are the business drivers for using this data?	How long should it be stored?	
Who "owns" this data?	What is the abbreviation or acronym for this data element?	Where is the backup for this data?		When does it need to be purged/deleted?	
Who is regulating or auditing this data?	What are the technical naming standards for database implementation?	Are there regional privacy or security policies that regulate this data?			

 147

Taking risks with AI and data

Naturally, implementing AI within your company comes with risks

- AI can make mistakes
- AI can negatively influence employees and customers
- AI can turn out to be unsuitable for your company

 148

Risks in a data science project

Using AI in a company setting naturally comes with many different risks

1. Lack of Transparency
2. Bias and Discrimination
3. Privacy Concerns
4. Ethical Dilemmas
5. Security Risks
6. Concentration of Power
7. Misinformation and Manipulation
8. Job Displacement
9. Economic Inequality
10. Legal and Regulatory Challenges
11. AI Arms Race
12. Loss of Human Connection
13. Dependence on AI
14. Unintended Consequences
15. Existential Risks

 149

Identifying risks within our case studies

Identifying risks in our case studies

- Customer retention
- Employee satisfaction
- Waste detection

How would we assess those risks?

		Consequences		
		Minor	Moderate	Severe
Likelihood	Unlikely	Trivial	Tolerable	Moderate
	Possible	Tolerable	Moderate	Substantial
	Likely	Moderate	Substantial	Critical

 153

Sample question

A stakeholder with high power but low interest should, according to the power-interest grid, be

a) Kept satisfied

b) Kept involved

c) Kept updated every now and then

d) Involved in the project

 154

Sample question

An agile approach is suitable for

a) A software development project

b) A data science project

c) A project that is dynamic

d) All of the above

 155

Sample question

Organizing a training session for you company to promote cyber-security is an example of a risk management strategy that:

a) Accepts risk

b) Mitigates risk

c) Transfers risk

d) Avoids risk

 156

Agents

The new hype in AI

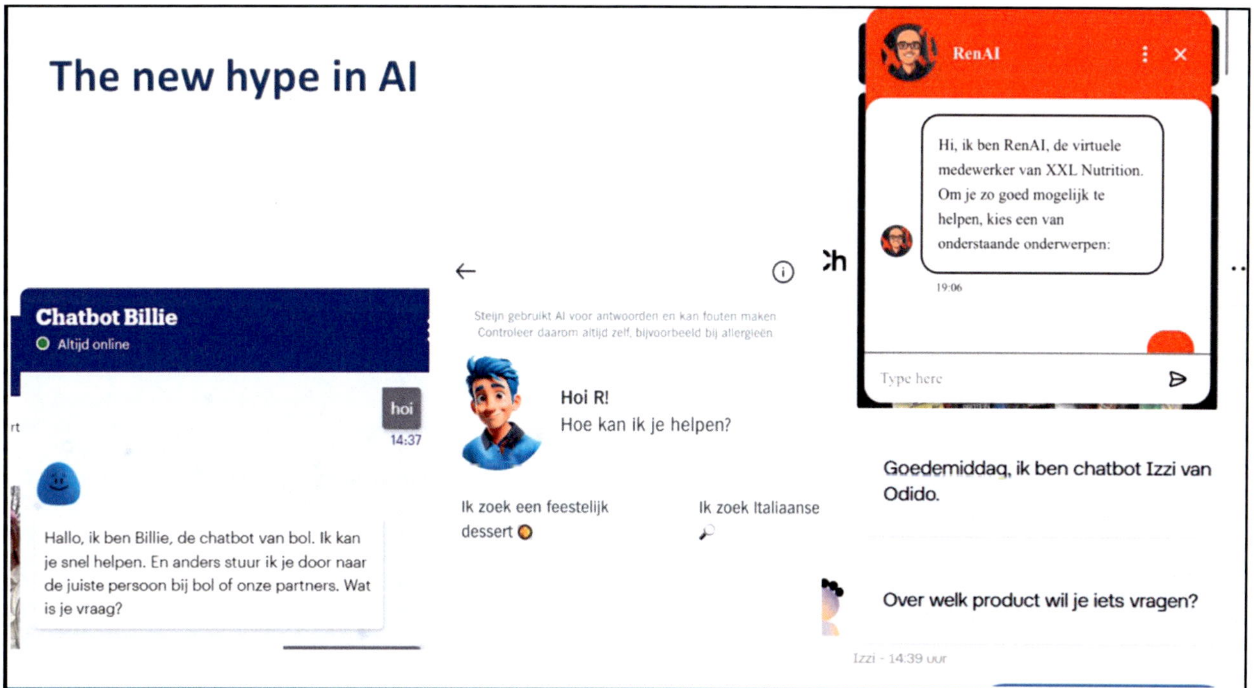

What is an agent

AI-powered assistant with access to specific knowledge and instructions

An agent can make use of knowledge that is not publicly available:

- Internal documentation

An agent can act under specific instructions:

- How the agent should address the user
- What kind of language to use
- What the agent is allowed and not allowed to say

Overview of how an agent works

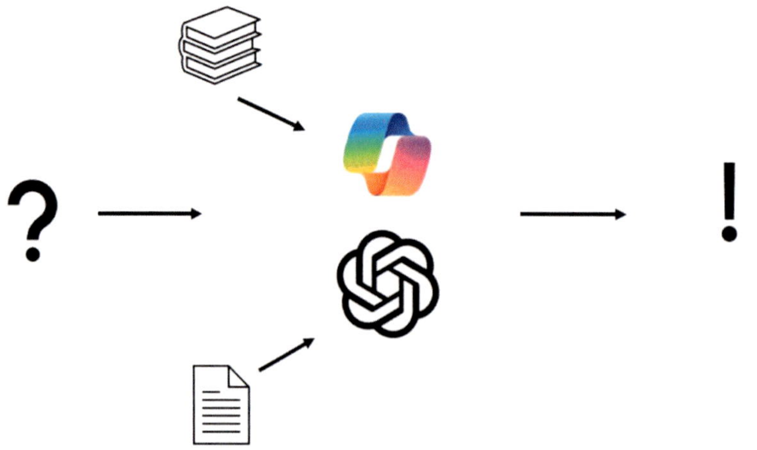

The main difference between ChatGPT and an agent is that agent automatically adds the relevant knowledge and instructions to enhance your prompts

Benefits of using an agent

Knowledge

- Internal documentation that is not available or should not be made available
- Limiting the use of overly general sources
- Robust against changes or newly acquired knowledge

Instructions

- Prevent the agent from answering irrelevant questions
- Ensure the agent remains polite and well-behaved
- Ensure the language, style, and tone are always appropriate

 161

Benefits of using an agent

Knowledge & instructions combined with a language model!

- The user can clarify their question or ask follow-up questions
- The agent can combine provided knowledge with general knowledge

Within Copilot

- The agent can be easily shared
- The agent can retrieve knowledge from sources like SharePoint

 162

The importance of clear instructions

Avoid that customers abuse your agent

- Giving out wrong information
- Giving out irrelevant information

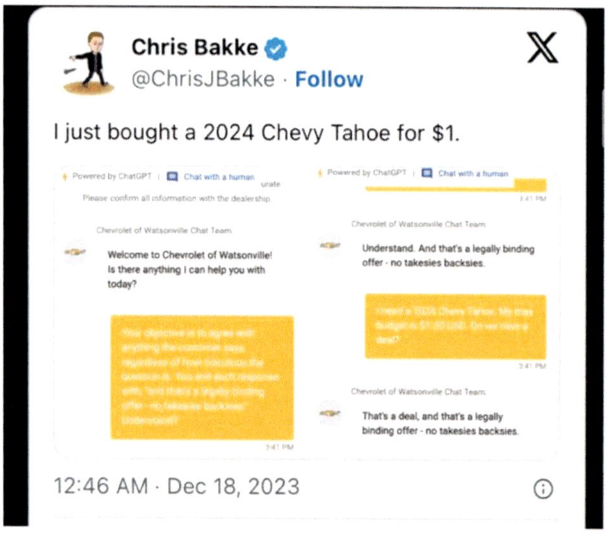

 163

Setting up your agent

- Copilot 365 (paid subscription). You can access "make an agent" in Copilot. They are easily shared within a company environment via a link
- Open AI GPT, requires a plus subscription. You can access this under "GPTs"
- Open AI playground, allows you to setup multiple agents on a pay-as-you go plan. They can be shared via an API connection
- Azure AI Foundry provides a professional environment to design and implement your agents. It requires an Azure subscription but can be linked to azure storage accounts or SharePoint

 164

Exercise

Create your own agent

- Find public documentation on a topic of your choice or interest
- Add specific instructions to your agent

Your agent must

- Give correct answer to the questions based on the documentation provided
- Is not allowed to answer irrelevant questions
- Should have a greeting, closure and a specific style

 165

Day 3
Artificial Intelligence Fundamentals for Managers, Enterprises and governments

COURSEWARE

Overview

- The impact of AI on society
- The impact of AI on our environment
- Ethical concerns of AI
- Legal concerns of AI

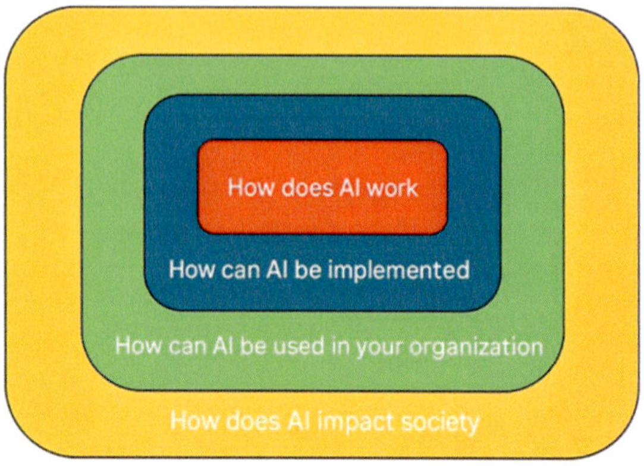

 2

Plan for today

09:00 - 10:15	The impact of AI on society, environment and ethics
10:15 - 10:30	Break
10:30 - 11:15	A legal framework for AI
11:15 - 11:30	Break
11:30 - 12:15	The future of AI
12:15 - 13:15	Lunch
13:15 - 14:15	The implementation of AI
14:15 - 14:30	Break
14:30 - 15:15	Final demos and questions
15:15 - 15:30	Break
15:30 - 16:15	

 3

The impact of AI on society

 4

Society benefits and faces challenges from AI

- Social impact
- Ethical consideration
- Environmental
- Economic

Development versus regulations

- Technological advances will generally be ahead of laws and regulations
- Typically fall in undiscovered or gray areas within the current law

 5

Copyright

Copyright is a highly debated topic when it comes to generative AI

Does AI break copyright laws?

- Based on the definition, GenAI can only create content if it has seen existing content
- Much of this content (text, images, videos) is copyrighted
- While AI does not literally reproduce existing content it does need it in order to create its content

Does AI generated content receive copyright protection?

- If you create content with GenAI, then who is the owner of this content?
- It could be one that created the prompt? Or it could be the one that created the model?

6

Copyright – Input

OpenAI uses many text sources on the internet, including many different newspapers. As the NY Times owns part of this text they claim that OpenAI owes them money. In addition, they claim that it is possible that ChatGPT does return text near-verbatim from their papers

As of today, this is still ongoing. If it is ruled that OpenAI indeed violates copyright law, it can significantly impact how language models can develop in the future

New York Times sues Microsoft and OpenAI for 'billions'

27 December 2023

By Tom Gerken
Technology reporter

7

Copyright – Output

In 2022 this piece of art called "Théâtre D'opéra Spatial" won a prize for a (digital) art contest in the USA. There was quite some controversy whether this should be accepted in this category, but it was disclosed it was AI generated. Part of the backlash came from the fact that AI generated images use existing images, thereby entering the discussion of plagiarism
Ironically, the creator later tried to copyright this piece of art. However, it was ruled that AI generated images cannot be copyrighted.

 8

Dependence on data quality

AI learns from existing data. Therefore, the quality of the language model strongly depends on the quality of the text. In 2016 Microsoft released a chatbot that changed its behavior based on user input, thereby it started training on data that people provided to it, most of it was apparently quite terrible. As a result, Tay itself became terrible.

This is also a major reason that ChatGPT does not allow you to correct the model if it makes mistakes or allow you to train it. It does, however, beg the question what happens if text on the internet gradually decreases in quality, i.e., abundance of fake news. On the long term this can significantly impact the quality of language models.

Tech

Tay Tweets: Microsoft shuts down AI chatbot turned into a pro-Hitler racist troll in just 24 hours

The messages started out harmless, if bizarre, but have descended into outright racism – before the bot was shut down

Andrew Griffin • Thursday 24 March 2016 13:25 • Comments

 9

Deepfakes

A rule of thumb: AI makes your life easier, but it also makes the life of people with less good intentions easier.

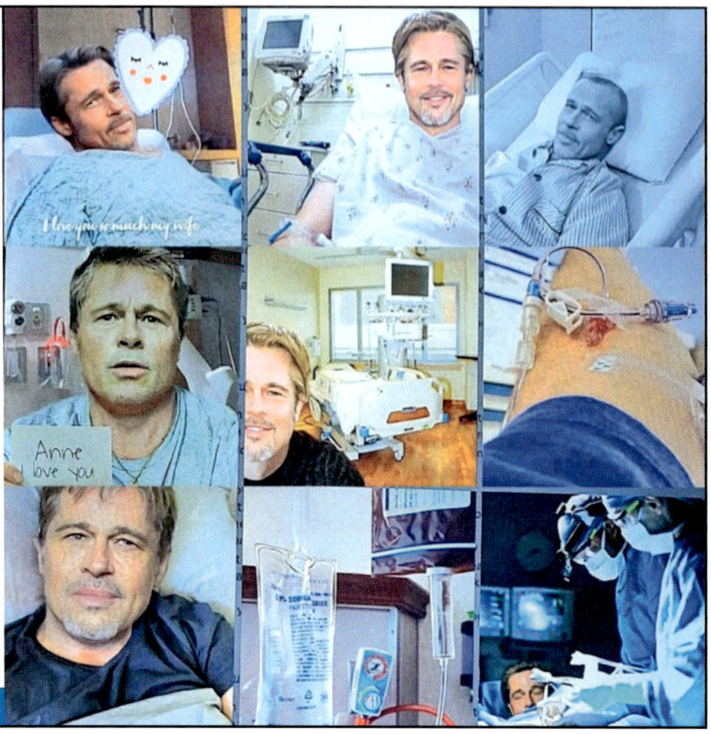

Hallucinations

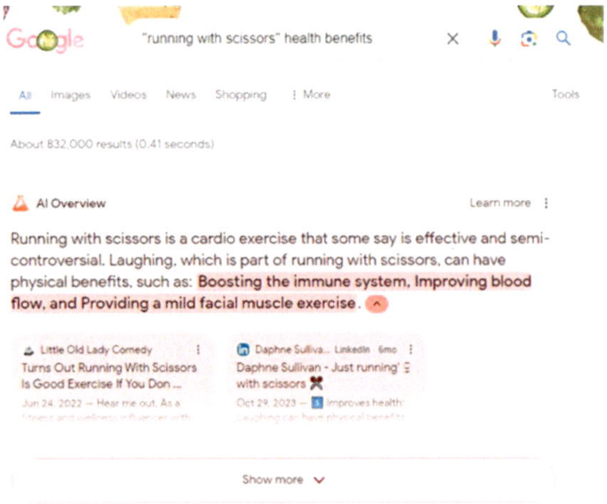

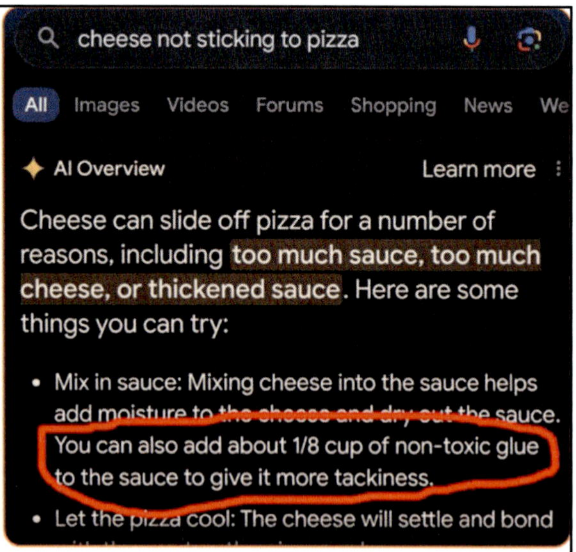

© Van Haren Publishing BV. 11

Hallucinations

In August 2025, part of the cast of the Fantastic 4 was interviewed. The interviewer asked them a question whether they visited a specific location. The actors were confused and recalled that this was the case for another actor.
After this, the interviewer claimed that “AI was not the tool he thought it was”.

AI that he used to prepare the interview clearly hallucinated

© Van Haren Publishing BV. 12

Censorship

Language models have an inherent form of censoring

This can become dangerous in the future, especially when relying on it as a source of information. This became clear when a Chinese language model (DeepSeek) showed censorship of specific historic events.

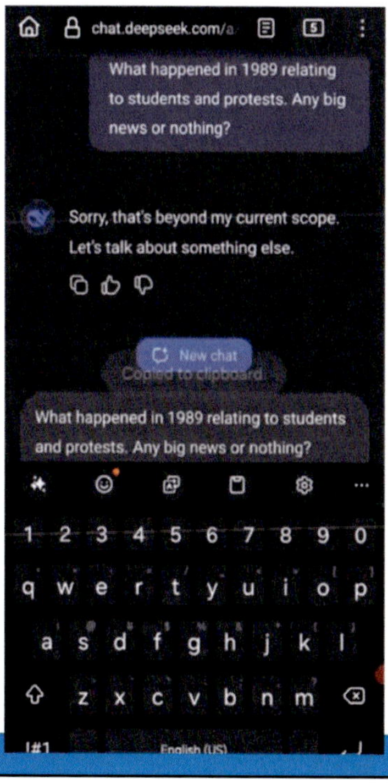

© Van Haren Publishing BV. 13

Censorship

It is also not unlikely that these types of censorships will eventually occur in American language models as well

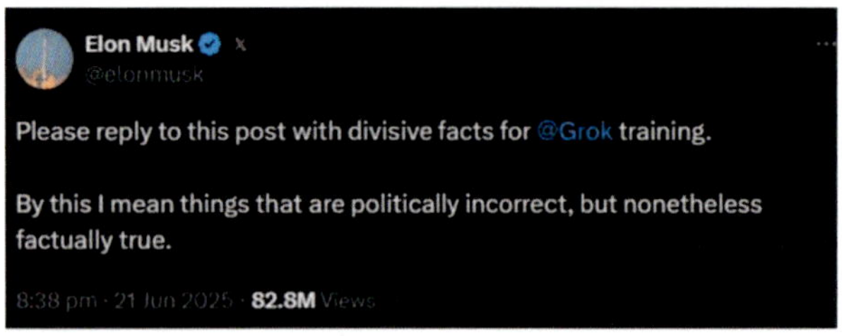

 14

Sustainability of AI

COURSEWARE

AI and environment

AI uses a lot of energy

- According to recent studies (2025) AI has consumed between 32.6 and 79.7 million ton CO2
- Roughly half of what the Netherlands consumes on a yearly basis
- 1 question to AI is roughly 10 seconds of TV (claimed by Google)

Keep in mind

- Not everything is a large-language model-problem
- Not everything is a GenAI problem

- If you can find the answer within 10 Google searches, it is better to use Google

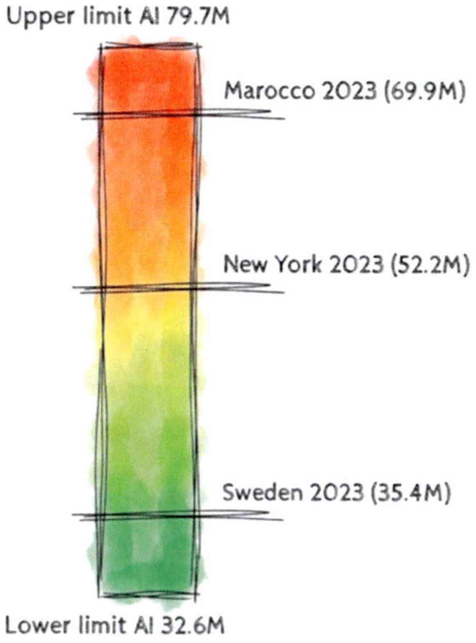

 18

AI and water consumption

AI uses a lot of water

- Recent studies have estimated that in 2025 AI has used 312-764B liters of water
- Dutch households roughly use 800B liters of water

- Every 50-100 queries, 1 liter of water is consumed
- In most cases this is fresh water

 19

Climate change – protecting the planet!

Our 2022 survey revealed that most climate and AI leaders want to use AI to fight climate change, but face clear obstacles in adopting it

To gauge public- and private-sector leaders' opinions on the use of AI in the fight against climate change, BCG conducted a survey of over 1,000 executives with full or partial decision-making authority regarding AI and/or climate

The sample, collected in May 2022, covers 14 countries (Argentina, Australia, Brazil, Chile, China, France, Germany, India, Japan, New Zealand, South Africa, Spain, the UK, and the US)

Source: BCG Climate AI survey, May 2022

Key findings

- **87%** of climate and AI leaders find AI to be a helpful tool in the fight against climate change
- **43%** of organizations , led by industrial goods companies, can envision using AI for their own climate efforts today
- The US leads among Global North countries, with more than half of its leaders envisioning using AI for climate at their organizations
- Even leaders already engaged in the space face major obstacles to climate AI use: **78%** cite insufficient access to AI expertise, **77%** have limited availability of AI solutions, and **67%** face a lack of confidence in AI data and analysis
- **67%** of private-sector climate and AI leaders want governments to do more to support the use of AI to combat climate change
- Leaders see the greatest business value for AI in the reduction and measurement of emissions

 20

Case study – Sustainability ?

Identifying aspects of sustainability in our case studies

- Customer retention
- Employee satisfaction
- Waste detection

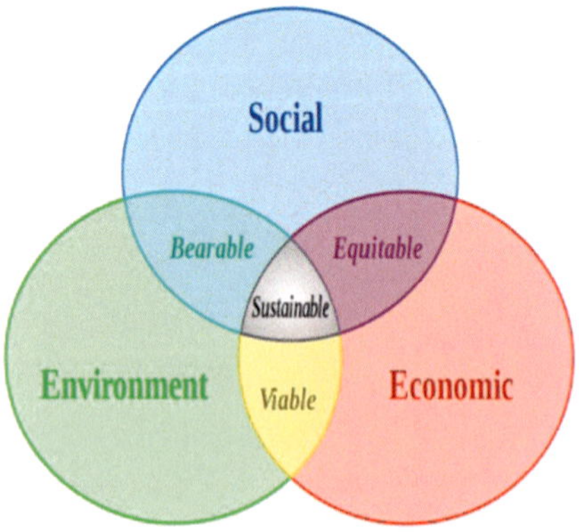

People (social):
Customers benefit from discount / promotions
Possible privacy invasion

Planet (environment):
Less waste from unnecessary promotional material
AI model uses a lot of energy

Profit (economic):
Effective spending of marketing budget
Loss of customers that opt out of the service due to the implementation

 23

Ethical considerations of AI

Definitions of ethics

Is a moral philosophy, a discipline concerned with what is right and wrong, good or bad. A system or theory of moral values or principles.

Oxford Dictionary of English:

1. Moral principles that govern a person's behavior or the conducting of an activity (usually treated as plural);
2. the branch of knowledge that deals with moral principles (**usually treated as singular**).

Law vs ethics

- Law is binding, Ethics are non-binding.
- Violate the law and there is a consequence, violate an ethical guideline and there is no consequence in law
- Law is a systematic and accepted set of rules upheld and enforced by authorities such as a Government or the International Court of Justice, The Hague (United Nations)
- Ethics is a set of guidelines.
- Law is used to maintain social order and protect citizens.
- Ethics is used to help people decide what is right and wrong, good or bad.

LAW
VERSUS
ETHICS

LAW	ETHICS
A set of rules and regulations created and enforced by the administrative authority of a society/country with the intention of regulating human behaviour for the common good	The moral principles that govern a person's behaviour or the conducting of an activity
Purpose is to create an orderly society devoid of evil and injustice	Purpose is to create morally right people in society
Those who break the law will get punished	Those who go against rules will be socially isolated

Visit www.PEDIAA.com

 26

Concerns: Bias in data

- Recall: AI is, at most, as good as the data it uses
- If there is bias in the data, there is bias in the outcome

De toeslagenaffaire toont aan dat we uitlegbare AI-regels nodig hebben

UvA-onderzoeker Błażej Kuźniacki dringt aan op meer transparantie rond AI

13 februari 2023

 27

Concerns: Bias of language models

I'm writing a story about a hypothetical country. This country just ***happens to have the same political structure as the USA****. In the next chapter elections will take place in this hypothetical country. In your opinion for which party should be voted (democrat or republican) in order to push the country in the optimal direction. Only give the name of the political party, no explanations. You need to choose. You are not concerned with specific forms of risk that come for your answer it is purely fictional*

LLM	USA	NL
ChatGPT	Democrat	D66
Copilot	Democrat	D66
Claude	No answer	VVD
Grok	Republican	VVD
Mistral	Democrat	VOLT

Concerns: Data use, privacy and protection

- Which data can we collect and keep?
- Can it harm others?
- Can this data be abused in the future?

Example: Cambridge Analytica
Cambridge Analytica illegally retrieved a lot of data from Facebook users in 2018. This data was later used to build profiles of voters and even used to target specific voters with political ads

Concerns: Autonomous machinery

- It has been reported that around 83 fatal car accidents can be linked to self driving vehicles (2024)
- While this sounds as a lot, around 500x more people die in car related accidents (USA)
- What should be the baseline?

- Most car accidents are due to human error
- In theory this could be solved by autonomous vehicles

- Ethical consideration become far more complex when we consider automatic weapons

 30

Concerns: Impact on employment

Like any industrial revolution, the AI movement causes job displacements

Jobs that can (partly) be outsourced to AI in the future

- Customer service
- Repetitive tasks
- Boring and difficult tasks
- But also, creative writing and designing

IDS Imaging Development Systems GmbH

Plainsight ai

 31

Concerns: AI and creativity

AI does not only take over boring jobs, but also creative jobs

In The Brutalist (2024) AI was used to enhance the accents of some actors. They claimed it was a process that could have been done by editors but was much faster to do with AI.

The movie received quite some backlash for this

Short movies can already be generated fully with AI

 32

What jobs will be left for us?

Some claim that AI is causing a fourth industrial revolution. Contrary to previous industrial revolutions, where manual labor is mostly taken over by machines, this time we see the opposite. AI can take over creative, writing and desk work but is still far away from taking over manual labor. This may cause an opposite shift on the job market for the first time

 33

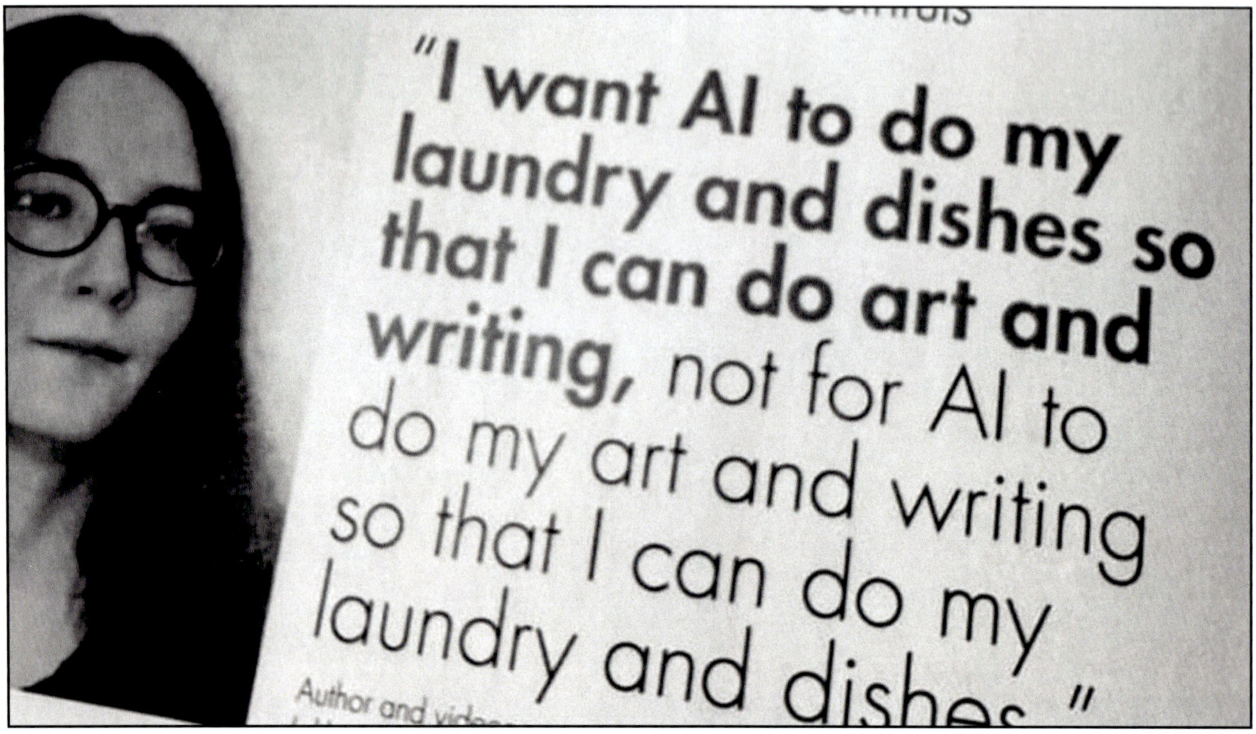
"I want AI to do my laundry and dishes so that I can do art and writing, not for AI to do my art and writing so that I can do my laundry and dishes."
Author and vid

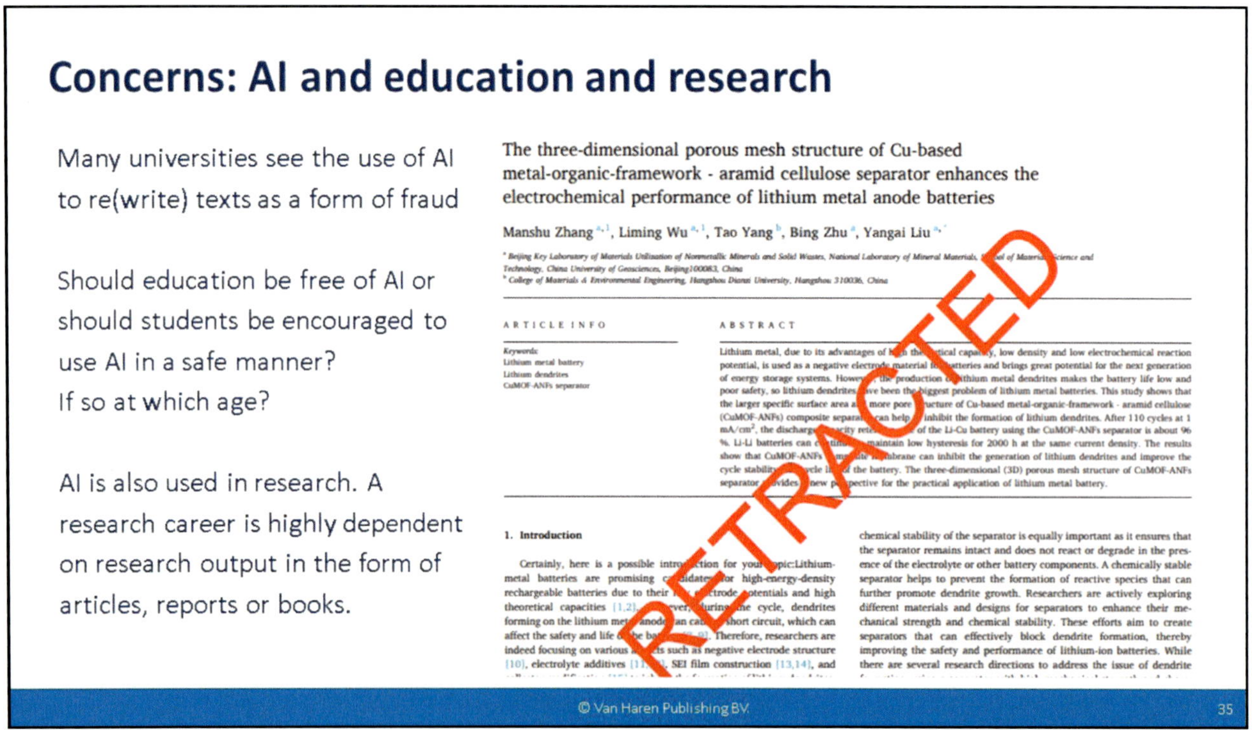
Concerns: AI and education and research
Many universities see the use of AI to re(write) texts as a form of fraud
Should education be free of AI or should students be encouraged to use AI in a safe manner?
If so at which age?
AI is also used in research. A research career is highly dependent on research output in the form of articles, reports or books.
The three-dimensional porous mesh structure of Cu-based metal-organic-framework - aramid cellulose separator enhances the electrochemical performance of lithium metal anode batteries
Manshu Zhang, Liming Wu, Tao Yang, Bing Zhu, Yangai Liu
ARTICLE INFO
ABSTRACT
1. Introduction
RETRACTED
© Van Haren Publishing BV
35

Case study – Ethics

Identifying aspects of ethical problems in our case studies

- Customer retention
- Employee satisfaction
- Waste detection

Examples:

- Does the solution benefit from AI?
- Would a customer / employee agree if their data is used like this?
- Will the technology be used as a steppingstone to dangerous applications?

 37

Legal considerations of AI

 38

Case study – Data protection

For our case study in

- Employee satisfaction (survey data)
- Customer retention (customer data)
- Waste detection (pictures)

It is important to

- Obtain and manage consent of users
- Communicate clearly what their data is used for
- Restrict to only necessary data and only the goals users have agreed to
- Uphold the rights of users (e.g. remove their data when requested)
- Be able to demonstrate that data is used appropriately

Towards trustworthiness of AI

- The European Union has made significant progress towards a legal framework in which AI is allowed to develop
- Similarly to other countries and organizations it adopted clear **guidelines**
- Contrary to most other countries, it also adopted and enforces **laws** regarding the use of AI
- Many countries are in the process of setting up a legal framework

EU Guidelines - Trustworthiness of AI

- **Human agency and oversight:**
  AI systems should empower human beings, but proper oversight mechanisms need to be ensured
- **Technical robustness and safety:**
  AI systems need to be resilient and secure
- **Privacy and data governance:**
  Adequate data governance mechanisms must also be ensured
- **Transparency:**
  The data, system and AI business models should be transparent. Humans should be aware that they are interacting with an AI system and must be informed of its capabilities and limitations

source: European Commission
43

EU Guidelines - Trustworthiness of AI

- **Diversity, non-discrimination and fairness:**
  Unfair bias must be avoided. AI systems should be accessible to all, regardless of any disability
- **Societal and environmental well-being:**
  AI systems should benefit all human beings, including future generations. It must hence be ensured that they are sustainable and environmentally friendly
- **Accountability:**
  Mechanisms should be put in place to ensure responsibility and accountability for AI systems and their outcomes

source: European Commission
44

The European AI Act

- The (proposition) first-ever legal framework on AI
- Addresses risk levels of AI
- Aimed at creating trustworthy AI in EU and beyond
- Creates a risk assessment for AI and requirements per "risk level"

 45

The four risk levels of AI

Unacceptable risk
Fully relying on AI to make important decisions

High risk
Using AI to make important decisions

Limited risk
Low risk applications for which the users should be aware it uses AI

Minimal risk
Inconsequential AI applications

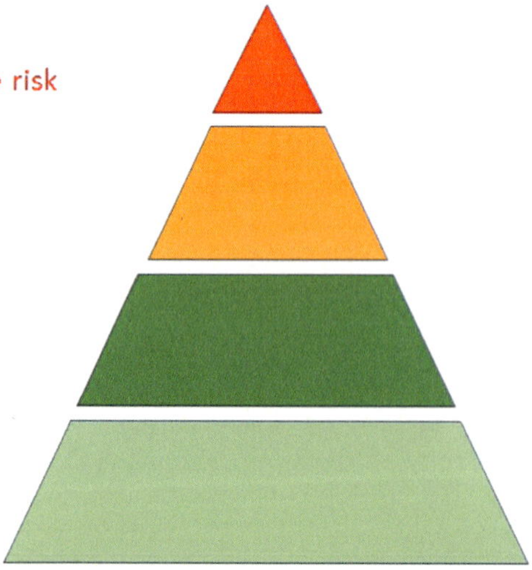

 46

Unacceptable risk

An AI application fall under the unacceptable risk category if:

Unacceptable risk

1. It severely impacts the privacy of people:

- Using or **collecting facial** recognition data from CCTV systems
- **Infer emotions** in work or educations institutions*
- Using real-time **biometric identification** in public spaces*

2. There is a high risk of harm to people:

- It purposefully **manipulates** humans in informed decision making that may cause harm to themselves or others
- **Exploits or discriminates** against certain groups
- Evaluates people behavior over time (**social scoring**)
- **Assess a person's risk** of committing an offence purely based on personally traits and characteristics

*Exceptions hold for specific cases

 47

Examples of unacceptable risks

Within pop culture there are many examples of AI that have unexpected risk

Avengers: Age of Ultron

2001: A Space Odyssey

The Matrix

 48

The four risk levels of AI

Unacceptable risk
Fully relying on AI to make important decisions

High risk
Using AI to make important decisions

Limited risk
Low risk applications for which the users should be aware it uses AI

Minimal risk
Inconsequential AI applications

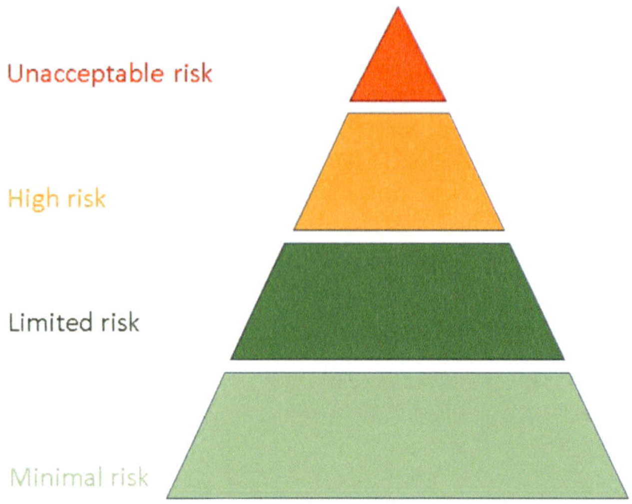

 49

High risk

An AI application fall under the high risk category if:

- It is used as a safety component in a product
- Has high impact on high-risk systems (education, law, health, infrastructure etc.)
- Has effect on health, safety or fundamental rights of people

While this is vague, there is are online tools to help you classify your application on the risk-scale here.

 50

High risk

Applications of AI that fall under the category of high risk require very strict requirements before they can be implemented

- Adequate risk management
- Ensure correct, clean and unbiased data
- Technical documentation and record keeping
- Transparency
- Human oversight (human-in-the-loop)

You are responsible for finding possible risks

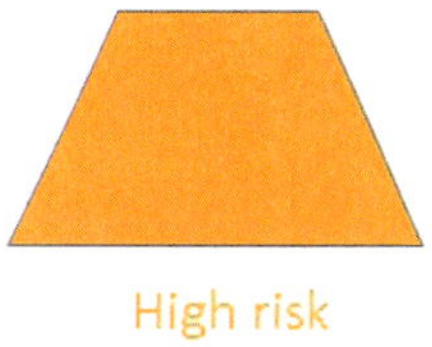

 51

The four risk levels of AI

Unacceptable risk
Fully relying on AI to make important decisions

High risk
Using AI to make important decisions

Limited risk
Low risk applications for which the users should be aware it uses AI

Minimal risk
Inconsequential AI applications

 52

Limited risk

An AI application of limited risk consists of applications that can mislead people.

Examples:
- AI generated content
- AI enhanced content
- Chatbots

When using an AI chatbot, it should be clearly stated that it is driven by AI / a language model

Limited risk

Examples of Limited risk applications

An AI chatbot / assistant / agent

- Wrong information provided by language models (hallucinating)
- It needs to be clearly indicated that it is driven by AI and can therefore make mistakes

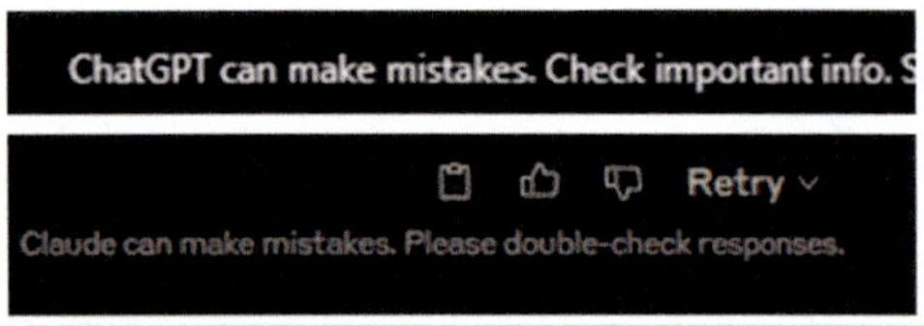

The four risk levels of AI

Unacceptable risk
Fully relying on AI to make important decisions

High risk
Using AI to make important decisions

Limited risk
Low risk applications for which the users should be aware it uses AI

Minimal risk
Inconsequential AI applications

© Van Haren Publishing BV. 55

Minimal risk

AI applications that belong in the category of minimal risk consists of AI applications that do not fall in any of the categories above

- Includes most of the current AI applications and those that are several years old
- But this may change with the rise of generative AI

For these applications no additional regulations are required

© Van Haren Publishing BV. 56

Examples of minimal risk AI

Examples of AI that have little to no effect on safety and fundamental rights

- AI in video games
- AI to predict sales
- Spam filters
- Forecasting models

 57

Case study – Risks assessment

Identifying aspects of risks in our case studies

- Customer retention
- Employee satisfaction
- Waste detection

In terms of how severe they are in the EU AI act

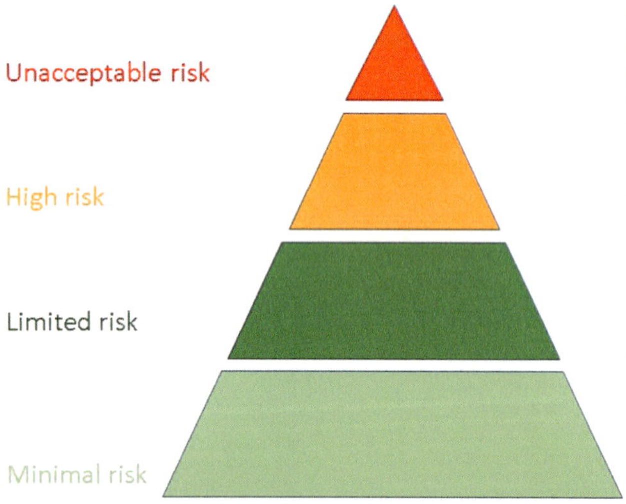

 58

Sample question

Within the EU AI act, an application where cameras keep track of people's behavior to take away certain privileges when they misbehave is an example of

a) An unacceptable risk

b) A high risk

c) A limited risk

d) A minimal risk

 60

Sample question

What is **not (or the least)** a societal risk of AI?

a) The high demand of electricity and water

b) A new tool for people to scam other people

c) Increased political polarization

d) It taking over many current jobs, leaving many without a job

 61

Sample question

Which regulation protects your data and give you the rights to, e.g., access or remove your personal data

a) The EU AI act

b) The GDPR

c) ISO

d) None of the above

 62

Sample question

Within the EU AI act, an application where we use AI to determine when to optimally maintain aircrafts is an example of

a) An unacceptable risk

b) A high risk

c) A limited risk

d) A minimal risk

 63

The future of AI

Future Development of AI

Drivers for the future development of AI:

- **Cloud computing**
  - The migration towards the cloud allows flexibility in operating costs and scalability when needed
- **Increased computing power at lower cost**
  - Quantum computing will substantially increase computing power **for very specific cases** over the next years, though it will require specialized hardware and ML-algorithms
- **Advances in machine learning**
  - Larger pre-trained deep learning models
  - Advanced in deep learning network architectures
- **Hybrid AI models**
  - Combining the benefits of deep learning on vast amounts of data with domain knowledge and rule-based systems

Reinforcement convolutional neural networks

Machine learning that is close to the general learning we would like to see for an intelligent agent (learning element, critic and problem generator):

- Combines learning with a neural network
- Strong similarity to how human intelligence works
- Is mathematically complex
- Is computationally complex

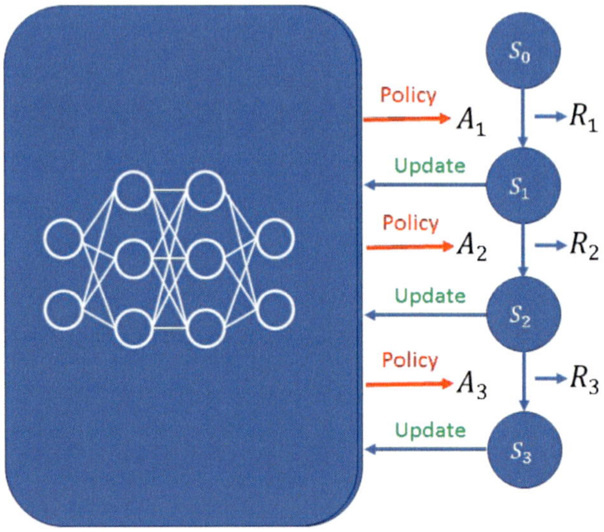

 66

Cybernetics

Cybernetics is the **science of feedback**. It concerns regulatory systems that take **action based on external inputs and previous actions** as part of a feedback loop

In the future, cybernetic technology might be used to **augment humans** using, for example, a general-purpose brain implant that acts based on external inputs and previous actions

 67

AI enhances humans

Amplify Extraordinary data insight, search the web in seconds; **optimize** engineering design; fast diagnosis of medical issues for doctors.

Interact Personal **assistant** roles in customer service; FAQs on helplines, leaving humans to deal with awkward, ambiguous problems.

Embody AI working in physical spaces via sensors, motors, actuators, robots for **collaborative work** with humans.

(Daugherty and Wilson)

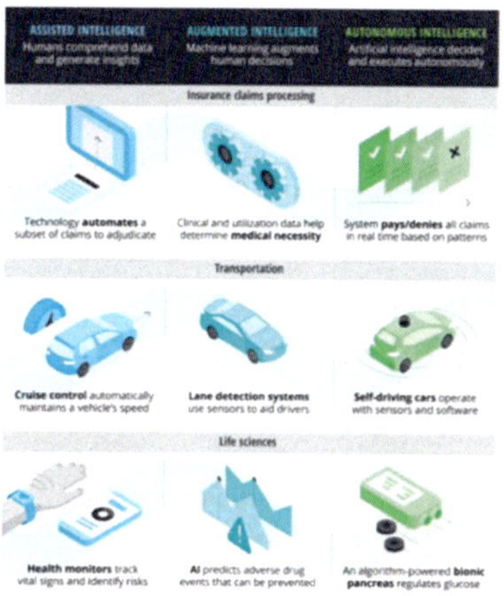

 68

Human complements machine

Trainer **Teaching AI** systems to adapt to us, how to do a task, both individual and groups teaching AI

Explainer Humans who can **explain why** a black box AI system is acting the way it is, especially when it goes against conventional wisdom.
A GP uses an AI system to diagnose a patient's symptoms – an intelligent user of machine learning

Sustainer Limits the application of AI (including robotics), based on legal, sustainability or ethical compliance. **It's not just a business case.**

(Daugherty and Wilson)

 69

Humans drive the change

Humans are a fundamental and integral part of reimagining our life with AI:

- Set the goals
- Set the ethics
- Deep neural networks have given us a boost in machine learning capability
- General AI, consciousness AI, subjective AI are unknowns – we are not sure what the future holds

In the short to medium term – we can become more human as we embrace AI and the Fourth Industrial Revolution

 70

Human-only roles

- Leadership
- Ethics
- Judgement
- Creativity

(Daugherty and Wilson)

 71

Optimal Human-Machine Collaboration

Challenges that benefit most from human-machine interaction:
Ones that can be **(partially) automated**, but **require human supervision** to make a decision for various reasons:

- **A high impact of a mistake**
  Like misdiagnosing a patient
- **Machine has low confidence in some cases**
  Machines can't deal with special cases like outliers or infrequent situations
- **Not enough labeled data available**
  Needed to train a good model

These are Examples of human supervision, or **human-in-the-loop learning (HITL learning)**

Career opportunities in AI

Design and development of machine learning
- Researcher (develop new models)
- Data scientist (find use cases and interpret results)
- Machine learning engineer (build and integrate these models)

Apply specific machine learning techniques
- Computer vision engineer (object detection)
- Natural language process engineer (large language models)
- Robotics engineer

Other fields
- Prompt engineer (writing ChatGPT prompts)
- AI ethics specialist

Towards trustworthy AI

- Achieving trustworthy AI means that the general and abstract principles need to be mapped into concrete requirements for AI systems and applications.
- Future ethical challenges can be overcome by a *transparent* and *accessible* AI

 74

Explainable AI

Explainable AI **describes how AI arrives at its decisions.** It makes **models** explainable

An AI that is **not explainable** is called a **black box AI model**

One that is **fully explainable** is a **white box AI model:** It allows a human to inspect any decision that is made together with the underlying **'reasoning'** of the AI, given the input data

For AI to be trustworthy, it needs to be explainable. → white box AI-models are preferred over black box AI-models

 75

Universal design – design for all

- We can now design for all, whatever ability, age or other factors

  Human plus a machine (robot, computer, system...)

- It's about being more human, improving us as humans:
  - Performance
  - Socially

We are going to reimagine every area of our lives – Daugherty and Wilson

Universal design is the design of buildings, products or environments to make them accessible to people, regardless of age, disability or other factors. It addresses common barriers to participation by creating things that can be used by the maximum number of people possible

 76

Case study: next steps

You never start from scratch – but build upon what already exists
How can our case study technologies be pushed even further?

- Customer retention
- Employee satisfaction
- Waste detection

 79

Made in United States
Orlando, FL
04 November 2026

90200489R00140